Foucault and Lifelong Learning

Over the last twenty years there has been increasing interest in the work of Michel Foucault in the social sciences and in particular with relation to education. This, the first book to draw on his work to consider lifelong learning on its own, explores the significance of policies and practices of lifelong learning to the wider societies of which they are a part.

With a breadth of international contributors and sites of analysis, this book offers insights into such questions as:

- What are the effects of lifelong learning policies within socio-political systems of governance?
- What does lifelong learning do to our understanding of ourselves as citizens?
- How does lifelong learning act in the regulation and reordering of what people do?

The book suggests that understanding of lifelong learning as contributory to the knowledge economy, globalization or the new work order may need to be revised if we are to understand its impact more fully. It therefore makes a significant contribution to the study of lifelong learning.

Andreas Fejes is a Senior Lecturer and Postdoctoral Fellow in Education at Linköping University, Sweden. His research explores lifelong learning and adult education in particular drawing on poststructuralist theory. He has recently published articles in *Journal of Education Policy*, *Educational Philosophy and Theory*, *International Journal of Lifelong Education* and *Teaching in Higher Education*.

Katherine Nicoll is a Senior Lecturer in Education at the Institute of Education, University of Stirling, Scotland. Her research explores post-compulsory and professional education and policy in particular drawing on poststructuralist theory. She has recently published *Rhetoric and Educational Discourse: Persuasive Texts?* (with R. Edwards, N. Solomon and R. Usher, 2004) and *Flexibility and Lifelong Learning: Policy, Discourse and Politics* (2006).

Foucault and Lifelong Learning

Governing the subject

Edited by Andreas Fejes and Katherine Nicoll

Routledge
Taylor & Francis Group

LONDON AND NEW YORK

First published 2008
by Routledge
2 Park Square, Milton Park, Abingdon, Oxon OX14 4RN

Simultaneously published in the USA and Canada
by Routledge
270 Madison Avenue, New York, NY 10016

*Routledge is an imprint of the Taylor & Francis Group,
an informa business*

© 2008 selection and editorial matter: Andreas Fejes and
Katherine Nicoll; individual chapters: the contributors

Typeset in Garamond by Keyword Group Ltd
Printed and bound in Great Britain by Antony Rowe Ltd, Chippenham,
Wiltshire

British Library Cataloguing in Publication Data
A catalogue record for this book is available
from the British Library

Library of Congress Cataloging-in-Publication Data
Fejes, Andreas.
   Foucault and lifelong learning: governing the subject / Andreas Fejes &
   Katherine Nicoll.
      p. cm.
   Includes bibliographical references and index.
   ISBN 978-0-415-42402-8 (hardback) – ISBN 978-0-415-42403-5 (pbk.) –
   ISBN 978-0-203-93341-1 (ebook) 1. Adult education–United States.
   2. Continuing education–United States. 3. Foucault, Michel, 1926–1984.
   I. Nicoll, Kathy, 1954-II. Title.

   LC5251.F4 2008
   374'.001–dc22   2007026841

ISBN 10: 0-415-42402-X (hbk)
ISBN 10: 0-415-42403-8 (pbk)
ISBN 10: 0-203-93341-9 (ebk)

ISBN 13: 978-0-415-42402-8 (hbk)
ISBN 13: 978-0-415-42403-5 (pbk)
ISBN 13: 978-0-203-93341-1 (ebk)

Contents

SECTION 3
Governing subjects 191

Preface

A book on Foucault and lifelong learning

Today, the question that emerges for educators, educational researchers and scholars is how to engage in lifelong learning at a time when it has become a greater focus for policy at local, national and supranational levels and where it has become a theme, force or lever for change in learning and teaching contexts and practices. There is no doubt that in real terms lifelong learning has been taken up and deployed by politicians within postindustrialized societies as a means to spread learning across populations, in efforts for increasing and widening participation in learning and for the skilling and upskilling of populations. At the same time, there has been an increasing questioning within the scholarly literature that is concerned with the analysis of policy and lifelong learning as to what they might be within the contemporary period, and how analysis might best approach its work of engagement; what theories, methodologies and methods should it use and what questions should it ask? Policy and educational analysts have identified and discussed various research approaches in terms of the meanings of policy and lifelong learning that they produce, their productivities and limitations. Arguments for alternative and more critical approaches have arisen forcefully, with related questions about just what these might most appropriately be.

As contributors to a book on lifelong learning we have all in one way or another asked ourselves such questions and found ourselves taking up theoretical resources from the work of Michel Foucault as our response. For us then, the significance of putting exemplars of our work together as a book is that we can explicate something of lifelong learning in ways that we feel are important. Ours of course are not the only ways to take up Foucauldian resources for the analysis of lifelong learning (for there are other scholars who also do this kind of work). However, we do not want to suggest that for this reason this work is incomplete, because it does not contain all that is going on in this area of research. To suggest this, might be to imply that we think that a unity – a complete and exhausted theory – would be possible or even desirable. Rather, we want to displace at the outset any perhaps common-sense notion that we are engaged in constructing a unifiable theory. What you find here are examples that are intended to be taken only as fragments of theorization. We do not intend you to read them as a body of work that can somehow be synthesized to create a singular picture that will tell the truth of what lifelong learning really is, in terms of governance or subjectivity, or indeed in any terms. Rather, we hope that you will read these chapters as alternative 'tales' of lifelong learning. Alternative, that is, in relation to those narrations that we hear so often from policy makers and indeed practitioners, and alternative from those that we might read within the research and scholarly literature that tell us about lifelong learning but begin with other theories and methodological assumptions and questions. We intend that our chapters are to some extent illustrative of what can be done by drawing upon Foucauldian resources and that they work actively to critique and to undermine dominant notions of what lifelong learning is and does. But they are in no way intended as exhaustive.

Over the last fifteen to twenty years, there has been increasing interest in the work of Michel Foucault in the social science in general and in relation to education in particular. Since the groundbreaking work of Stephen Ball (1990a), there have been many texts which have explored the significance of Foucault's work for education. However, most of these have focused on the significance of Foucault for schooling and for higher education and less on adult education or lifelong learning. It is arguable that in the same period, as the interest in Foucault has grown, so has the policy interest and research focus on lifelong learning. This book therefore sets out explicitly to explore the significance of Foucault's work for our understanding of the policies and practices of lifelong learning, in particular focusing on and exploring his concepts of governmentality and discipline. It draws upon work produced for an international symposium, funded by the Swedish Research Council, which brought together many of the leading academics in the field in February 2006 to discuss Foucauldian perspectives on lifelong learning. This book is intended as a focal point for developing scholarship and research in this area.

A poststructuralist positioning within studies of education is of course not new. With the increasing emphasis on the discursive construction of reality, resources already exist to engage with questions of discourse. Indeed a recent edition of *Journal of Education Policy* was given over specifically to poststructuralism and policy analysis (Peters and Humes 2003) and a recent issue of *Educational Philosophy and Theory* was given over to a Foucauldian, discursive and governmentality analysis of the learning society (Simons and Masschelein 2006). This book is positioned to some extent in relation to these and to the work of policy analysts such as Stephen Ball (1990a, 1994), James Joseph Scheurich (1994) and Norman Fairclough (2000). Also in some kind of relation with post-compulsory education analysts such as Sandra Taylor *et al.* (1997) and Richard Edwards (1997), and is of course in continuity with the work of the editors (cf. Edwards *et al.* 2004; Fejes 2006; Nicoll 2006). However, the focus within this book on lifelong learning locates it somewhat differently.

Since his death in the mid-1980s (and even before) there have been some lively debates and discussions in the academic world about ideas from Michel Foucault's work. These have emerged mainly within the social sciences. Although this interest in Foucault has increased, it took a long time before scholars in education started to take up his ideas. One might consider this remarkable, as several of these concepts (discipline, surveillance, technologies and so forth) are specifically talked about in relation to education. However, although he mentioned the school (1991) as an example of a modern institution where disciplinary power was produced and exercised, he never did specifically enter the educational arena in his research. Before 1990 the use of his ideas was almost completely absent in educational research (Olssen 2006). One of the exceptions was Hoskin (1979, 1982), who drew on ideas from *Discipline and Punish* (Foucault 1991) when analysing the prehistory of the examination. It was only in the late 1980s and early 1990s that people started to use Foucault's ideas extensively and they have become a major inspiration in educational research during the last decade. A wide variety of phenomena have been studied, with numerous approaches.

A first collection of work on the theme of Foucault and education was published in 1990 (Ball 1990b) where the focus was on education and its relationship to politics, economy and history in the formation of humans as subjects. Most of the contributions drew on ideas from *Discipline and Punish* (Foucault 1991), especially the idea of dividing practice; how school in many different forms divides pupils into the normal and the abnormal. The book could be seen as a groundbreaking piece of work as it introduced Foucault in a broad sense to research on education. After this book was published, there was a major increase in the use of Foucault in educational research. Several collections of work have since been published on the issue and with a change of focus from the idea of subjects as objects and docile bodies to a greater interest in Foucault's later work and the modes through which subjects construct themselves, as technologies of the self, and to the idea of governmentality.

In *Foucault's Challenge*, Popkewitz and Brennan (1998) argued that the use of Foucault in educational research had been sparse, probably because it requires a shift from the modernist and progressive discourses which dominate education. By introducing chapters by authors from different disciplines that drew on Foucault in relation to education they wanted to revise these dominating discourses in education. A major concern for their book and several of the chapters was to produce a genealogy of the subject by analysing systems of reason in making specific subjectivities possible. Concepts such as genealogy and governmentality were central and the reader was presented with detailed analyses of how systems of reason in different cultural settings shape different subjectivities.

In the collection *Dangerous Coagulations*, Baker and Heyning (2004) also engaged in a conversation with research on education where Foucault was used. The authors wanted to avoid ending up in a discussion on the correct way to use Foucault. Their book can be seen as a collection of different ways of using Foucault in relation to education. The dominant contributions are those of historicizing approaches and a more sociological Foucault where concepts such as governmentality and technologies of the self are used.

We could say that the ambition in this book is similar to Baker and Heyning (2004) in so far as we want to focus on different uptakes of Foucault in educational research. However, our focus is on other cultural practices which are related to lifelong learning and governing of the subject. Our book, then, contributes to a reconceptualizing of lifelong learning. This, in itself, produces certain possibilities for reflexive criticism, both of the limitations of this book and of the work of others. It is sufficient to say that Foucault (1980) points to the requirement for forms of political analysis and criticism that may prove productive within contemporary contexts of globalization. These are contexts which are characterized by the reconfiguration of economic, social and political relations of power; for our purposes, in part through policy themes of lifelong learning. He suggests that productive strategies are those that may modify and coordinate the modification of power relations within the contexts of their operation.

... A Politics

This book is not neutral, nor apolitical. It seeks to undermine and make vulnerable discourses of lifelong learning by pointing out that these have been inhibited by attempts to think in terms of totality and truth. By this we are pointing to the quite general tendency (whether of educators, policy analysts, the public or the media) to ask questions over whether or not lifelong learning is this or that, is it or is it not a good thing, or what it is, or, what it means, as if there were any one straightforward and correct answer. The problem is in assuming that totalizing questions and answers over the truth of lifelong learning are the appropriate ones. By seeking these, other important questions and answers are missed out. For example, what are the effects of lifelong learning as true discourse and of questions of it regarding its truth or totality? If one refuses to begin from a starting assumption that lifelong learning is either a good or bad thing, or has a singular significance or meaning, if one refuses to think like this, then it becomes possible to formulate questions over the means for its constitution, and the significance and effects of lifelong learning as totality and truth. How does lifelong learning come to be dominantly taken as (and with regard to questions of) totality and truth within a society at a particular time? What is the significance of lifelong learning as totality and truth? What are its effects?

Furthermore, there is an argument that, by researching lifelong learning through any approach at all, we help to make it more widely and commonly accepted as a 'real' object, which has, as it were, in advance, a real meaning. This is an effect of the way that we generally tend to think of language.

Language is taken as denotative of objects; the term 'lifelong learning' thus names a real object, existing out there in the real world (as when we say 'stone' or 'chair' we expect the word to correspond to some equivalent reality of a stone or chair). Language can, alternatively, be regarded as connotative; we 'make up' – constitute – forms of social and human life through our language and social practices. In this case, language and social forms constitute objects such as lifelong learning. Of course if our argument that by researching lifelong learning we help to constitute it as something that is taken by others to be real is to work logically, then people (apart from ourselves) need to read our research papers (and very probably, not many do). But it does not require that they agree with what we write. Merely reading about or entering into a conversation about lifelong learning (and this does not of course need to be a research text or conversation) leads to the reinforcement of lifelong learning as a real object, suitable to be talked about and generally discussed and criticized within the social formation. Thus, by researching lifelong learning in any way at all, we are complicit in making it potentially more widely accepted as some 'thing' that is real. This is precisely what we are trying to avoid.

Having said this, by beginning our argument with a rejection of what we suggest is a dominant assumption that we are looking for totalizing answers or truths over the meaning of lifelong learning, any suggestion that the work of theorizing and examination that follow within subsequent chapters could offer definitive or generalizable answers – 'truths' – to questions of lifelong learning is eroded. However, poststructuralist analyses drawing upon various resources from Foucault's work do allow for the production of alternative meanings. These are not by any means meant as replacements for others. They are just other kinds of meanings. We suggest they are a variety that may act to 'counter' relations of power within and between policy and more dominant approaches to lifelong learning and lifelong learning analysis at this time. As a 'beginning' or starting point, therefore, we are less concerned with the substance of lifelong learning than with exploring different approaches to analysis and their possible relationships in the constitution of meanings of lifelong learning.

Explorations of the means by which lifelong learning is brought forth within policy discourses and how it takes effect, will help formulate a notion of lifelong learning as a form of governance of the subject that can potentially be changed. Rather than simply engage in a struggle over truth, which we have seen may be counterproductive, we can bring out how lifelong learning comes to be persuasive and powerful.

The book starts with a chapter in which we engage with questions of the contribution of Foucault to research on lifelong learning. Thereafter, the book is divided into two main parts. The first part introduces chapters which analyse the subjectivities shaped and governed by policy. In the second part chapters are introduced that focus on how the pedagogical subject is shaped through different educational practices. The book ends with a chapter which reflexively engages with the book in its entirety, drawing out some of the lines of discussion that have variously and productively emerged and considering their limitations.

References

Baker, B.M. and Heyning, K.E. (eds) (2004) *Dangerous Coagulations: The Uses of Foucault in the Study of Education*, New York: Peter Lang.

Ball, S. (1990a) *Politics and Policy Making in Education. Explorations in Policy Sociology*, London: Routledge.

Ball, S. (ed.) (1990b) *Foucault and Education: Disciplines and Knowledge*, London: Routledge.

Ball, S. (1994) 'Some reflections on policy theory: a brief response to Hatcher and Troyna', *Journal of Education Policy*, 9: 171–82.

Edwards, R. (1997) *Changing Places? Flexibility, Lifelong Learning and a Learning Society*, London: Routledge.

Edwards, R. (2003) 'Ordering subjects: actor-networks and intellectual technologies in lifelong learning', *Studies in the Education of Adults*, 35: 55–67.

Fairclough, N. (2000) *New Labour, New Language?*, London: Routledge.

Fejes, A. (2006) *Constructing the Adult Learner: A Governmentality Analysis*, Linköping: Liu-Tryck.

Foucault, M. (1980) *Power/knowledge: Selected Interviews and Other Writings 1972–1977*, Brighton: Harvester Press.

Foucault, M. (1991) *Discipline and Punish: The Birth of the Prison*, Harmondsworth: Penguin.

Hoskin, K. (1979) 'The examination, disciplinary power and rational schooling', *History of Education*, 8: 135–46.

Hoskin, K. (1982) 'Examination and the schooling of science', in R. MacLeod (ed.), *Days of Judgement: Science, Examinations and the Organization of Knowledge in Late Victorian England*, Driffield: Nafferton Books.

Nicoll, K., Solomon, N. and Usher, R. (2004) *Rhetoric and Educational Discourse. Persuasive Texts?* London: RoutledgeFalmer.

Nicoll, K. (2006) *Flexibility and Lifelong learning: Policy, Discourse and Politics*, London: RoutledgeFalmer.

Olssen, M. (2006) *Michel Foucault: Materialism and Education*, London: Paradigm Publishers.

Peters, M. and Humes, W. (2003) 'Editorial: the reception of post-structuralism in educational research and policy', *Journal of Education Policy*, 18: 109–13.

Popkewitz, T. and Brennan, M. (eds) (1998) *Foucault's Challenge: Discourse, Knowledge and Power in Education*, New York: Teachers College Press.

Scheurich, J. (1994) 'Policy archaeology: a new policy studies methodology', *Journal of Education Policy*, 9: 297–316.

Simons, M. and Masschelein, J. (2006) 'The learning society and governmentality: an introduction', *Educational Philosophy and Theory*, 38: 417–30.

Taylor, S., Rizvi, F., Lingard, B. and Henry, M. (1997) *Educational Policy and the Politics of Change*, London: Routledge.

Acknowledgements

This book is based on a symposium entitled *Foucault and Lifelong Learning/Adult Education* held at Linköping University, Sweden, 7–11 February 2006. The editors and contributors to the book would like to convey their thanks to the Swedish Research Council for financing the symposium and the Department of Behavioural Sciences and Learning at Linköping University for organizing it. Without their help and support of our discussion of mobilizations of the work of Michel Foucault this book would not have emerged.

Contributors

Helene Ahl is Associate Professor and Research Fellow at the School of Education and Communication at Jönköping University, Sweden. Her current research concerns discourses on lifelong learning. Her previous work includes studies on motivation, gender and entrepreneurship and entrepreneurship education.

Per Andersson is Associate Professor and Senior Lecturer in Education at Linköping University, Sweden. His main research interest is educational assessment, and particularly the recognition of prior learning. He has published extensively on this topic. Recent books include *Re-theorising the Recognition of Prior Learning* (co-edited with J. Harris, 2006) and *Kunskapers Värde* (with A. Fejes, 2005).

Liselott Assarsson is a Senior Lecturer in Education at Linköping University and analytical expert at the Swedish Agency for Flexible Learning, Sweden. The focus of her thesis is how identities are construed in adult education. Her main research interest is discourses of lifelong and flexible learning, currently concerning vocational education/training and particularly learning careers.

Gun Berglund is a PhD student and Lecturer at the Department of Education at Umeå University, Sweden. She is currently completing her doctoral thesis on lifelong learning discourses in Sweden, Australia and the US. She teaches mostly within the HRM programme and leadership courses.

Gert Biesta is Professor of Education at the Institute of Education, University of Stirling, and visiting Professor at Örebro University and Mälardalen University, Sweden. Recent books include *Derrida & Education* (co-edited with D. Egéa-Kuehne, 2001), *Pragmatism and Educational Research* (with N. C. Burbules, 2003) and *Beyond Learning: Democratic Education for a Human Future* (2006) (for more information see www.gertbiesta.com).

Richard Edwards is Professor of Education at the University of Stirling, Scotland, UK. He has researched and written extensively on adult education and lifelong learning from a poststructuralist perspective. His current research interests are in the areas of globalization, policy and literacies.

Andreas Fejes is a Senior Lecturer and Postdoctoral Fellow in Education at Linköping University, Sweden. His research explores lifelong learning and adult education in particular drawing on poststructuralist theory. He has published recently in articles *Journal of Education Policy*, *Educational Philosophy and Theory*, *International Journal of Lifelong Education* and *Teaching in Higher Education*.

Marinette Fogde is a doctoral student in Media and Communication Studies at Örebro University, Sweden. She is currently completing her doctoral thesis on the governing of job seeking subjects by examining contemporary job search practices of a Swedish trade union.

Jan Masschelein is Professor of Philosophy of Education at the Catholic University of Leuven, Belgium. His primary areas of scholarship are educational theory, political philosophy, critical theory and studies of governmentality. Currently his research concentrates on the 'public' character of education.

Katherine Nicoll is a Senior Lecturer in Education at the Institute of Education, University of Stirling, Scotland, UK. Her research explores post-compulsory and professional education and policy in particular drawing on poststructuralist theory. She has recently published *Rhetoric and Educational Discourse: Persuasive Texts?* (with R. Edwards, N. Solomon and R. Usher, 2004) and *Flexibility and Lifelong Learning: Policy, Discourse and Politics* (2006).

Mark Olssen is Professor of Political Theory and Education Policy in the Department of Political, International and Policy Studies at the University of Surrey, UK. He is the author of many books and articles in New Zealand and England. More recently he has published the book *Michel Foucault: Materialism and Education* (2nd ed. 2006).

Ulf Olsson is Associate Professor in Education at the Stockholm Institute of Education, Sweden. His research is concerned with the history of present, political thought and technologies in different discursive and institutional practices, principally Public Health and Teacher Education.

Kenneth Petersson is Associate Professor in Communication Studies at the Department of Social and Welfare Studies, Linköping University, Sweden. His research is concerned with the history of present, political thought and technologies in the field of criminal justice and in other different discursive and institutional practices.

Thomas S. Popkewitz is Professor at the Department of Curriculum and Instruction, the University of Wisconsin-Madison, USA. He studies the systems of reason that govern educational reforms and research. His book *Cosmopolitanism and the Age of School Reform* (2008) explores changing pedagogical theses about the child as a history of the present and its processes of inclusion and abjection.

Maarten Simons is Professor of educational policy at the Centre for Educational Policy and Innovation, Catholic University of Leuven, Belgium. His research interests are in educational policy and political philosophy with special attention for governmentality and schooling, and the 'public' character of education.

Nicky Solomon is Associate Professor at University of Technology, Sydney, Australia. Her research interests are in the area of work and learning, focusing on the development of workplace learning policies and practices in Australia and the UK.

Katarina Sipos Zackrisson is a Senior Lecturer in Education at Linköping University and analytical expert at the Swedish Agency for Flexible Learning, Sweden. The focus of her thesis is how identities are construed in adult education. Her main research interest is discourses of lifelong and flexible learning, currently concerning digital literacy and learning regions.

Chapter 1

Mobilizing Foucault in studies of lifelong learning

Katherine Nicoll and Andreas Fejes

Lifelong learning is an important contemporary theme within many countries and international organizations, in particular within the European Union and the Organization for Economic Co-operation and Development (OECD). It is promoted through national and international policies as a solution to the particular challenges of the contemporary age that must be overcome. It is used as a means to promote change and in this it promotes further change, within socio-political systems of governance, institutions for education and training and in our very understanding as citizens within society. Lifelong learning is therefore a significant phenomenon of our times and one that warrants close scrutiny. This book thus takes up questions of lifelong learning and the significance of such change. Drawing upon the work of Foucault it is possible to address such issues, in particular examining lifelong learning as part of the practices of governing in the twenty-first century, exploring the techniques through which such governing takes place and the subjectivities brought forth.

In this chapter, we outline how the work of Michel Foucault can be useful in the analysis of lifelong learning. We argue that he provides valuable tools that help us to understand our contemporary world and its discourses of lifelong learning in ways that are quite different from any other kind of analysis. These are helpful in promoting a critical attitude towards our present time and to the truths promoted today through and around lifelong learning. They show us how there has been and will always be other truths and ways of acting upon others and ourselves, thus pointing to the possibility of other ways of governing and constructing subjectivities.

Lifelong learning

The specific focus on lifelong learning within this text is undoubtedly timely and important. Lifelong learning is promulgated within contemporary national and international policies as a truth, as a required response to an increasing pace of change, the economic and social pressures of globalization and uncertainty over the future. Policies argue that if economies are to remain competitive within global markets and societies continue to cohere, then lifelong learning as a capacity and practice of individuals, institutions and educational systems must be brought forth in the construction of learning societies. They suggest that if nations do not join the race for a learning society, then all may be lost. Lifelong learning is thus promoted as a powerful policy lever for change within contemporary societies, and as such it requires our serious contemplation.

Lifelong learning is not promoted everywhere. It does, however, emerge within contemporary policies of many post-industrial nations and intergovernmental agencies. For example, lifelong learning and the learning society are promoted within the UK (Kennedy 1997; NAGCELL 1997, 1999; NCIHE 1997; DfEE 1998, 1999; SE 2003; DfES 2006), in Australia (DEETYA 1998), in Sweden (Fejes 2006) in Germany and from the Dutch, Norwegian, Finnish and Irish governments (Field 2000). Lifelong learning has been taken up strongly within the United Nations Education, Scientific and Cultural Organization (UNESCO 1996, 1997) and by the European Commission (1996, 2000). In the United States, the National Commission on Teaching and America's Future (1996, see Popkewitz this volume) promotes learning through life. There is a sense that lifelong learning is being promoted as 'the' solution within a new policy rationality of capitalism, whereby those who do not conform will be left out of the next phase. The question of who is included and excluded is therefore significant – for whosoever rejects this new rationality may potentially miss, as the policy narrative goes, the economic boat. Questions over what lifelong learning is and what it does, therefore become urgent. Together with this, as we will argue later on in this chapter, questions over the kinds of questions asked of lifelong learning are equally important.

Lifelong learning is not a uniform or unitary theme within policy. It has emerged at differing times and in different nations over the last years, with differing emphases. John Field (2000) traces how policies of lifelong education, rather than learning, for example, emerged within European policies during the 1960s and 1970s, and were taken up by intergovernmental agencies such as UNESCO and OECD. Lifelong education appeared again in 1993, within the European Commission in Jacques Delors' White Paper on competitiveness and economic growth (European Commission 1993). It emerged as lifelong learning in 1996 within European and national policy vocabularies, after the European Commission declared that year as the European Year of Lifelong Learning.

Three orientations to lifelong learning within policy have been suggested by Kjell Rubenson (2004) over the period from the 1970s until now – humanist, strong economistic and soft economistic. During the 1970s, discussion on lifelong learning was humanist in orientation. In his reading of the Faure report, published by UNESCO in 1972, written by the International Commission on the Development of Education and entitled *Learning to Be: The World of Education Today and Tomorrow*, Biesta (2006) sees this humanistic orientation as 'remarkable' for its vision of a generalized role for education in the world, for its reflection of the optimism of the 1960s and early 1970s in the possibility of generalized progress, and in its contrast with policies and practices of lifelong learning today. Edgar Faure at that time identified four assumptions underpinning the position of this report on education, 'the existence of an international community' with a: 'fundamental *solidarity*'; a shared 'belief in *democracy*'; the aim of development as the '*complete fulfillment of man*' and that 'only an *over-all, lifelong education* can produce the kind of complete man the need for whom is increasing with the continually more stringent constraints tearing the individual assunder' (Faure *et al.*, in Biesta, 2006: 171, emphasis by Biesta).

During the 1980s and until the late 1990s this vision for lifelong learning was replaced by an orientation with a strong economic focus (Rubenson 2004). Highly developed human capital, and science and technology were identified as important means to increase productivity. Instead of humanistic ideas concerning equality and personal development, concepts such as evaluation, control and cost efficiency became important. A qualified workforce with the necessary skills and competences was central to arguments for lifelong learning. Over the last few years a third orientation to lifelong learning has emerged – a soft version of the ecomonistic paradigm. The economic perspective is still conspicuous, and the market has a central role, but civil society and the state have entered the arena to a higher degree within policy discourse. Here, the responsibility for lifelong learning is divided between the market, state and civil society, and the individuals' responsibility for learning is the focus.

Rather than viewing these orientations as discrete or as distinct phases of policy interest in lifelong education and lifelong learning across time, Biesta (2006) argues for a multi-dimensional, triadic 'nature' of lifelong learning – with personal, democratic and economic functions. He suggests that for the authors of the Faure report an economic function of lifelong learning was in evidence, but was subordinated to a democratic and to a lesser extent a personal function. Thus, he proposes that there is a generalized polyvalence in and around economic, personal and democratic functions of lifelong learning within policy representations, and that this may help to contribute to its continued success as a policy theme and to its capacity for mobilization across social formations. More recently, however, for example, within the 1997 OECD report *Lifelong Learning for All*, the emphasis has been switched and the previously subordinated economic function has come to the fore and has taken on a different meaning in terms of value.

We can see that in more recent approaches the economic function of lifelong learning has taken central position, and we might even say that in the current scheme *economic growth* has become an *intrinsic value*: it is desired for its own sake, not in order to achieve something else. (The idea that economic development is an aim in itself is, of course, one of the defining characteristics of capitalism.)

(Biesta 2006: 175, emphasis original)

Now, it appears that the economic function of lifelong learning is dominant within policy discourses and that this is increasingly promulgated as being of intrinsic value for societies. Personal and democratic functions are still there, but they take a subordinate role.

The analyses proposed by Rubenson and Biesta are created through different theoretical resources than those taken up within this book, but they point to important features of and distinctions between lifelong learning policy discourses during different periods of time. For us, the focus on the economic function of lifelong learning within contemporary discourses needs to be analysed as produced within specific historical and discursive conditions – conditions which must be carefully made visible as a way to destabilize our 'taken-for-granted' notions of lifelong learning. Such analysis will point to the work of power and how it discursively shapes, fosters and governs specific subjectivities, an issue that we will return to later on in this chapter.

Why Foucault and lifelong learning?

But we are getting ahead of ourselves already. Why do we then think that it is helpful to use ideas from the work of Michel Foucault for studies of lifelong learning? To us, it is first a question of perspective. Foucault's work offers us a quite different perspective through which to articulate what goes on through lifelong learning. It offers alternative ways to formulate the questions that we might ask and thus the answers that we might find. To explain this further we will need to talk a little more about this perspective and what it can offer.

The chapters within this book, you could say, in one or other way, although certainly in very different ways, explore questions of power. They explore *how* (the means by which) lifelong learning is promulgated as power within the contemporary period, and *what happens* in the modification and co-ordination of power relations through lifelong learning. We know that to explore lifelong learning in these terms may mean that we ultimately find that we must put aside previous assumptions that we know what it is we do when we engage with lifelong learning either as policy makers, researchers, teachers or learners, and this is what we want. Foucault points out to us that although people can be quite clear about what they are doing at a local level, what happens in terms of the wider consequences of these local actions is not coordinated: 'People know what they do; they frequently know why they do what they do; but what they don't know is what what they do does' (Foucault, in Dreyfus and Rabinow 1982: 187). It is these wider means and effects of lifelong learning as it is embroiled with and intrinsic to relations of power that we are interested to explore.

Such an analysis puts a specific focus on *relations of power*, a power that is not acknowledged in the everyday policy making and practices of lifelong learning or often within research into it. By posing such questions we are able to show, for example, how the ambition to 'be inclusive' through lifelong learning has exclusionary practices as one of its effects. Now, we may have already known that practices of inclusion in school and further education colleges leads to exclusion, but lifelong learning may well exacerbate rather than ameliorate this situation as it becomes increasingly 'necessary' in all walks of life.

Lifelong learning is then, through a Foucauldian perspective, intrinsic to contemporary political technologies and strategies of power. However, to say this, it is not necessary to see these as emanating from any particular person, group or indeed strategist. Indeed, Foucault specifically encourages us to give up these ideas. People who are engaged in lifelong learning practices act knowingly and may have strategic purposes. However, it is possible that when those who are involved see the wider consequences of a multiplicity of actions that take place locally, they may also see that there are unintended consequences in what both they and others do. Actions may not 'join up' (to use a commonly used policy phrase) to produce the effects that we had in mind within our localities. For this reason alone we feel that we should look to the practices of lifelong learning, across its multiple locations, so as to explore the possibility of a 'grid of intelligibility' (Foucault, in Dreyfus and Rabinow 1982: 187) for it.

Through a Foucauldian approach it is therefore possible to ask questions other than those offered by positivism or by alternative interpretative perspectives. Instead of focusing on lifelong learning as something that is effective or ineffective in terms of policy or other aims, is essentially good or bad, or as something which can free people from constraints, we pose quite other questions. Thus, we (as authors) hope in one way or another to destabilize those things which we and others might otherwise take for granted about lifelong learning in the present time. Such destabilization is to introduce a certain kind of awkwardness into the very fabric of our experience, by making our narratives of such experiences 'stutter' (Rose 1999).

Positivist and some kinds of interpretative research into lifelong learning aim to produce generalizable 'truths' about it. Foucault (1983) helps to show how this may be dangerous, as discourses of truth generally are. We can see this in that our research can have the effect of producing the things that we want to destabilize, undermine, oppose or counter within relations of power. As an example, here, the concept of 'Bildung' has been centrally used by critical theorists and has significantly informed policies and practices of education in many European nations over the last years (cf. Gustavsson 2002). It is an idea about the purpose of education as that which develops the ability of the human to be reflective (on themselves and their surroundings) as a means of emancipation from social conditions and constraining relations. Bildung is a narrative about freeing oneself through learning as self-autonomy and critique. Such a construction, however, is 'troubled' through a Foucauldian approach as that which is made possible by, and reinforces, that which it opposes – constraint (Masschelein 2004). By believing that we are free we can accept and act within conditions of constraint. Thus, the autonomous, self-reflective life does not overcome power relations. Instead, it is a particular kind of historical 'figure of thought' of self-government through which we become traversed by power relations even as we believe ourselves to be free. This approach thus permits questions about our discourse of Bildung and what the effects of this are. Where lifelong learning is dominantly considered to signify freedom from power through self-autonomy and critique, Foucault helps us to 'read' it alternatively as a mechanism of power whereby the individual governs themselves within relations of power. Thus, through this, we see how our generalized narrations of freedom as a 'truth' can be dangerously misguided.

We are also particularly interested in the notion of *governmentality* and the kind of analyses that it can offer. If we look at research conducted in education, and to some extent about lifelong learning, using different 'uptakes' of Foucault's work (see Solomon, within this text for her theorization of this notion), we can see how there has been a shift from the uptake of Foucault's earlier work (*Discipline and Punish, Power/Knowledge*) to favour his later work (*Governmentality, Genealogy, History of Sexuality*). Further, we can see how there is an emphasis on a sociological uptake of Foucault, where the notion of governmentality is central and the interest is directed towards an analytics of government. For sociologists of governance the object of investigation is the pattern or order that emerges within a society from relations between actors and groups who aim to influence or steer such relations in some way (Rose 1999). By contrast the analytics of government, taken up here, aims not for description and unification, but for *diagnosis* of the fragmented and serendipitous, complex and contradictory lines of action and thought, and agents that seek to govern conduct, so as to better understand how we come to act and think as we do within the present: 'the heterogeneity of authorities that have sought to govern conduct, the heterogeneity of strategies, devices, ends sought, the conflicts between them, and they ways in which our present has been shaped by such conflicts' (Rose 1999: 21).

One of the strengths of this notion of governmentality is that it displaces our rather common-sense and commonly used concept of 'government' with a perspective, rather than another concept or theory. Rather than government as that which is concerned with governing through law-making, the police, decisions in governmental organizations and so forth, government concerns our everyday life, all the relations of power that we are involved in, not least our relations to ourselves. This displacement of our generally accepted notion of government is made possible through Foucault's (1980) displacement of our concomitant notion of power. There is not somebody, such as an employer, or something, such as a nation-state, state authority or government who has used and uses power against someone else. Power is not the property of a person or object. Rather, power is relational and discursive. It circulates everywhere, through networks of relationships, operating through relations of power. Taking such a stance makes it possible for us to approach governing as something other than the 'government' and in such a way that we do not presuppose it. It allows us to relate activities for the government of ourselves, the government of others and the government of the state (Dean 1999), which makes it possible to show the complexity of the conduct of government. The focus is not on social, economic and political circumstances that shape thought (for example, of our narrations of lifelong learning), instead, the focus is on how thought (of lifelong learning) operates within the taken-for-granted ways that we do things.

Government and governmentality

Drawing then on resources from the work of Michel Foucault allows us a specific focus for the analysis of lifelong learning as an element in the exercise of relational power. To appreciate the implications of this it is necessary to see just how different Foucault's notion of power is from the one that we generally use in our everyday conversations and thought, and see just how carefully he constructs it to avoid some pitfalls that he identifies in our more generally accepted version. From there it becomes possible to appreciate just how different a perspective on government is in Foucauldian terms and how different the sorts of questions over lifelong learning are that we are then able to take forward.

For Foucault, our generally accepted or dominant idea of power – ' "le" pouvoir' – is something that does not exist (Foucault 1980: 198). He suggests that this is a notion of power as a substance that is located at or emanating from a given point. It is one that for him is to be rejected on a number of accounts. First, it is based on analysis that does not account for a number of very real social phenomena, for example, that of the organization of people into groups and hierarchies within social formations. Second, it is a notion of power that is faulty in that it constructs a theory of power with various prior assumptions as its starting point. Here assumptions that people are essentially equal or that power is exercised where individual or collective rights are taken away are intrinsic to our common understandings of what power is; whether the latter is the moment of an historical invasion of a population or a hypothesized juridical event whereby the rights of an individual to freedom or equality are taken away by imprisonment. Third, there are consequences of these assumptions. The problem here, for Foucault, is that by starting with these assumptions it is always going to be necessary to point to that particular moment when power over a population or individual begins and to deduce its existence – its 'reality' – from the moment where it starts.

Power and the conduct of conduct

Foucault suggests an alternative starting point in our consideration of power. He proposes that the reality of power is that of relations – 'In reality power means relations, a more-or-less organized, hierarchical, co-ordinated cluster of relations' (Foucault 1980: 198). The approach to power must be that which makes it possible to analyse such clusters of relations through some sort of grid of analysis. To avoid the problem of metaphysical or ontological questions of power, to avoid what he identifies as the 'what' and 'why' (later 'where') and 'how' questions of power that bind us in searches for the qualities of origin, essence and manifestation of power, he suggests an alternative. This is not, he is careful to explain, to *avoid* questions of metaphysics or ontology themselves, but *is* to cast suspicion on them and reframe them by asking whether these three qualities of origin, essence and manifestation, as those that describe power and reify it, are legitimate questions (Foucault, in Dreyfus and Rabinow 1982). It *is* to ask whether there are specific and complex realities of power that are being avoided through the obviousness to us of the double question – What is power? and where does it come from? Foucault proposes a 'how' question that is quite different from that which we might normally suppose we might ask, and which allows us to question our prior assumptions that we know what power is:

> To put it bluntly, I would say that to begin the analysis with a 'how' is to suggest that power as such does not exist. At the very least it is to ask oneself what contents one has in mind when using this all-embracing and reifying term.
>
> (Foucault, in Dreyfus and Rabinow 1982: 217)

A 'how' question of this sort is one of the *means* by which power is exercised, and over *what happens* in situations were people say that power is being exerted over others: 'The little question, What happens? although flat and empirical, once it is scrutinized is seen to avoid accusing a metaphysics or an ontology of power of being fraudulent; rather it attempts a critical investigation into the thematics of power' (Foucault, in Dreyfus and Rabinow 1982: 217).

This is then an analytics of power that does not presuppose it and does not attempt to form a unified theory. To draw upon resources from the work of Michel Foucault is to then begin from a different place within the power relations that produce questions of the metaphysics and ontology of power as those that should be asked. The question of the 'how of power', in terms of 'by what means is it exercised' and 'what happens?', for Foucault is one that focuses on the means and effects of power in situations when people say that power is being exerted. For us then, to position our work in this way is to avoid the problems of any assumption that we have a theory of power as a starting point in our analysis of lifelong learning, to take up resources from Foucault's own critical investigations into the thematics of power and to approach lifelong learning as in some way embroiled within power relations.

Power, then, is relational and does not exist except through action; it is the way in which actions modify other actions within relationships between individuals or groups. This power is quite separate from any relinquishing of freedom or rights between these individuals or groups, although it is possible that such relinquishing results in the formation of a relationship of power. The possibility of the exercise of power does, however, depend upon the maintenance of 'the other' as an active subject, 'free', with a whole range of possible actions available to it and able to be invented.

> [T]he exercise of power ... is a total structure of actions brought to bear upon possible actions; it incites, it induces, it seduces, it makes easier or more difficult; in the extreme it constrains or forbids absolutely; it is nevertheless always a way of acting upon an acting subject or acting subjects by virtue of their acting or being capable of action. A set of actions upon other actions.
>
> (Foucault, in Dreyfus and Rabinow 1982: 220)

A power relationship is always a question for Foucault of the conduct of conduct (this is a play by Foucault on the double meaning of the verb in French; to lead or drive and to behave or conduct oneself, see translator's note in Dreyfus and Rabinow 1982: 221) and this is one of government: 'For to "conduct" is at the same time to "lead" others (according to mechanisms of coercion which are, to varying degrees, strict) and a way of behaving within a more or less open field of possibilities' (Foucault, in Dreyfus and Rabinow 1982: 220–1).

This is not government as we have come to know it quite commonly today as 'our government'; the group of people who represent us within political positions, or even to those within state structures that provide us with 'welfare'. Rather, it is a notion of government that Foucault suggests was more familiar to people in Europe during the sixteenth century, encompassing the governing of conduct right across a social formation.

> Government [in the sixteenth century] ... designated the way in which the conduct of individuals or of groups might be directed: the government of children, of souls, of communities, of families, of the sick. It did not only cover the legitimately constituted forms of political or economic subjection, but also modes of action, more or less considered and calculated, which were destined to act upon the possibilities of action of other people. To govern, in this sense, is to structure the possible field of actions of others.
>
> (Foucault, in Dreyfus and Rabinow 1982: 221)

The exercise of power through the governing of conduct presupposes and requires an active and free subject. There is then a relationship between power and freedom that is mutually constitutive. To put this in another way, if the exercise of power is replaced by factors that *determine* action, then there is no longer an exercise of power; it has been supplanted by a situation of constraint – the action of the subject is constrained or determined. Freedom thus is a pre-requisite and necessary condition for the exercise of power and is found in the 'agonism' (Foucault, in Dreyfus and Rabinow 1982: 222) of relations of power – there is always on the one hand an incitation to act in a particular way and on the other the possibility of acting willfully in disregard of this incitation.

Even although Foucault's early work suggests the necessity of the study of the micro-physics of power (in terms of power relations at the micro-level), in later work he begins to consider questions of how micro-relations of power become more widely articulated: 'how do diverse power relations come to be colonized and articulated into more general mechanisms that sustain more encompassing forms of domination and ... how are they linked to specific forms and means of producing knowledge?' (Jessop 2007: 36).

Rose (1999) puts it in another way when he uses the term 'translation' to explain the constantly changing links between the micro-physics of power and the objectives of government: 'In the dynamics of translation, alignments are forged between the objectives of authorities wishing to govern and the personal projects of those organizations, groups and individuals who are the subjects of government' (Rose 1999: 48).

To reject power as a unified theory, and as emanating from a particular point, is of course to reject theorizations of the state as the source of a power to which we give up our freedom: 'I do, I want to, and I must pass on state theory – just as one would with an indigestible meal' (Foucault, in Jessop 2007: 35). How then are we to understand government and the institutions of the state through which we are governed? The modern idea of the universal state is now displaced. The power and control of the modern state is to be identified in 'social norms and institutions and distinctive forms of knowledge rather than sovereign authority' (Jessop 2007: 35). The state, as the subject, is decentred. There is no pre-given construction of a state as actor or as essence. Instead, the state can be seen as an epistemological pattern of assumption about governing (Hultqvist 2004), thus shifting the focus from an analysis of the state to a focus on how power and knowledge operate within the taken-for-granted ways we perceive our present time – the how and what of power.

Of course systems and institutions of education involve the exercise of power as the conduct of conduct and the organization of people into groups and hierarchies. Indeed these are pre-eminent characteristics within institutions of education, in the sense that they not only involve leading and channelling the conduct of teachers and students, and organization of these people into groups and hierarchies, but also produce people to fit into wider sorts of roles and organizations. In this is an implication that power relations involve some sort of calculative strategy over how the leading or directing of how the conduct of conduct might be done (Dean 1999).

However, to consider 'strategy' in relation to power is not to restrict it to an idea that is derived from the state or institutions themselves. Rather, 'the state is nothing more than the mobile effect of a regime of multiple governmentalities' (Foucault, in Jessop 2007: 36) and strategy is a means for the coordination of power relations that is derived in some way from them. Strategy might be employed in three ways that come together within a power relation (Foucault, in Dreyfus and Rabinow 1982: 224–5):

- through a rationality that is aimed to achieve specific ends as the outcome of action;
- through the way in which a subject acts in terms of what he or she considers the action of another is likely to be and what the other thinks the subject will do, in order to gain advantage; and
- in the procedures used to reduce the possibility of the struggle and confrontation of the other.

To consider lifelong learning in this way is in part to examine what it might be as a strategy that brings forth empirical change within prior relations of power. Thus we are engaged in the analysis of lifelong learning in terms of how it is exercised as power, and what happens empirically in situations where people say that lifelong learning is involved in the reconfiguring of educational relations and in the construction of new ones that may have nothing to do with those that went before.

Governmentality

The notion of governmentality is taken up in two main ways within work drawing upon Foucault and in attempts to understand the significance of changes in contemporary life (Dean 1999; Edwards and Nicoll 2007). One is as a framing within which to analyse practices of governing. Here there is a focus on the different forms of power in society: sovereign power invested in the monarch, disciplinary power invested in nation-states that has as its object the disciplining of individuals within a territory, and governmentality (bio-power) that regulates populations as resources to be used and optimized. For Foucault, discipline and regulation signify the ways in which life has become a matter of care in the exercise of power, they cover 'the whole surface that lies between the organic and the biological, between body and populations'. According to Foucault (2003a), bio-power emerges at a particular moment within the modern state as a coherent political technology based on disciplinary power, as a concern for the human species and interest in the body as an object to be manipulated. Through the emergence of science (e.g. statistics) the interest in the body changed from its reproductive function to the possibility of manipulating it. For example, through bio-power education emerged as a public effort between the state and the individual. The population was to be regulated in accordance to the need of society through schooling in which power operated on the body (discipline) as to shape it in specific ways.

As a second way of drawing upon a notion of governmentality (cf. Dean 1999), liberal modes of government are distinguishable as governing through the freedom and capacities of the individual and this requires and forms a particular and technical 'mentality' within advanced liberal democratic states. Here 'It … [governmentality] … deals with how we think about governing, with the different mentalities of government' (Dean 1999: 16, parenthesis inserted). 'Thinking' here is conceived as a collective activity that draws from 'the bodies of knowledge, belief and opinion in which we are immersed' (Dean 1999: 16); mentalities as in some sense a 'condition' of thought are not usually open to question by those who use them. Mentalities may be derived, at least in part, from the disciplines of the human sciences but they are not in any way dependant upon these. To take up governmentality in this sense within an analysis is to be concerned with the way in which mentalities become joined up and channelled effectively through relations of power as a means for the conduct of conduct and within regimes of practices or government:

> The analysis of government is concerned with thought as it becomes linked to and is embedded in technical means for the shaping and reshaping of conduct and in practices and institutions. Thus to analyse mentalities of government is to analyse thought made practical and technical.
>
> (Dean 1999: 18)

Here the emphasis is on regimes of practice or government. Such regimes of course involve those practices of the production of knowledge and truth, and knowledge and truth are drawn upon in the constitution of those mentalities that we use to inform our activities. Regimes of practice, knowledge and truth, mentalities and activities are thus dependant upon and require each other within a circular arrangement.

As we have been outlining it here, government concerns the conduct of conduct and requires an active and free subject. As we have seen above: '[i]t therefore entails the possibility that the governed are to some extent capable of acting and thinking otherwise' (Dean 1999: 15). For Dean (1999: 15), liberal modes of government are those that try to work through the freedom and capacities of those who are governed, and may indeed conceive of freedom as the technical means to secure the aims of government: 'To say this is to say that liberal mentalities of rule generally attempt to define the nature, source, effects and possible utility of these capacities of acting and thinking'. Here different notions – 'mentalities' – of freedom attempt to shape the field of possibilities for the exercise of freedom, although they can never fully determine it. As Dean (1999) points out, Adam Smith's notion of liberty as a natural attribute of *Homo oeconomicus* differs from that of Friedrich Hayek as that of the exercise of the rational choice of the individual within the market. As we see then, this is not to assume that 'the governed' exist in any real way, 'only multiple objectifications of those over whom government is to be exercised, and whose characteristics government must harness and instrumentalize' (Rose 1999: 40).

Focusing on the governability of subjects Foucault (2003a) asks the question – What rationalities of governing are constructed in specific historical spaces? The focus of his analysis is on the emergence of the modern social state, the forms of modern exercise of power and its different expressions. Through the modern state the exercise of power has become more finely meshed, expanded and scattered. The result is an increased governability, through regulation and the standardization of peoples' conduct (Hultqvist and Petersson 1995). We could say that in a governmentality analysis one links a micro-analysis of power relations as they are played out in its extreme point of exercise (Foucault 1980) in different practices shaping the self-organizing capacities of individuals, to analyses of practices deemed political and aimed at the management of large-scale characteristics of populations and territories (Rose 1999). For example, lifelong learning can be analysed as a political technology aimed to shape learning citizens in the name of national prosperity. Such a political practice is linked to different micro-practices in which the learning citizen is fostered, e.g. in job-seeking enhancement (see Fogde in this book), in academic writing (see Solomon in this book) and in recognition of prior learning (see Andersson in this book).

Today, for many in a time of a neoliberal governmentality, we can see how governing is practiced through alliances between different authorities that seek to regulate the economy, social life and the life of the individual (Hultqvist and Petersson 1995) as a contrast to the natural and spontaneous order of Hayekian liberalism (Peters 2001). Thus, freedom has been reconceptualized. Now, we are defined as autonomous and active individuals who seek self-realization in the name of freedom. Neoliberalism thus constitutes a particular relationship between government and the governed. The governed are subjects of their own lives who practice freedom as a form of self-governance (Burchell 1996). One could say that neoliberalism promotes a specific form of freedom as a way of integrating the self-conduct of the governed into the practices of government. Freedom has become a specific form of resource for government, where the citizen's expression of their freedom coincides with the political ambition to govern – freedom has become both the instrument and the effect of governing. It is possible to relate such a practice to the changes in governing during the twentieth century, for example, as a shift from a social state, governing through institutional legislation during the early twentieth century, to an enabling state governing through each citizen's choices (Rose 1996). Neoliberal rule is based on and supports each citizen's freedom to choose while regulating behaviour.

Governing the subject

As governing attempts to shape, foster and maximize the capacities of the population and each citizen, the target of governing practices becomes the 'thing' to be governed – the subjects. Or to phrase it differently, in a governmentality analysis the interest is directed towards the specific ways human beings are made objects of knowledge and their subjection through different techniques in specific historical practices. In such an analysis subjects are not seen as a priori entities with specific characteristics and agency. Instead, in line with Foucault (2003b), the subject is decentred and analysed as being shaped in specific ways in different historical practices. Thus, instead of studying subjects as agents (a priori), the focus is on studying the specific historical practices, the discourses (lifelong learning, for example) produced by and producing these practices and what different subject positions are constituted through them. In a decentring of the idea of the unified, coherent self, there is potential for a multiplicity of subjectivities, multiple and partial uptakes, constraints and elisions.

As we have mentioned, for government to operate it requires knowledge about the 'thing' that is to be governed. Thus, knowledge discursively defined as legitimate forms the basis for the operation of government. For Foucault (1980), power and knowledge are not external to each other, nor are they identical. Instead, they are intertwined in a correlative relationship, which is determined in its historical specificity. For power to operate, it needs to be grounded in knowledge about the things it operates on and in relation to. Knowledge about the subject is the basis for the operation of power and power defines what knowledge is legitimate. Thus, a study of government also includes a study of what is possible and not possible to think in different historical practices, the regimes of truth concerning the conduct of conduct, the way one may speak, who is authorized to speak etc. For example, what possible ways are there to speak about the participant in adult education (see Fejes in this book), its characteristics (see Ahl in this book) or the child (see Popkewitz in this book) and what has made such speech possible?

In his writings, Foucault presented several ideas about how subjectivity is fabricated, but all in some way relating to the idea of the decentring of the subject. He argued that the goal of his work has been to:

> [C]reate a history of the different modes by which, in our culture, human beings are made subjects. My work has dealt with three modes of objectification that transforms the human beings into subjects. The first is the modes of inquiry that try to give themselves the status of sciences .... In the second part of my work, I have studied the objectivizing of the subject in what I shall call 'dividing practices' .... Finally, I have sought to study – it is my current work – the way a human being turns him/herself into a subject.
>
> (Foucault 2003b:126)

Thus, for Foucault there is no project of trying to construct a general history of the human subject. People have been represented as subjects in a whole variety of ways throughout history. Instead, the focus is to try and map out and to make visible the discursive conditions which make possible the emergence of specific subjectivities, the techniques which operate to shape such subjectivities and the practices in which we turn ourselves into what is deemed desirable – to govern ourselves – the conduct of conduct. For example, the 'lifelong learner' is a particular neoliberal form of just such a subjectivity. The lifelong learner requires correlative practices and techniques of objectification and subjectification in order that it may be governed as one of 'the people' of today. Thus, in an analysis of the lifelong learner through an analytics of governmentality, it becomes central to ask a question of the subjectivities that are brought forth. Put another way, what kind of objects are constructed as governable subjects within discursive practices? Instead of studying lifelong learners as if we know what they already are, the focus is on studying the subjectivities that are 'made up', both made possible or constrained and elided through such discourses.

To study how subjectivities are being shaped, an analytics of governmentality analyses the specific technologies, techniques and tactics which operate in discourse as to shape desirable subjectivities. Technologies do not have any essence and they are not the direct linear output of a specific will to govern or any intention. Instead, they are assemblages of aspirations, beliefs, knowledge, practices of calculations etc., which aspire to shape specific subjectivities (Rose 1999). Foucault (2003a: 237) expresses it:

> [T]he finality of government resides in the things it manages and in the pursuit of the perfection and intensification of the processes it directs; and the instrument of government, instead of being laws, now come to be a range of multiple tactics.

If we return to the lifelong learner, one example of such technology operating as to shape such subjectivity is confession. In educational practices, educational guidance is a function which aims to support the pupil in their choices. For example, the adult learner in Sweden who wishes to enter adult education will meet the educational counsellor to discuss, through dialogue, what kind of education they wish to enter, with what pace of study, with which educational organizer, during which hours of the day etc. (Fejes 2006). In such practice, confession operates as to shape a specific subjectivity – an individual who is responsible for their education and whose will to learn is being shaped. Through expressing one's inner desires to the confessor (educational counsellor) one's self becomes an object of knowledge (visible for calculation), at the same time there is a process of subjectification. To acknowledge the confessional practice means that you also acknowledge the legitimacy of such practice. Thus, the learner being guided has accepted being positioned as a specific kind of learner – one who constantly learns and whose learning is never finished (see Edwards in this book). Further, in such practice, the dialogue pedagogy and the creation of a study plan (a form of contract in which the pupil and the counsellor agrees on what the pupil will study, in what forms etc.) operate as techniques or tactics which shape the subjectivity of the lifelong learner as one who desires to learn all the time, and one who takes responsibility for her/his own learning.

To summarize, in a governmentality analysis questions of interest might be:

*   What rationalities of governing are constructed?
*   What subjectivities are brought forth?
*   How is governing conducted?
*   What is the teleos of government (cf. Dean 1999)?

By a focus on the how and what of power we are able to take a critical attitude towards and to question our present by making visible how power operates and what the effects of such operations are. This is a normative task as it does not offer any prescription of what the result of such questioning might be – an exemplary criticism instead of foundational critique and prescription (cf. Dean 1999). However, as will be seen, the chapters in this book have different uptakes of Foucault. Thus the issues of normativity and prescription are handled differently.

... And so further

Explorations of the means by which lifelong learning is brought forth, and exercised and promulgated as power within discourses, and the effects of this, will help formulate understandings of lifelong learning in the governance of the subject. Rather than simply engage in a struggle over truth, which we have seen may be counterproductive, we can bring out how lifelong learning comes to be persuasive and powerful, and how the narrations of it that we come to take as truthful might be made to stutter or be countered.

References

Biesta, G. (2006) 'What's the point of lifelong learning if lifelong learning has no point? On the democratic deficit of policies for lifelong learning', *European Educational Research Journal*, 5: 169–80.

Burchell, G. (1996) 'Liberal government and techniques of the self', in A. Barry, T. Osborne and N. Rose (eds), *Foucault and Political Reason: Liberalism, Neo-Liberalism and Rationalities of Government*, Chicago: The University of Chicago Press: 19–36.

Dean, M. (1999) *Governmentality: Power and Rule in Modern Society*, London: Sage Publications.

DEETYA (1998) *Learning for Life, Final Report: Review of Higher Education Financing and Policy*, Canberra: DEETYA.

DfEE (Department for Education and Employment) (1998) *The Learning Age: A Renaissance for a New Britain*, London: Stationary Office.

DfEE (1999) *Learning to Succeed: A New Framework for Post-16 Learning*, London: Stationary Office.

DfES (2006) *Further Education: Raising Skills, Improving Life Chances*, London: DfES.

Dreyfus, H. and Rabinow, P. (1982) *Michel Foucault: Beyond Structuralism and Hermeneutics*, London: Harvester Weatsheaf.

Edwards, R. and Nicoll, K. (2007) 'Action at a distance: governmentality, subjectivity and workplace learning', in S. Billett, T. Fenwick and M. Summerville (eds), *Work, Subjectivity and Learning: Understanding Learning Through Working Life*, Dordrecht: Springer.

European Commission (1993) *Growth, Competitiveness, Employment*, Luxemburg: Office for Official Publications of the European Communities.

European Commission (1996) *Teaching and Learning: Towards a Learning Society*, Luxembourg: Office for Official Publications of the European Communities.

European Commission (2000) *Commission Staff Working Paper, Memorandum on Lifelong Learning*, Brussels: European Commission.

Fejes, A. (2006) *Constructing the Adult Learner: A Governmentality Analysis*, Linköping: Liu-Tryck.

Field, J. (2000) *Lifelong Learning and the New Educational Order*, Stoke on Trent: Trentham Books.

Foucault, M. (1980) *Power/Knowledge: Selected Interviews and Other Writings 1972–1977*, New York: Pantheon.

Foucault, M. (1983) 'On the genealogy of ethics: an overview of work in progress', in H.L. Dreyfus and P. Rabinow (eds), *Michel Foucault: Beyond Structuralism and Hermeneutics*, Chicago: The University of Chicago press.

Foucault, M. (2003a) 'Governmentality', in P. Rabinow and N. Rose (eds), *The Essential Foucault: Selections from the Essential Works of Foucault 1954–1984,* New York: The New Press.

Foucault, M. (2003b) 'The subject and power', in P. Rabinow and N. Rose (eds), *The Essential Foucault: Selections from the Essential Works of Foucault 1954–1984*, New York: The New Press.

Gustavsson, B. (2002) 'What do we mean by lifelong learning and knowledge?' *International Journal of Lifelong Education*, 21: 13–23.

Hultqvist, K. (2004) 'The traveling state: the nation, and the subject of education', in B.M. Baker and K.E. Heyning (eds), *Dangerous Coagulations? The Uses of Foucault in the Study of Education*, New York: Peter Lang.

Hultqvist, K. and Petersson, K. (eds) (1995) *Foucault: Namnet på en Modern Vetenskaplig och Filosofisk Problematik*, Stockholm: HLS Förlag.

Jessop, B. (2007) 'From micro-powers to governmentality: Foucault's work on statehood, state formation, statecraft and state power', *Political Geography*, 26: 34–40.

Kennedy, H. (1997) *Learning Works: Widening Participation in Further Education*, Coventry: FEFC.

Masschelein, J. (2004) 'How to conceive of critical educational theory today?', *Journal of Philosophy of Education*, 38: 352–67.

NAGCELL (National Advisory Group for Continuing Education and Lifelong Learning) (1997) *Learning for the Twenty-first Century, First Report of the National Advisory Group for Continuing Education and Lifelong Learning*, Sheffield: DfEE.

NAGCELL (1999) *Creating Learning Cultures: Next Steps in Achieving the Learning Age, Second Report of the National Advisory Group for Continuing Education and Lifelong Learning*, Sheffield: DfEE

NCIHE (National Committee of Inquiry into Higher Education) (1997) *Higher Education in the Learning Society: Summary Report*, Norwich: HMSO.

National Commission on Teaching and America's Future (NCTAF) (1996) *What Matters Most: Teaching for America's future*, Washington, DC: National Commission on Teaching and America's Future.

Peters, M. A. (2001) *Poststructuralism, Marxism and Neoliberalism: Between Theory and Politics*, Lanham: Rowan & Littlefiedl Publishers, INC.

Rose, N. (1996) 'Governing "advanced" liberal democracies', in A. Barry, T. Osborne and N. Rose (eds), *Foucault and Political Reason: Liberalism, Neo-liberalism and Rationalities of Government*, Chicago: The University of Chicago Press.

Rose, N. (1999) *Powers of Freedom: Reframing Political Thought*, Cambridge: Cambridge University Press.

Rubenson, K. (2004) 'Lifelong learning: a critical assessment of the political project', in P. Alheit, R. Becker-Schmidt, T. Gitz-Johansen, L. Ploug, H. Salling Olesen and K. Rubenson (eds), *Shaping an Emerging Reality – Researching Lifelong Learning*, Roskilde: Roskilde University Press.

Scottish Executive (Scottish Executive – SE) (2003) Life Through Learning: Learning Through Life. The Lifelong Learning Strategy for Scotland www.scotland.gov.uk/Resource/Doc/47032/0028819.pdf (accessed 9 September 2007).

UNESCO (1996) *Learning: The Treasure Within, Report to UNESCO of the International Commission on Education for the Twenty-first Century*, Paris: UNESCO.

UNESCO (1997) *Open and Distance Learning: Prospects and Policy Considerations*, Paris: UNESCO.

Section 1

Governing policy subjects

Chapter 2

Actively seeking subjects?

Richard Edwards

Discourses are powerful and some are more powerful than others. States and governments are powerful. Through political and policy-making processes, they attempt to inscribe certain practices with particular kinds of meanings and position actors as having particular roles and dispositions, thereby shaping the institutional climate within which people work and live. Institutions, such as churches/mosques and universities, through their practices traditionally authorized certain discourses, thus making them more powerful than others. In exploring the discourses of lifelong learning, there is therefore a need to explore the ways in which certain of them have become more powerful than others and how these are intertwined with wider practices in the social order. This also involves examining the exercises of power within which they are entangled.

The multiplicity of discourses of lifelong learning does not come from nowhere, nor are their uptakes arbitrary. It is important therefore that lifelong learning has emerged as a significant policy discourse, predominantly in certain of the Organization for Economic Co-operation and Development (OECD) countries, at a time of rapid economic and social change with all the consequent insecurities and uncertainties that are invariably identified as an aspect of the impact of globalizing processes. What do lifelong learning discourses mean in this context, where lifelong learning and globalization co-emerge?

There have been many tracings and translations of the discourses of lifelong learning with a multiplicity of meanings generated from these analyses. Like the postmodern, lifelong learning with its current concern for developing human capital means for some an abandonment of the traditional significance for education of the struggles for personal development, justice and social equality. However, the complexity of practices that fashion the social order suggests the need for caution in trying to explain the discourses of lifelong learning simply in terms of the codes of 'the knowledge economy', 'capitalism', 'globalization' or 'the new work order'. This is not to say that these codes are unimportant. However, their importance rests more in their semiotic positioning of certain social practices within particular discursive domains than in their description and explanation of what is 'truly' going on. They are not merely commentaries on politics and policy but integral to the discursive struggles to inscribe certain meanings rather than others in the language games of lifelong learning. How powerful they are remains an open question.

Foucault's (1979, 1980, 1981, 1991) accounts of power and the historical changes in its mode of deployment in ordering the social opens up possibilities for exploring the significance of the discourses of lifelong learning in changing conditions. In so doing, it provides the possibilities for analysis without reducing lifelong learning to a mere epiphenomenon of some deeper underlying structure(s) of meaning. In this chapter, I am particularly interested in Foucauldian conceptions of power and their possible relation to those practices within which lifelong learning is assembled and the forms of subjectivity with which it is associated. I do not pretend that Foucault is the only voice providing useful insights, nor that his work provides a full set of answers to the questions we may pose. However, it does offer useful positionings in the discursive struggles in which we engage.

Discourse and the disciplining of individuals

It is now well known that Foucault's (1979, 1980) work challenges certain general assumptions of the separation of knowledge from power. Power and knowledge, power-knowledge, are always found embedded together in discursive regimes of truth. According to Foucault, a discourse is a structuring of meaning-making whose major characteristic is its disciplinary and hence regulatory power. Foucault's argument is that in every social order the production of discourse is at once controlled, selected, organized and redistributed according to certain rules and structures. Any social order requires that people are not free to say or do anything, whenever and wherever they like. It is the risk of this that requires discourse, in its everyday sense, to be corralled, controlled and channeled, and it is 'discourse' in Foucault's sense that does this. A Foucauldian discourse therefore defines what can be included and what is prohibited. It covers objects that can be known and spoken about, rituals that must be carried out and the right to speak of a particular subject, who can speak, from what institutional base and about what. These prohibitions and possibilities interrelate, reinforce and complement each other, forming a complex web, continually subject to modification. Discourse fashions subjects in terms of social positioning, subjectivity and voice. Thus it is powerful, both productively and in prohibiting. A 'discourse' is a unit of human action, interaction, communication and cognition, not just a unit of language. It is not simply a way of expressing a pre-existing reality, nor a reference to things that pre-exist statements about them. Discourse is *constitutive* of knowledge, rather than simply the neutral expression or representation of something outside language. It fashions *representations* and shapes *actions*, making different ways of knowing the world and of acting within it possible.

Discourse is a way of representing knowledge about a particular domain at a particular historical moment, for example, madness at the beginning of the nineteenth century, sexuality at its end and, here, lifelong learning at the beginning of the twenty-first century. Discourse defines the domain and produces the objects of knowledge within that domain. It also influences how ideas are put into practice and used to regulate conduct. This means that meaning is fashioned *through* discourse. Here meaning performs, with discourse merging into *praxis*, in the process subverting the common-sense distinction between talking and doing. Foucault traces the emergence of discourses that have shaped modern institutions such as the prison, the asylum and the hospital. It is from these institutional sites that discourse is authorized and from and through which individuals are regulated.

Discursive practices render particular aspects of existence meaningful in particular ways, which then become thinkable and calculable and thus amenable to intervention and regulation, with documentation, computation and evaluation as the main instruments or technologies for achieving this. It is through these practices that power is exercised and where it takes particular forms. In relation to the institutions emerging with the modern nation state, the dominant form of power is discipline, displacing the coercive power of sovereign monarchies and where lifelong learning sits within this framing and its institutionalization are two of the questions that need to be addressed.

Pedagogic practices have always been associated with the incorporation of individuals into such discursive regimes of truth. People are regulated through these regimes but also through their actions support their reproduction. Most importantly, knowledge links to power, not only assuming the authority of 'the truth' but also with the power to *make itself* true. All knowledge, once co-implicated with action, has real *effects*, and in that sense *becomes* true, or more accurately *counts* as true.

Given this analysis, for lifelong learning to be mobilized as meaningful, it is necessary that disciplinary practices emerge in correlative power-knowledge formations embedded in discourse(s) that define truth. To put it another way, truth-making practices of lifelong learning need to take hold. Such practices operate through technologies that draw upon and perpetuate a mind/body dualism, inscribing the educated/uneducated, the trained/untrained, the skilled/unskilled, the competent/incompetent, and through these inscriptions allowing the construction of standards and the deployment of normalizing judgement. Here we see the means that realize the performance of what Foucault referred to as the disciplinary practices in training and re-shaping 'docile bodies'.

However, these docile bodies must also be *active subjects*, because discipline does not turn people simply into passive objects. Indeed, discipline as a form through which power is exercised cannot work unless subjects are *capable of action*, even if this capacity is not the same as that identified by those who insist on human free will. It is through mobilization into discursive regimes that people become active subjects inscribed with certain capacities to act. Here the meaning of human agency does not entail an escape from power, but consists rather of a specific exercise of power – one is empowered in particular ways through becoming the subject of, and subjected to, power. Thus, even social movements entail exercises of power, even as they might oppose the power of governments. Capacities are brought forth and evaluated through the disciplinary technologies of observation, normalization, judgement and examination, the extent, criteria and methods for which are provided by the discourses in play. Here to become inscribed within certain discourses of lifelong learning is to become an active subject of a particular sort, one for whom care of the self – the ways in which we conduct ourselves – through the technology of learning becomes an expression of (self-)discipline.

The relationship between education as a discursive regime of truth, with an associated set of disciplinary practices, and other discursive regimes is of interest here. The latter themselves entail a range of pedagogical practices to effectively do the work they do. For instance, the academic discipline of social work provides a regime of truth for induction into the practice of social work and in defining what it means to be a social worker. Implicit within this is a range of pedagogical practices that in part are explicitly educational. The discursive regime of social work thereby has an implicit pedagogy which traditionally is either not itself an explicit part of the discourse of that (academic) subject or sits at the margins of disciplinary discourses. What this means is that for Foucault, the modern disciplined, normalized social order is underpinned by a set of pedagogical practices which at one and the same time are explicitly the concern of educational discourse, but which are practiced in *all* social organizations and institutions. However, educational discourse usually identifies the practices of education as an institution. This wider understanding of pedagogy across the social order and within other disciplines is denoted through the emergence of the discourse of lifelong learning. In this sense, discourses of lifelong learning can fashion and mobilize a range of embodied subjectivities within and through the wider disciplines. These subjectivities are not a natural 'given', but are themselves effects of discursive practices. It is partly the extent to which these come to be mobilized that lifelong learning becomes a site for explicit pedagogic debate and practice, even as it challenges the exclusivity of educational institutions as pedagogical institutionalizations of disciplinary power. Shifts within education, such as shifts towards and within the framing of lifelong learning, therefore provide the possibility for disturbing the pedagogical practices that form and maintain other discursive regimes and, with that, the subjectivities of individuals and, in the case of lifelong learning, their subjectivity precisely as *learners*. 'Lifelong learner' therefore in part displaces the docile body of disciplinary practices, as both a response to wider changes and a contributor to them.

Undoubtedly, the significance of Foucault's work poses a paradox for many educators. Many understandings tend to view education as the slow unfolding of knowledge and truth, a humanizing and developmental process, one which results in individual and social progress, enlightenment and emancipation. However, what are we to make of the ever more extensive knowledge generated in and about learning, and those further dimensions of the learner to be framed for pedagogical intervention? Wherever there are social practices, so increasingly learning seems to be identified as taking place (Chaiklin and Lave 1996). At the same time, disciplinary practices seem to be ever more intrusive, the technologies for 'governing the soul' provocatively referred to by Rose (1989). Could this be part of the powerful significance of contemporary discourses of lifelong learning?

In Foucault's terms, wherever and whenever learning takes place, those learners are required to bring forth their subjectivities for disciplining so that they can become a particular type of person. In becoming subject to particular disciplinary regimes, people also become active 'subjects'. Yet discipline was not the only form of power explored by Foucault. As well as discipline, the discourses of lifelong learning can also be positioned in relation to contemporary forms of governmentality.

Governmentality and populations

In recent years, there has been increasing interest in developing Foucault's later ideas on power associated with the concept of governmentality. Governmentality is 'an ensemble formed by the institutions, procedures, analyses and reflections, the calculations and tactics, that allow the exercise of this very specific albeit complex form of power' (Foucault 1991: 20). There are two main senses in which he is interpreted as using this notion. One is as a framing within which to analyse the practices through which governing in general takes place alongside other forms of power. In addition to disciplinary power invested in nation states, which has as its object the regulation of individuals within a territory, there is also sovereign power invested in the monarch and *biopower* which involves a governmentality that regulates populations as resources to be used and optimized. The legitimacy of governmentality derives from its capacity to nurture individual life by integrating bodies, capacities and pleasures into a productive force. The training of bodies requires the development of healthy populations and vice versa. Discourse comprises an ensemble of practices indispensable to governmentality, in the sense of governing that is not confined to the state and its institutions but is spread throughout the social order. What is identified here is that governing is about increasing productivity or capacities rather than simply training to be docile. To achieve this, subjects again need to be known, a knowledge that forms the basis of efficient management and the maximization of productive capacity in all parts and levels of the social order. Without this knowledge the risks that are inevitably involved in the process of maximizing productivity would be too great for this project to be successfully realized. Thus with governmentality, it is essential that subjects become empowered in the sense of their capacities being maximized. Governing is distributed and at a distance from the state.

On this reading, the policy discourses of lifelong learning are not only exercises of power but also signal a change in the ways in which power is being exercised and the social form thus ordered. For Foucault (2003), discipline and regulation identify the ways in which the exercise of power in life has become a matter of self-care. Here, since power is enmeshed with regulation, there is a process of self-regulation where subjects accept a regulation which is self-imposed though the internalizing of the regulating gaze. With governmentality subjects are still fashioned within power-knowledge relations, but this is now brought about by inciting people to talk about their desire and to signify themselves as subjects of desire, a desire which includes a *desire for learning*. Reflecting on oneself signifies the uncovering of a hidden truth about the self. Subjectivity is fashioned around this uncovering which reveals and enables the fulfillment of desires. Stern self-improvement through discipline is supplemented and displaced by the play of desire as a sign of learning.

For Foucault then, governmentality is concerned with the conduct of conduct and this involves regarding 'the forces and capacities of living individuals, as members of a population, as resources to be fostered, to be used, to be optimized' (Dean 1999: 20). Thus, as Dean suggests, 'to analyze government is to analyze those practices that try and shape, sculpt, mobilize and work through the choices, desires, aspirations, needs, wants and lifestyles of individuals and groups' (Dean 1999: 12). Government then is the disciplining into a form of life *freely accepted* that works by shaping subjectivity through the 'educating' of subjects who would otherwise remain 'undisciplined' and therefore unproductive. This mode of shaping becomes increasingly important within cultures where disciplining through force, coercion or intrusive regulation meets with increasing disapproval. In contemporary culture therefore, governmentality involves a non-coercive *pastoral power* that works through infiltrating regulation into the very interior of the experience of subjects (Rose 1989). Subjects 'educate' or fashion themselves, a process where subjective experiences are simultaneously shaped and yet paradoxically remain uniquely one's own.

Governing therefore does not so much *determine* people's subjectivities, but rather elicits, fosters, promotes and attributes it. It is not oppressive in any obvious sense, but instead it works on, through, and with, *active* subjects by promoting working on oneself through, among other things, processes of reflection and reflexivity. Thus, the changing exercises of power are coded by changing discourses of learning, with greater emphasis placed on the fashioning of reflective spaces through which to do the work required in the care of the self. What this suggests is that the regulation of populations combines with the disciplining of individuals to mobilize subjects who may combine differing aspects and combinations of docile bodies and active subjectivities, and where notions of reflection become more the order of the day. Here reflection is not simply a more humane or empowering form of pedagogic practice. It is still a form of regulation, but one that is more subtle and apparently less intrusive, enabling individuals to have more space so that they can act upon and for themselves and express desires.

This is a view explored by Barry (2001), who uses changes in the pedagogical practices of museums as analogies for the changing exercises of power in governing more generally. He posits what he rightly indicates is a too simplistic dichotomy of, on the one hand, discipline that aims to produce docile bodies with the imperative to learn. Here museum visitors are positioned to engage in passive contemplation of static displays. On the other hand, Barry posits interactivity, which encourages flexibility and offers the possibility of discovery. Here visitors are positioned to participate interactively with dynamic displays and simulations. This position is embedded in certain pedagogic discourses of reflection and experiential learning. It is not hard to see how these ideas about changing forms of governing relate to the policy discourses of lifelong learning more widely, where elements of docility and the imperative to be active by learning (or else!) are to be found alongside the encouragement to become flexible, adaptable, enterprising and invitations to discover. Both identify exercises of power, but the practices associated with them and the possibilities for a multiplicity of positions and shaping of subjectivity differ as they ebb and flow. This therefore provides possibilities for multiple meanings of lifelong learning.

Through the elaboration of the interstices between these forms of power and their differing practices, we may illuminate the complexities of contemporary mobilizations of lifelong learning in ways which go beyond some of the over-generalized discourses that currently fashion its meaning(s).

Actively seeking subjects

One influential argument that has been put forward is that the shifts in governing aim to fashion active subjects through the norms and values associated with 'responsible' consuming and enterprise. Here, subjectivities are themselves re-fashioned to elicit a particular image of human beings:

> The self is to be a subjective being, it is to aspire to autonomy, it is to strive for personal fulfillment in its earthly life, it is to interpret its reality and destiny as a matter of individual responsibility, it is to find meaning in existence by shaping its life through acts of choice.
>
> (Rose 1998: 151)

It is the ethos of enterprise that helps to re-shape subjectivity through self-fashioning. This enterprise, usually coded in discourses of flexibility, adaptability and innovation, can be found in many policies concerning employability and competitiveness. For Foucault, ethics are not formalized moral codes, abstract senses of right and wrong. They are construed as the practices through which one evaluates and acts upon oneself, what Foucault refers to as 'technologies of the self' (Foucault 1988). These are the devices that enable the fashioning of personal identity, or a means by which people fashion themselves as subjects. Technologies, including those of the self, are the means whereby subjects come to accept, value, desire and strive to achieve congruence between their personal objectives and those objectives external to themselves – an internalization of external objectives.

Insofar as enterprise, flexibility and innovation are positioned as essential to the 'good life', a range of technologies, or pedagogic practices, are deployed through which human beings are positioned as enterprising, innovative and flexible learners. Organizational technologies (involving the exercise of power) and technologies of the self (the fashioning of subjectivity) become aligned with technologies of success (motivation and enterprise). The organizationally desirable (more productivity, flexible working, increased efficiency, maximization of outputs) counts as the personally desirable (greater self-fulfillment through performing excellently and being recognized as such). In this way, subjects are brought forth who are (self-) fashioned and positioned as active learners *and* as self-regulating subjects, where the subjectivity stimulated is one that regards the maximization of capacities and dispositions appropriate to maximizing their own productivity as both necessary and desirable. Subjects with an enterprising relationship to the *self* are framed in certain discourses of learning, a self that exhibits qualities of autonomy, self-management and personal responsibility, and reflectiveness.

This work of acting upon oneself is supported by 'experts of organizational life, engineering human relations through architecture, timetabling, super-visory systems, payment schemes, curricula, and the like' (Rose 1998: 154). The social order is itself positioned as a learning order and different actors are mobilized to be worked upon to enhance their desire for learning to choose and choosing to learn in order that they become enterprising and flexible. At the same time, however, it is important to emphasize that these technologies can only *shape* rather than determine, because once people become active subjects there is also brought forth the capability to fashion different meanings and to code their practices differently.

Du Gay (1996) argues that the ethos of enterprise is crucial to the development of discourses of flexibility among nations, organizations and individuals in support of economic competitiveness. Here the discourses ascribe particular meanings to practices which actually perform that flexibility. Thus, in workplaces, workers are subject to practices of management, appraisal and development that attempt to position them as enterprising subjects, engaged in an 'enterprise of the self'. In this position,

> no matter what hand circumstances may have dealt a person, he or she remains always continuously engaged ... in that one enterprise ... In this

sense the character of the entrepreneur can no longer be seen as just one among a plurality of ethical personalities *but must rather be seen as assuming an ontological priority*.

(du Gay 1996: 181, emphasis in original)

Exposure to the risks and costs of these activities are constructed as enabling workers to take responsibility for their actions, signifying a form of empowerment and success within the organization. Nor is this restricted to careers alone, as the whole of life is inscribed with this ethos of enterprise. Here 'certain enterprising qualities – such as self-reliance, personal responsibility, boldness and a willingness to take risks in the pursuit of goals – are regarded as human virtues and promoted as such' (du Gay 1996: 56). Fashioning people's values, norms, desires and dispositions therefore becomes a key dimension of organizational change through the recoding of the meaning of work and its significance in people's lives. We might then want to position change agents in organizational and political life as *discourse technologists* whose task is to re-code the meaning of practices. Here the directions and processes of change are formed through the attempted production of a shared ethic, in effect a set of shared meanings, that both exposes all to the risks of failure and failing to change (the 'or else' mentioned earlier), but also inscribes shared desires, goals and aspirations.

The ethos of enterprise is both prescriptive and powerful and the practices through which it is fashioned are many and varied. As Rose (1999) indicates, one of the calculations in which an enterprising self engages is that to do with its own learning. There is a felt need to adopt an active learning approach to life and to calculate the learning needed to enhance one's freedom and self-reliance. Learning therefore becomes a more explicit actor, a positioning congruent with attempts at different forms of social order:

The new citizen is required to engage in a ceaseless work of training and retraining, skilling and reskilling, enhancement of credentials and preparation for a life of ceaseless job seeking: life is to become a continuous economic capitalization of the self.

(Rose 1999: 161)

This mobilization of active, enterprising and flexible subjects of learning can be thought of as part of the wider mobilizations in the social order, in which the range of interactivities and actors involved will vary but where the desire to learn will be forthcoming.

Confessional practices and lifelong learning

Central to Foucault's position is the emergence of the self to be worked upon as part of the processes of fashioning the productive self. Pivotal to this work are confessional practices. These are a form of discursive practice that elicit one's self as an object of knowledge, with one's inner life as the terrain to be explored. The assumption is that there is deep hidden meaning buried 'inside', which once discovered, opens the door to happiness, psychic stability and personal empowerment. To confess is to discover the 'truth' about oneself. The emphasis then is on talking about oneself, being 'open', in effect, being prepared to share with total strangers the most intimate details of one's 'private' life. Telling all is the thing to do, making ourselves the plastic object of self-work a species of moral obligation.

The burgeoning self-help literature, as well as a plethora of courses, seminars and workshops are signs of the widespread incidence of confessional practices. They are also to be found in the growing use of portfolios and student-centred learning and the requirement in education to reflect upon one's self and one's performances. The characteristic of confessional practices is that they are never-ending. There is always more to know, one can never finally realize all one's potential. In living one's life, one creates more data about which to confess. Personal change becomes identified as something that is constantly needed. Confession involves practices that generate meanings about the need for lifelong learning and for particular kinds of learning on an ongoing basis.

Foucault (1981) refers to confession as the process of fashioning one's subjectivity as an object of learning. In relation to sexuality, for example, he argues that the confessional practices of the Christian church were about the discursive transformation of desire in order that sex could be 'policed' rather than suppressed/repressed. This process now encompasses not only sexuality but also health, lifestyle, well-being and career development, becoming central in the ordering of the social, where externally imposed discipline has given way to the self-discipline of an autonomous and desiring subjectivity. Confession has now less to do with salvation and much more to do with self-regulation, self-improvement and self-development. In other words, confession actively codes a subject as productive and autonomous, but a subject who is *already* governed through participating in confessional practices. The practice of telling all, or telling our own story, has become a means of identifying individuals and establishing and enforcing their location within power-knowledge networks. Confessional practices involve self-interventions into those aspects of the self that have hitherto remained unspoken and therefore unregulated. They are positioned as the super-highway to empowerment and self-change.

> The confession has spread its effects far and wide. It plays a part in justice, medicine, education, family relationships, and love relations, in the most ordinary affairs of everyday life, and in the most solemn rites ... One confesses in public and in private, to one's parents, one's educators, one's doctors, to those one loves ...
>
> (Foucault 1981: 59)

As well as something to confess, in order to confess then there must be someone to whom one confesses. It is in the very process of confessing that people become positioned as speaking and desiring subjects, even as they are enfolded in power where they become subject to the authority and authoritative discourse of the confessor – priest, therapist, counsellor, adviser or teacher – within the transaction. These confessors generate material spoken or 'performed' by the confessing subject, material which is constituted into a body of knowledge that inscribes subjects in particular ways, for example, as a 'case' (Foucault 1979). By this means subjects are positioned as a legitimate site of intervention by the expert-as-confessor. Through the expertise of this 'guide', subjects become enfolded within a discursive matrix of practices that bring forth their 'learning needs' and define their desires and paths of self-development.

In guiding subjects to recognize themselves as learners in need of further development through learning, they have to accept that they are indeed *learners* and have to position themselves as a particular kind of learner – a learner whose learning is never complete. Yet even as confession has become a sign of modern forms of governing, its status as a regime of truth, a particular power-knowledge formation, is precisely one *not* identified as powerful. There is a cloaking in apparently objective expertise and an internalization of the humanistic discourse of helping and personal empowerment. This mode of exercising power works relationally and rhizomatically by spreading and entwining throughout the capillaries of the social order. The obligation to confess is relayed through so many different points, is so deeply ingrained in us, that we no longer perceive it as the effect of a power that constrains us. On the contrary, it seems that truth, lodged in our most secret nature, demands only to surface; that if it fails to do so, this is because a constraint holds it in place, the violence of a power weighs it down, and if it can finally be articulated it appears as a kind of liberation.

The processes of governmentality are both inscribed *and* contested in the subjectivities of subjects. Through confessional practices and techniques of confession people's inner lives are brought into the domain of power. It is in the very process of confessing that people are fashioned as active subjects, yet at the same time are enfolded in power as they become subject to confessional discourses and therefore sites for intervention. Here, to realize oneself, to find the truth about oneself becomes both personally and economically desirable – 'individuals, themselves ... can be mobilized in alliance with political objectives, in order to deliver economic growth, successful enterprise and optimum personal happiness' (Miller and Rose 1993: 102). Confessional practices, both within and outside education, and where desire and economics interact, are central to this form of governing. Here lifelong learning is positioned as a *moral* obligation. Confessional practices function to incite people to recognize their moral obligations by accepting their responsibility *as individuals* in all domains of life. Here the self becomes objectified or commodified. It is targeted as a self that is lacking, one that has a duty to affirm and reaffirm its worth by perpetual learning – in many cases through training and retraining. To stand still, to fail to update oneself, is to move backwards, and therefore fail to fulfill one's obligations or responsibilities.

Fashioning lifelong learning

What is suggested in this chapter is that there is a requirement to look at lifelong learning as co-emerging with changing forms of governing and identifying different forms of the exercise of power. Discourses of lifelong learning are ascribed particular meanings and with them come certain practices of learning and subjectivities amenable to learning on a lifelong basis. Of course, none of this is monolithic, but what is clear is the way in which certain pedagogies are coded as forms of power-knowledge that play a significant part in ordering the social. As lifelong learning is fostered outside as well as inside specific educational institutions, the practices through which specific networks are formed become more complex, often involving hybrid mobilizations of disciplinary and governmental power. The resulting networks through which the exercise of power is dispersed and deployed are fluid and rely on the practices of mediation between different objects/subjects within the network. Thus, even as there are attempts to mobilize lifelong learning in specific ways, these will be subject to diverse and unexpected shifts and changes, as the spaces for reflection precisely provide possibilities for critique and alternative meanings. This might involve a challenge to the very notion of lifelong learning, if we take learning to be a cognitive category, and the assertion of the semiotic as a way to challenge both that idea and the coding of, for instance, the workplace as one of enterprising selves. Totalizing the diversity of social practices under a single sign of 'lifelong learning' does not in and of itself do justice to the variety of meanings translated and ordered in specific contexts. Following Foucault, as a regime of truth, lifelong learning may need to be decentred in order that we can look again at the meanings it has and the work it does. Whether it has established itself as a regime of truth also remains a question to be explored.

References

Barry, A. (2001) *Political Machines: Governing a Technological Society*, London: The Athlone Press.

Chaiklin, S. and Lave, J. (eds) (1996) *Understanding Practice*, Cambridge: Cambridge University Press.

Dean, M. (1999) *Governmentality: Power and Rule in Modern Society*, London: Sage.

Du Gay, P. (1996) *Consumption and Identity at Work*, London: Sage.

Foucault, M. (1979) *Discipline and Punish*, Harmondsworth: Penguin.

Foucault, M. (1980) *Power/Knowledge*, Brighton: Harvester.

Foucault, M. (1981) *History of Sexuality: An Introduction*, Harmondsworth: Penguin.

Foucault, M. (1988) 'Technologies of the self', in L.H. Martin, H. Gutman and P.H. Hutton (eds), *Technologies of the Self: A Seminar with Michel Foucault*, Amherst, Mass: University of Massachusetts Press.

Foucault, M. (1991) 'Governmentality', in G. Burchell, C. Gordon and P. Miller (eds), *The Foucault Effect: Studies in Governmentality*, London: Harvester.

Foucault, M. (2003) *Society Must Be Defended*, London: Penguin.

Miller, P. and Rose, N. (1993) 'Governing economic life', in M. Gane and T. Johnson (eds), *Foucault's New Domains*, London: Routledge.

Rose, N. (1989) *Governing the Soul*, London: Routledge.

Rose, N. (1998) *Inventing Ourselves*, Cambridge: Cambridge University Press.

Rose, N. (1999) *Powers of Freedom: Reframing Political Thought*, Cambridge: Cambridge University Press.

Chapter 3

Understanding the mechanisms of neoliberal control

Lifelong learning, flexibility and knowledge capitalism[1]

Mark Olssen

I wish to demonstrate in this chapter that Foucault's conception of governmentality provides a powerful tool for understanding developments in relation to learning and education which links the organization of learning to both politics and economics in developed Western societies. My thesis will be that the radicalness of Foucault's own is much greater than many writers on Foucault seem to realize. For what is offered by Foucault's conception I will argue is a new version of 'superstructural sociology'[2] that provides a means of understanding how educational and economic practices mutually condition and adapt to each other, while avoiding the excesses that plagued Marxist analyses in the later twentieth century that represented such processes as the outcome of a necessary determination. In this context I will argue that Foucauldian concepts of governmentality and state reason enable a more powerful understanding of relations between discursive patterns of a society and the dominant institutional forms of economic and political power than Marxism did. While I will identify lifelong learning as a specifically neoliberal form of state reason in terms of its conception, emergence and development, which has manifested a uniformly consistent – albeit not exclusive – concern of serving the dominant economic mode, the prospects for moving beyond it depend, I will claim, on whether the structures of learning created can be harnessed for other ends; that is, whether embryonic within the discursive programme of lifelong learning is the possibility of linking the discourse to a progressive emancipatory project based upon egalitarian politics and social justice. Is it indeed possible that we can all be inhabitants of a genuinely learning society? And what would such a society look like?

By way of structure, my chapter will comprise the following sections: first, an elucidation of Foucault's concept of governmentality; second, an outline of neoliberalism as a distinctive mode of governmentality; third, a consideration of the inherent dangers afflicting lifelong learning programmes of being harnessed in the interests of neoliberal reason, through discourses of flexibility or flexible specialization; and fourth, the need for a normative analysis in order to separate learning from its neoliberal capture, transforming it away from discourses of neoliberal flexibilization to representing discourses of democratization and social justice. A final section will then trace some further implications of this, linking the ideas raised back to a consideration of the concept of lifelong learning.

Foucault's concept of governmentality

Foucault's concept of governmentality refers to the structures of power by which conduct is organized and by which governance is aligned with the self-organizing capacities of individual subjects. It deals with particular models of governing individuals. Foucault developed this conception of power in the late 1970s in his courses at the Collège de France in order to provide a more macro-dimension to enable him to theorize models of power which dealt with collective governance. While in his genealogical studies he had analysed micro- and disciplinary dimensions of pastoral power and bio-power, giving shape to modern institutions such as schools, prisons and hospitals (partly no doubt as a response to the sorts of criticisms that Luccio Trombadori levelled at him in the interviews of 1978, concerning the overly 'localistic' nature of his analysis of power and rendering it impossible to insert individual events within a broader political perspective), Foucault shifted his analysis to represent the collective dimensions of governmental power as manifested by such agencies as the modern state (cf. Foucault 1991b: Ch. 6). His aim was not, however, to ascertain the legitimacy to state power, or the management of states, but to understand the nature of governmental rationalities as specific forms of state reason, linked to specific technologies in terms of *how* collective power was exercised over individuals. '"How", not in the sense of "How does it manifest itself?" but "By what means is it exercised?" and "What happens when individuals exert (as they say) power over others?"' (Foucault 1982a: 217).

This is what Foucault meant by government, which referred to a form of activity aimed to guide and shape conduct. To govern thus designates 'the way in which the conduct of individuals or of groups might be directed ... [it] is to structure the possible field of action of others' (Foucault 1982a: 221). In 'The Subject and Power' (1982a: 221) essay Foucault alludes to the equivocal nature of the term conduct as it pertains to power relations. For, on the one hand, it pertains to 'lead[ing] others (according to mechanisms of coercion which are, to varying degrees strict)' and, on the other, 'a way of behaving within a more or less open field of possibilities' (Foucault 1982a: 220–1).[3] Hence, he says, 'The exercise of power consists in guiding the possibility of conduct and putting in order the possible outcome'. And this is what makes the issue of power, 'less a confrontation between two adversaries ... than a question of government' (Foucault 1982a: 221).

To speak of government or power is to presuppose that '"certain people exercise power over others", which is to speak of "relationships"' (Foucault 1982a: 217). In this sense, power relations are distinct from 'objective abilities' as well as from 'relations of communication', yet they can be 'grasped in the diversity of their logical sequence, their abilities, and their interrelationships' (Foucault 1982a: 219). What is important to see here is that for Foucault power is not an *entity*, but rather a *relation of forces*. What constitutes the specific nature of power is that it is a 'set of actions upon other actions'; that is, it is:

> a total structure of actions brought to bear upon possible actions; it incites, it induces, it seduces, it makes it easier or more difficult; in the extreme it constrains or forbids absolutely; it is nevertheless always a way of acting upon an acting subject or acting subjects by virtue of their acting or being capable of action.
>
> (Foucault 1982a: 220)

What is also important is that power is exercised strategically only over free subjects. By the word *strategy* Foucault means three things:

> First, to designate the means employed to attain a certain end, it is a question of rationality functioning to arrive at an objective. Second, to designate the manner in which a partner in a certain game acts with regard to what he thinks should be the action of the others and what he considers the others think to be his own; it is the way in which one seeks to have the advantage over others. Third ... it is a question ... of the means used to obtain victory.
>
> (Foucault 1982a: 224–5)

A power strategy then is 'the totality of means put into operation to implement power effectively or to maintain it' (Foucault 1982a: 225). To the extent that such relations of power are open and fluid, there is a degree of instability permitting the possibility of reversal or modification. In this sense, while hegemonies exist, they exist precariously. To the extent to which relations of power have become congealed, or fixed, it represents a 'strategic situation, more or less taken for granted and consolidated by means of a long-term confrontation between adversaries' (Foucault 1982a: 226).

In a 1978 lecture at the Collège de France, Foucault (1991a) introduces the term *governmentality* to supplement pastoral power and bio-power. Governmentality has dual functions as *individualizing* and *totalizing*, in shaping both individuals and populations, in order to understand the collective exercise of power. If 'bio-power' referred to disciplinary power introduced in the early modern period in order to rationalize the problems afflicting populations, governmentality pertains to the specificity of power relations with its concern to shape conduct as part of a broader issue involving the *political* exercise of power. It includes 'techniques and procedures for directing human behaviour' (Foucault 1997b: 81). It pertains, he says (Foucault 1991a: 87–8), to 'a concern with the art of government ... of how to be ruled, how strictly, by whom, to what end, by what methods, etc.' In addition, the concept can be applied to the family, religion, the economy, as well as the state. In its most general sense it pertains to the 'problematic of government in general' (Foucault 1991a: 88) and articulates 'a kind of rationality' (Foucault 1991a: 89). In this sense, at it most simple level, governmentality expresses itself as an *art* and is a form of *state reason* (*raisson d'etat*).

For Foucault (1991a: 90), the art of government is also concerned with the issue of *security*, of stabilizing the fragile link between ruler and the ruled, of rendering it legitimate, 'to identify dangers ... to develop the art of manipulating relations of force that will allow the Prince to ensure the protection of his principality'. The concept of *security* is, along with governmentality, a central concept for Foucault, and is concerned with the issue of how the state deals with unpredictable events, how it evaluates and calculates the costs and consequences, and how it manages populations within constraint rather than through the imposition of rule. Indeed, 'one need[s] to analyze the series: security, population, government' (Foucault 1991a: 87) as part of a combined approach. While sovereignty is concerned with the problem of rule through the imposition of law, security is concerned with the management of populations. The intersection of security and government occurs with the concern for the 'regulation of populations' and the search for 'mechanisms capable of ensuring its regulation' (Foucault 1997a: 67). While the issue of security is relevant in all periods of history, it became of increased concern in the eighteenth century and affected the form and practice of government.

Lifelong learning as a neoliberal reason of state

In Foucault's sense, lifelong learning represents a model of governing individuals in their relation to the collective. In this sense it constitutes a distinctively neoliberal governmentality. As governmentality constitutes a reason of state in a practical sense it also constitutes a technology of control. Its specific governmental significance can be seen in the EU which has declared lifelong learning as a central educational project in its quest to integrate 25 populations into a new European identity. The European Commission has stated: 'Lifelong learning is an overarching strategy of European co-operation in education and training policies and for the individual. The lifelong learning approach is an essential policy strategy for the development of citizenship, social cohesion, employment and for individual fulfillment' (European Commission 2002: 4). As in the Lisbon Memorandum on lifelong learning, the European Commission established lifelong learning, both in its informal and formal senses, as a major asset for the European Union, especially related to the tasks of regional development and integration, modernization and the promotion of human capital and employability (Commission for European Communities 2000).

To understand the dangers and possibilities associated with recent models of learning in order to understand the sense in which theories of learning and power interact, we must understand Foucault's analysis of neoliberalism. Neoliberalism refers to a particular economic model which in the context of this chapter pertains to the way that practices of economics and discursive patternings of knowledge and learning interact. As a particular model of power it emerged as a revision of classical economic liberalism in the 1970s in the US and Britain as a response to stagflation and the collapse of Bretton Woods system of international trade and exchange, leading to the abolition of capital controls in 1974 in America and 1979 in Britain (Mishra 1999; Stiglitz 2002). These policies made it extremely difficult to sustain Keynesian demand management. Exchange rates were floated and capital controls abolished, giving money and capital the freedom to move across national boundaries. Far from being a necessary process reflecting the inevitable post-Fordist determinations of the economic, neoliberalism must still be understood as the deliberate policy of those in power. As Paul Hirst (2000: 179) states, the creation of markets has been engineered by particular policies. It was public policy, not market pressures, that led to the deregulation of capital markets and the removal of exchange controls in the late 1970s and early 1980s. As he states, 'What is supposed to be an inevitable market-driven global process is actually substantially a product of public policy ... It was influential economic policy elites and state officials in advanced states that shaped the deregulatory free-market vision of world trade' (Hirst 2000: 179).

The important message here is that the forms of governmentality that are shaping learning have been directly engineered as a consequence of the neoliberal revolution since the 1970s.

Lifelong learning as an instrument of flexible governmentality

In this context lifelong learning can be represented as a particular technology of power in the same sense, indeed the same way, that public choice theory agency theory or cost-transaction economics can be seen as technologies of power. Whereas the latter are global discourses pertaining to the management of public enterprises in market terms, lifelong learning represents a global discourse for the flexible preparation of subjects. There is a parallel, then, to the 'old' Marxist sense of 'superstructures' whereby social and institutional domains such as education are rendered compatible to the imperatives of economic management. While my basic theoretical model is not narrowly functionalist, or economistic, it can be observed that at a certain level of analysis, a functionalist explanation works: lifelong learning constitutes a specific technology which makes both the tertiary and non-tertiary labour force subject to a new form of flexible rationalization which under national systems of Keynesian welfare nationalism never actually existed, which is to say, as Robert Boyer (1988: 258) has put it, that under Keynesian modes of regulation, the free development of global economies was 'delayed because of a lack of social and technical means of controlling workers'. It is the global production of infinitely knowledgeable subjects that the technology of lifelong learning enables. It thus represents a specifically global and non-Keynesian means of constituting workers as knowledgeable subjects.

The emergence of the technology serves in these senses as both cause and effect. It enables both the individualization of responsibility for education or learning on the one hand and the abolition of welfare obligations of states on the other. In this sense, the technology of lifelong learning enabled a downgrading of social rights within any particular national territory in preference for a global-level playing field characterized by equality of opportunity. Its main strength is that it constitutes a flexible technology in a number of senses. First, it enables businesses and governments to avoid direct responsibility. Second, it enables the adaptability of workers in terms of their mobility within the workforce between businesses and countries. It thus enables workers to move from one job to another within a given overall production process, or within a production process that can switch between products and skills and which can itself be transitory. This kind of flexibility requires skill and competence of a potentially short-term nature, features which did not characterize Taylorism or Fordism.[4]

The key strategy, of which lifelong learning is a component, is that of 'workforce versatility' which enables high levels of job mobility, premised on a high level of general and technical training and a ready ability to add new skills in order to make change possible. The lifelong worker thus equates directly with Proudhon's 'ideal worker' (*l'ouvrier proudhonien*). As a strategy, then, lifelong learning enables a relaxing of legal restraints over conditions of work and employment, especially dismissal, within particular national boundaries. It translates as a proposal to reduce controls over employee rights and safeguards with regard to job security or protection, ensuring an automatic mechanism of worker adaptability which reduces workers ties to a particular company or business by making the employment contract itself more flexible. A new regulatory environment is produced which increases the mobility of capital, lessening its dependence on the traditional employment contract and absolving the establishment or company of responsibility for security and welfare. A new technology of flexible adaptation ensures that responsibility for employment tenure belongs to individuals themselves, ensures the possibility for companies to offset responsibility for social and fiscal payments and enhances the freedom of business in a global environment. Paradoxically, such flexibility, as Robert Boyer (1988: 227) states, helps maintain the stability of certain aspects of economic life. Hence discourses such as lifelong learning assist in stabilizing work-individual relations by enabling the system or sub-system to respond to a variety of disturbances. It substitutes for the rights of workers over education and entitlement to knowledge an automatic system based on the ready availability of information and skills. Thus lifelong learning involves a restructuring of the context of education in the interests of efficiency through flexibilization. As Tuschling and Engemann (2006: 460) state:

> The purpose is not to de-institutionalize but rather to inter-institionalize learning. [This involves] ... 1. changing the field of learning in order to totalize learning to all imaginable situations. 2. initiating a change in the self-performance of individuals that they act as learners in all imaginable situations. With these two components the learning individual is configured as an inter-institutional entity traversing situations and institutions, obliged to strategically show knowledge and skills. Especially non-formal and informal learning have to be presented as accessible and manageable. This is the task of the third component of inter-institutionalization: the techniques that allow both individuals and institutions to inscribe, store, process and transfer actions as learning. The main activities of the European Union in this field are centred around these techniques. It is within them that lifelong learning is getting a density and becomes most palpable.

Of central importance, then, is that strategies such as flexibilization must be seen as technologies of neoliberal governmentality with a direct benefit for the major economic actors involved.

Changes in the nature and management of knowledge: from collective to individual responsibility

Building upon the analysis above, as James Marshall (1996: 269) has noted, what is substituted in the neoliberal discourse of lifelong learning is knowledge for information: 'knowledge has been replaced by skills and *learning*. Everything which might have been seen as obtaining knowledge – an *object* of an activity – seems to have moved into an activity mode, where what is important is *process*'.

A link with 'process', rather than knowledge, means that education becomes concerned with skills and information. In this, as Bert Lambeir (2005: 350) notes, 'the bond between the information society and the learning society appears to be a very tight one'. As learning has been redefined in terms of process, and functions as information, it needs to be continuously relearned, readjusted and restructured to meet the needs of the consumer in the service information industry. Learning in this sense is an ongoing permanent addition of competences and skills adapted continuously to real external needs. As Lambeir (2005: 351) states, 'Learning now is the constant striving for extra competences, and the efficient management of acquired ones. Education has become merely a tool in the fetishisation of certificates'. The continual availability of information adapts learning and knowledge to the changing context of flexible production. In this sense, to echo Richard Edwards (1997: Ch. 2) it accommodates a world of constant change where the imperative or possibility of updating our knowledge and skills again and again in order to anticipate all possible transformation.

It is in this sense that the discourse of lifelong learning is a call for 'permanent education' (Lambeir 2005: 350). As Lambeir (2005: 350) continues:

> Lifelong learning is the magic spell in the discourse of educational and economic policymakers, as well as in that of the practitioners of both domains. The Flemish minister of education for example declares lifelong learning to be one of the government's priorities. She argues for equal learning opportunities for every individual, to encounter the threatening duality between those that did learn and still do, and those who do not use the educational facilities. In order to meet this goal individualised learning advice and support will be necessary. In this respect we might consider the following: first, learning activities must be presented as enjoyable, and related to the adult's curiosity and to the creation of new opportunities. Second, there is a need to set up a 'digital learning mall', a database which provides an overview of the learning opportunities offered in the country. Finally, the opportunity to use information and communications technology to offer more flexible and need-orientated learning facilities, must be explored.

Lifelong learning accommodates the global provision of education and skills on the basis of equality of opportunity, inclusiveness, emphasizing the importance of key qualifications, basic skills and primary knowledge. As Lambeir notes, this is provided on the basis of 'self-managed learning' incorporating a shift from 'offer-orientated' to 'question-orientated' education, or in Marshall's terms, from knowing *that* to knowing *how* in which learning becomes nothing more (or less) than the public collection of competencies offered in the labour market of learning opportunities. While many of these are useful, one can never have enough, and one can never have enough fast enough. In this sense, lifelong learning is a market discourse that orientates education to the enterprise society where the learner becomes an entrepreneur of themself. What she becomes depends solely on herself and the choices she makes. She is responsible for herself. Such a model requires skills of self-management and record keeping so that demonstrations of established learning are rendered transparent through audit. Ultimately lifelong learning shifts responsibility from the system to the individual whereby individuals are responsible for self-emancipation and self-creation. It is the discourse of autonomous and independent individuals who are responsible for updating their skills in order to achieve their place in society.

For Foucault lifelong learning would constitute a new technology of power and part of the mechanisms of control operating in our society. It is a discourse which aims at resolving the individual and the general – *omnes et singulatum*, in the interests of the smooth functioning of the whole. As well as constituting a strategy of government at the policy level, lifelong learning also constitutes a form of *bio-power* in that it aims to *discipline* subjects. Marshall (1995: 322) has proffered the term *busno-power* which can be represented as characterizing a particular form of *bio-power*. Busno-power:

> [I]s directed at the subjectivity of the person, not through the body but through the mind, through forms of educational practices and pedagogy which, through choices in education, shape the subjectivities of autonomous choosers ... this busno-power also impinges upon the population as a whole, as individual consumer activity 'improves' both society and economy.
>
> (Marshall 1995: 322)

Busno-power thus represents a distinctively neoliberal form of bio-power which constitutes individuals as autonomous choosers of their own lives. In this model, then, lifelong learning embodies new techniques of self-regulation and aims to minimize the 'time lag' between skills and individual development and economic and technological change (Kraus 2001, in Tuschling and Engemann 2006: 460).

While lifelong learning implies an active as opposed to a passive learner, when viewed in relation to neoliberal agendas it implies a shift in the control of authority for education from the collective to the individual, involving increasing responsibility of the individual for educational and work careers and the skills required and outcomes that ought to take place. Getting prepared is now more in the hands of the individual which entails greater risk in that the individual has to 'co-finance his own learning' (Commission of the European Union 2000, in Tuschling and Engemann 2006: 458). Hence, as Anna Tuschling and Christoph Engemann (2006: 458) note: 'lifelong learning means self determination and self-responsibility in educational tasks, including the financial aspects ... the lifelong learning discourse identifies a broad need to teach individuals to become autonomous learners'.

As such, say Tuschling and Engemann (2006: 458) citing Gerlach (2000), lifelong learning represents an 'internalized educational aspiration', where the individual is not only responsible for the content of the knowledge, but also for the levels and structures and process and organization. Essentially learners become the entrepreneurs of their own development. What the states provide are the tools that facilitate and audit the process. Not only must individuals learn, but they must learn to recognize what to learn, and what and when to forget what to learn when circumstances demand it, they say. They go on to cite Deleuze (1990) who characterizes the field of control in terms of 'limitless postponements', where 'perpetual training' replaces specified levels, in what are characterized as techniques of 'permanent self performance'. They then state:

> The ability to orientate oneself in such a manner is condensed in the second core concept of lifelong learning, the so-called social competences and key qualifications ... terms that point to basic self-organisational dispositions ... of being able to interpret their own circumstances, self-directed in a way that leads to learning.
>
> (Tuschling and Engemann 2006: 459)

Hence, there has been, I would claim, a change in the way knowledge is managed to accord with the new axioms of 'flexibility' demanded by the labour market. Individuals are increasingly rendered responsible for the appropriation of skills and knowledge in a perpetual and endless process. In this way the social costs of production are displaced on to the individual.

Learning for democracy

Must educational technologies such as lifelong learning inevitably serve the labour market? For 'old' Marxists, the answer seemed to be 'yes' for the institutions of the cultural superstructure, like education, were seen as necessarily expressing or reflecting the dynamics and imperatives of the 'capitalist' economic base. For Foucault, however, while possible interconnections and determinations must be an open field for analysis, the way the institutional realm is patterned does not necessarily reflect the base, or only those of the base, and this permits the possibility that educational institutions can themselves be designed to express more democratic normative aspirations. Although lifelong learning has quite clearly become a discourse of neoliberal governmentality in the present era, it cannot be disputed that many of the skills and opportunities for development, whether on computers, or language, or more specific goals, are clearly worthy as educational ideals. In one important sense, then, we are all, or should all be, inhabitants of a future learning society. The key question becomes for what purpose is learning to be readily available, what ends *should* it serve. If it is simply 'fast food for the brain' (Lambeir 2005: 354) or concerned narrowly with cognitive and metacognitive skills in the interests of adaptability to the world of work and the constantly changing demands of capital then it becomes a means of enabling business to minimize or avoid its social responsibilities by offloading the social and educational costs of production in a constantly changing technological environment.

The real question concerns, then, how can a model of learning which is not the servant of neoliberal reason be developed? At the risk of becoming naïvely prescriptive, the remainder of this chapter sets out to specify schematically some relevant normative criteria which any conception of learning should contain. That is, it aims, if only briefly, to establish a broad normative framework in order to safeguard learning from neoliberal appropriation, and link it to a conception of social justice and development. Partly, my message is that until a normative analysis is explicitly developed (rather than being left implicit as the unstated underside of critique) we run the distinct risk that conceptions of learning we are left to work with merely facilitate the ongoing reproduction of established economic and political relations.

The sort of learning society needed today is one that orientates learning and knowledge to survival defined as the security and well-being of all. The continuance of traditions and customs which enable individuals to function effectively as members of communities requires not the endless addition of skills and information for the labour market, but a progressive deepening of the political arts of democratic communication and negotiation through the skills of deliberation, contestation and debate. Learning must move away from a concern with quantitative addition of cognitive and metacognitive skills to a concern with qualitative transformation of the subject through their active engagement in the democratic process. Such a process does indeed involve accessing new information, adding new skills, but such a process must be in the context of active participation and engagement in the democratic structures through which the conflicts between individuals and society are accommodated and through which change and transformation are effected. This requires a theory of learning that teaches how powers are formed, harnessed and sustained; how compositions are brought into being, or avoided, how encounters are influenced and how institutional and collective politics are negotiated productively.

Clearly any meaningful idea of the learning society must embody and express principles that transcend the nation-state and the free development of all peoples. This can be represented as resting on the principles of *cosmopolitanism* which involves learning as a process of engagement with the 'other'. The commitment to cosmopolitanism incorporates a commitment to reason and human rights in equal distribution to the chances and prospects of survival. Self-organized learning certainly has a place in this scenario. But also essential are the twin values of freedom and participation as embodied, for instance, in Dewey's pragmatism, where learning rests upon a mode of life where reason is exercised through problem-solving, where the individual participates and contributes to the collective good of society and in the process constitutes their own development. In this model, the learning society is a global society of engagement. The learner is engaged in a process of action for change as part of a dialogic encounter rather than as a consequence of individual choice. Popkewitz *et al.* (2006: 433) refer to this project as founded upon an 'unfinished cosmopolitanism' where learning is talked about as 'planning one's biography as continuously solving problems, making choices and collaborating in "communities of learners" in a process of cultural innovation'. We use the term 'unfinished cosmopolitan' rather than the phrase 'lifelong learner' in order to historicize the present. Yet, it affects more than that, for just as it makes the individual inseparable from the collective, or rights inseparable from duties, so it makes learning inseparable from teaching and from community support. Hence learning is inseparable, as Wagner (1994: xiv) writes, from 'the substantive foundations of a self-realisation and of shifting emphasis between individualised entitlements and public/collective capabilities' (in Popketwitz, *et al.* 2006: 436). For Popkewitz *et al.*:

> The narratives of the unfinished cosmopolitan as the Learning Society embody new relations between individuality (the lifelong learner) and the social. The fabrication of the child as a problem solver no longer sediments responsibility in the range of social practices directed towards a single public sphere. The new individuality traverses diverse and plural communities to constitute the common good ... Reason is no longer for the perfection of the nation as the collective embodiment of the social good. Change, contingency and uncertainty in daily life are tamed through the rules and standards that place the problem solving child in diverse communities where the common good is formed ... The unfinished cosmopolitan ... is orientated to the future through unfinished processes that are viewed as expressing universal human attributes of reason, science and progress. The unfinished cosmopolitan problem solves to chase desire and works in a global world in which there is no finishing line.
>
> (2006: 437–8)

In this new field, say Popkewitz *et al.* (2006), the learning society no longer functions as an educational ideal, but as a political one. In this sense, learning is integrally related to community, as the systems of communication and language through which participation and learning take place are by their very nature social. Such a theme links directly to democracy as the mechanism through which individual and collective are mediated. As the techniques such as deliberation and contestation, which enable this mediating transference, are themselves only learnable in the context of participation and engagement, learning is itself a constitutive democratic project. If our substantive conception of democracy posits certain general ends, which allow for a degree of diversity and pluralism, our procedural view of democracy is as a multifaceted array of equally balanced institutions, mechanisms and processes instituted to ensure the *inclusion*, *security* or *safety* as well as *development* and *opportunities* of all individuals and groups. In this respect research on learning needs to focus on the means of *deepening* democracy to satisfy these goals.

Notes

1 I would like to acknowledge appreciation to the *International Journal of Lifelong Education* where an altered version of this paper was previously published (25 May–3 June 2006, 213–30).

2   The notion of 'superstructure' derives from Marx's *Preface* to *A Contribution to the Critique of Political Economy* (see Marx 1971: 20–1) and was extensively used in late nineteenth- and twentieth-century Marxist scholarship by most writers on Marxist issues. For instance, see Raymond Williams, 'Base and Superstructure in Marxist Cultural Theory' (in Williams 1980).

3   The English translator states that 'Foucault is playing on the double meaning in French of the verb *conduire* – to lead or to drive, and *se conduire* – to behave or conduct oneself, whence la conduite, conduct or behaviour' (cf. Foucault 1982a: 221, note 2).

4   Taylorism characterized wage/labour relations that slowly emerged in industry during the later years of the nineteenth century based on fragmentation and competition, while Fordism describes relations that became dominant since the 1950s, which prolonged the Taylorist mode through mechanization and factory organization (cf. Boyer 1988).

References

Boyer, R. (1988) *The Search for Labour Market Flexibility*, Oxford: Clarendon Press.

Commission for European Communities (2000) *Memorandum on Lifelong Learning*, Brussels, 30.10.2000, SEK (2000) 1832.

Edwards, R. (1997) *Changing Places? Flexibility, Lifelong Learning and a Learning Society*, London: Routledge.

European Commission (2000) *European Report of the Taskforce on Lifelong Learning*, Brussels.

European Commission (2002) *European Report on Quality Indicators of Lifelong Learning*, Brussels.

Foucault, M. (1982a) 'The Subject and Power: Afterword', in H.L. Dreyfus and P. Rabinow (eds), *Michel Foucault: Beyond Structuralism and Hermeneutics* (2nd edn.), Chicago: University of Chicago Press.

Foucault, M. (1982b) 'Le sujet et le pouvoir', in D. Defert, F. Ewald and J. Lagrange (eds), *Dits et Écrits IV 1980–1988*, Paris: Gallimard.

Foucault, M. (1991a) 'Governmentality', in G. Burchell, C. Gordon and P. Miller (eds), *The Foucault Effect: Studies in Governmentality*, Chicago: The University of Chicago Press.

Foucault, M. (1991b) *Remarks on Marx: Conversations with Duccio Trombadori*, trans. R.J. Goldstein and J. Cascaito, New York: Semiotext(e).

Foucault, M. (1997a) 'Security, territory, population', in P. Rabinow (ed.), *Michel Foucault: Ethics, Subjectivity and Truth*, London: Allen Lane/The Penguin Press.

Foucault, M. (1997b) 'On the government of the living', in Paul Rabinow (ed.), *Michel Foucault: Ethics, Subjectivity and Truth*, London: Allen Lane/The Penguin Press.

Hirst, P. (2000) 'Globalization, the nation-state and political theory', in N. O'Sullivan (ed.), *Political Theory in Transition*, London and New York: Routledge.

Kraus, K. (2001) *Lebenslanges Lernen. Karriere einer Letidee*, Bielefeld: W. Bertelsmann.

Lambeir, B. (2005) 'Education as liberation: the politics and techniques of lifelong learning', *Educational Philosophy and Theory*, 37: 349–56.

Marshall, J.D. (1995) 'Foucault and neo-liberalism: biopower and busno-power', in A. Neiman (ed.), *Philosophy of Education 1995, Proceedings of the Philosophy of Education Society*, IL: Philosophy of Education Society.

Marshall, J.D. (1996) 'Education in the mode of information: some philosophical considerations', in *Philosophy of Education 1996, Proceedings of the Philosophy of Education Society*, IL: Philosophy of Education Society.

Marx, K. (1971) *A Contribution to the Critique of Political Economy* (with an introduction by Maurice Dobb), London: Lawrence & Wishart.

Mishra, R. (1999) *Globalization and the Welfare State*, Cheltenham: Edward Elgar.

Popkewitz, T., Olsson, U. and Petersson, K. (2006) 'The learning society, the unfinished cosmopolitan, and governing education, public health and crime prevention at the beginning of the 21st century', *Educational Philosophy and Theory*, 38: 431–50.

Stiglitz, J. (2002) *Globalization and Its Discontents*, London: Penguin.

Tuschling, A. and Engemann, C. (2006) 'From education to lifelong learning: the emerging regime of learning in the European Union', *Educational Philosophy and Theory*, 38: 451–70.

Wagner, P. (1994) *The Sociology of Modernity*, New York: Routledge.

Williams, R. (1980) *Problems in Materialism and Culture*, London: Verso.

Chapter 4

Our 'will to learn' and the assemblage of a learning apparatus[1]

Maarten Simons and Jan Masschelein[2]

The word learning has come to be indispensable for speaking about ourselves, others and society. As employees in an organization, we recognize our need for the competencies necessary to do our job, and learning is regarded as a process or force to generate these competencies. Active citizenship and activities such as involvement and participation are regarded as necessary conditions for making democracy work, and in a similar way, it is argued that these democratic competencies can be learned. Moreover, activities in the so-called private sphere are regarded as competency-based or requiring specific skills. A range of activities, from child-rearing, having sex, eating or communication, to travelling and using free time, are regarded as being competency-based and in need of a prior learning process.

The aim of this chapter is to analyse the overwhelming importance of this idea of learning today. The point of departure of the analysis is the critical attitude that Foucault has labelled an 'ontology of the present' (Foucault 1984a). The main question could be formulated straightforwardly as follows: who are we, as people for whom learning is of major importance, who refer to learning as a way to constantly position and reposition ourselves? In short, learning is conceived as a kind of a 'singular, historical experience' emerging within a particular historical context (Foucault 1984b: 13). Further, it is our aim to analyse how this self-understanding and subjectivity emerges within present practices and discourses. For this analysis, we again draw on Foucault and in particular, his analysis of governmentality and the so-called studies of governmentality developed during the past decades. The aim of these studies is to analyse how a regime of government and self-government works (Dean 1999; Rose 1999; Foucault 2004a, b). The formula 'governmentalization of learning' points precisely at what is at stake today and what we would like to describe here: that learning has become a matter of both government and self-government (cf. Delanty 2003).[3]

In order to describe the governmentalization of learning and the assemblage of a 'learning apparatus' today, the first section of this chapter is a historical excursion that explains how the concept of learning, being disconnected from education and teaching, has been used to refer to a kind of *capital*, to something for which the learner herself is *responsible* and to something that can and should be *managed* (and is an object of expertise). The second section indicates how today these discourses are combined and play a crucial role in advanced liberalism that seeks to promote entrepreneurship. In the third section, the main role of entrepreneurial self-government within advanced liberalism will be explored further. We will explain that the entrepreneurship implies an adaptation ethics based on self-mobilization through learning and that advanced liberalism draws upon a kind of 'learning apparatus' to secure adaptation for each and all. In the last section, we will raise the critical question of whether learning indeed results in the freedom and collective well-being that is being promised in advanced liberalism.

Learning as both a problem and a solution

In order to be able to describe how learning comes to play a major role in the current governmental regime, it is necessary first to draw attention to older forms of problematization in which learning appeared as an important issue for reflection and thought; i.e. the 'historically conditioned emergence of new fields of experience' related to learning (Burchell 1996: 31). Hence, we will focus on the emergence of those fields of experience that involve the rationalization of problems as learning problems and regard the enhancement of learning as a solution (Foucault 1984a: 577). Three related fields of problems, shaped in the previous century, can be distinguished.

The capitalization of learning

At the end of the 1960s there was an interest in the development of a so-called knowledge society and knowledge economy. In this economy, knowledge functions as a 'central capital', 'the crucial means of production' and the 'energy of a modern society' (Drucker 1969: xi). It is argued that 'knowledge workers' are of major importance in an economy in which many activities imply a 'knowledge base'. Furthermore, it is argued that these developments require us to look at education in a new way: education (especially universities and research institutions) should be regarded as a 'knowledge industry', the main supplier for the new demand for a sufficient 'knowledge base' and useful 'knowledge workers' (Drucker 1969: 313).

Moreover, the logic of the knowledge economy – the logic of the development and technological application of knowledge – becomes the horizon for addressing the importance of 'continuing education' for 'knowledge workers': 'In a knowledge society, school and life can no longer be separate. They have to be linked in an organic process in which the one feeds back on the other. And this continuing education attempts to do' (Drucker 1969: 24). Continuing education is thus regarded as a solution to the need for a useful knowledge base, and economic problems are framed within an educational framework. Furthermore, and this is also related to the two other forms of problematization (see below), learning becomes disconnected from its traditional institutional context (school education, training) and conditions (teaching). While schooling and education have been regarded as an economic force for a longer time, against the background of the knowledge society learning itself is now regarded as a force to produce added value.

More specifically, against this horizon it is possible to address learning as that which links the employee to the process of production. Not just financial, physical and mental stimuli are required to establish this link, but also learning. At this point learning – as the ability to renew one's knowledge base or human capital – is regarded as a condition for economic development and productivity. In more recent discourses it is argued that for a knowledge worker, 'work ... is to a large extent learning' and that 'while learning, value is added to the existing human capital' (Bomers 1991: 5; Tjepkema 1996: 83). What is at stake, then, is a 'capitalization of learning'. In other words, what emerges is a field of experience in which learning appears as a force to produce added value.

Being responsible towards learning

For a second form of problematization we should consider the ideas of lifelong learning (éducation permanente), closely related to the concern for self-actualization and self-realization. The basic idea is that learning should not be limited to the school or other traditional institutions for education and to a particular time in people's life. What is needed is an integrated (educational) system or infrastructure that offers opportunities for lifelong learning and prepares 'mankind to adapt to change, the predominant characteristic of our time' (Faure et al. 1972: 104, 209). Regarded as self-realization and self-actualization, autonomy here means being able to meet our own needs, and since these needs are changing constantly, lifelong learning is required. Consequently, it is argued that 'the central mission of the school will be to teach the pupils to learn, to train them to assimilate new knowledge on their own' (Husén 1974: 23). Apart from this reconceptualization of the mission of schools, a field of experience emerges in which problems concerning individual well-being can be framed as educational and/or learning problems.

Part of this problematization of learning is the way adult education is reflected on. During the 1920s, Lindeman stressed the importance of learning for adults and the implication for education: against the background of 'education is life' and 'the whole of life is learning' it is argued that the situation of the learner should be the point of departure (Lindeman 1926: 4–5). Later on (and drawing upon humanistic psychology) the idea is that adult learning requires an attitude of self-direction towards learning. Knowles (1970), for example, describes self-directed learning as a process in which the learner takes the initiative (with the help of others if needed) to make a diagnosis of their learning needs, formulate learning goals, identify human and material resources for learning, choose and implement adequate learning strategies and evaluate learning results. Again, in view of the changing society and the need to be able to cope with changes the importance of self-regulation towards one's learning is stressed. This could be regarded as a 'responsibilization' towards learning.

Learning as object of (self-) management and (self-) expertise

Although related to the previous forms of problematization, the new educational and psychological expertise concerning learning processes offers a third form. First, learning is regarded as a kind of cognitive process, that is, a kind of process that is internal to someone who learns and that occurs incidentally or is planned. Change is a central theme here. Change, it is argued, can be the result of learning processes. This means that to understand these processes and to get a grip on them enables one to influence change (Gagné 1970). In short, learning as such becomes a domain of expertise. Expertise based on cognitive psychology reflects upon learning as processes of cognition, transforming information into knowledge (Mayer 1983). Knowledge, here, is the output of mental processes and as such the result of a 'construction' (von Glasersfeld 1995). The learner is addressed as someone in an environment and a social context in which knowledge is constructed on the basis of an input (experiences, information, problems ...) and where the existing knowledge base is reconstructed in order to bring about a new equilibrium.

Within this field of problematization where learning is objectificated as a process of construction within an environment, it is possible to focus on the abilities of the learner to get a grip on these processes: meta-cognition or knowledge about one's own cognition and active regulation of one's own learning processes (Flavell 1976). The learner is thus someone who can and should become aware of the learning processes and who should relate in an active, regulating way to these processes. Learners should become the 'managers' of their own learning, for example by developing their own learning strategy, monitoring the process and evaluating the results (Westhoff 1996: 21). In short, the expertise concerning learning presupposes that learners themselves can and should become the real experts (Shuell 1988). The result of this form of problematization is that learning is reflected upon as a fundamental process for coping with our environment and that the very 'management' or 'regulation' of this fundamental process can and should be learned. Thus what is at stake is the emergence of a kind of 'managerial' attitude towards learning; i.e. learning appears as a process of construction that could and should be managed, in the first place by learners themselves.

Learning and (self-) government

The aim of this section is to demonstrate how the initial forms of problematization identified in the previous section are being combined today and have become part of our present governmental regime that seeks to promote entrepreneurship. In order to describe some main features of the new governmental regime, we will start with some examples of the way in which people are addressed today as learners. The Belgian/Flemish and European context will offer these examples.

In the profiles for experienced and beginning teachers in Flanders that are prescribed by the Ministry of Flemish Community, teaching is regarded as an activity based upon competencies (MFC 1999). However, it is stressed that in order to remain a professional, it is important for a teacher to take care of their ongoing professional development. For this professional development or lifelong learning, teachers should have 'capacities for self-direction' (MFC 1999: 1). Teachers should regard their learning and the competencies generated during self-directed learning processes as a kind of capital or added value for their professionalism as well as for the productivity of the school and the educational system in general. Furthermore, companies or private and public organizations, too, are seen as having a learning capacity that they should develop and manage. An organization is regarded as having a 'collective brain function' and could and should develop this function in 'mobilizing the mental and creative capacities' of the employees (Bomers 1991: 4). Organizations are asked to focus not only on 'survival learning' or 'adaptive learning', but foremost on 'generative learning' – 'learning that enhances the capacity to create' (Senge 1990: 14). Good managers should therefore understand that their role is to a large extent an educative role, i.e. to offer learning opportunities or a learning network that combines the empowerment of individuals and the company.

Another example is the way in which policy and policy makers view society itself. Politicians in Flanders and the Netherlands claim that stimulating lifelong learning and offering facilities for learning should become a governmental aim for 'lifetime employability' (and a flexible labour market) as well as for individual self-realization – 'to become what you want' (Vandenbroucke 2004: 112). What is recommended is to stimulate an attitude in order to regard learning as something that is intrinsically motivated and that contributes in a fundamental way to the evolution of a learning society (European Commission 1995). It is argued furthermore that we should be aware that this 'will to learn' is not only a condition for our individual and collective well-being inside a state or inside the European Union, but is also required to remain competitive within an international environment.

For a final example that articulates this fundamental importance of learning in the way we come to think and speak about ourselves we could look at how problems in society are now dealt with as learning problems. An unemployed person, for example, is not just someone who is in need of an income, but could be regarded as someone in need of additional learning. In this context Giddens claims: 'The guideline is that, when possible, investment in human capital should have priority over offering immediate economic support' (Giddens 2000: 130). Poverty, and many other forms of exclusion, are now about the lack of adequate human capital, about irresponsibility towards one's learning capacity or about not being able to manage ones learning. In all these cases, so we can read, investment in human capital is required.

What these examples clarify is an interpellation at different places and levels in order to look at ourselves as having a learning capacity and as being responsible to use and manage this capacity. What accompanies this interpellation is the idea that the 'individual's place in relation to fellow citizens will increasingly be determined by the capacity to learn' and that this 'relative position, which could be called the 'learning relationship', will become an increasingly dominant feature in the structure of our societies' (European Commission 1995: 2). These examples enable us to describe more generally the new governmental regime of which we are part. In our opinion, *we*, addressed as learners, are no longer part of the social regime of government in the welfare state. While 'the social', 'social norms' and 'socialization' previously played a strategic role in governments' social regime, 'inclusion', 'capital' and 'learning' seem to be the strategic components nowadays. Being part of society is no longer about being socialized and developing a social, normalized relation to the self. Instead it is an ongoing task of managing one's learning process in order to produce the human capital and to be able to use social capital (or relations of trust) in order to be included (Edwards 2002: 353–65).

While the 'social citizen' refers to the form of self-government in the social regime, the figure of the 'entrepreneurial citizen' or 'entrepreneur of the self' refers to the form of self-government promoted and stimulated today.[4] Entrepreneurship here is about using resources to produce a commodity that meets needs and offers an income. But entrepreneurship, as economists have pointed out, is not just a mechanical process of allocation and production. It also involves an 'element of alertness', i.e. a speculative, creative or innovative attitude to see opportunities in a competitive environment (Kirzner 1973: 33). Entrepreneurship is a risky business. However, risk is not, as in the social regime, to be prevented, but instead is the condition for profit – a kind of 'stimulating principle' (Giddens 2000: 73, 129). Identifying actual self-government as entrepreneurship means that people are required to look at themselves as operating within an environment and having certain needs that they can satisfy through creatively producing goods.

While social citizens submit themselves to the social tribunal (and its social laws) in order to be free, a submission to the 'permanent economic tribunal' is a condition for entrepreneurial freedom or self-government (Foucault 2004a: 253). However, 'economic' in this expression should not be understood as being in opposition to 'social'. 'Economic' refers to the characteristics of entrepreneurship (needs, calculation, production, alertness, risk). Furthermore, against the background of entrepreneurship as a mode of self-government, social relations are re-coded as the result of entrepreneurship or reflected on as enabling entrepreneurship: relations towards one's friends and loved ones and relations of trust and networks with colleagues are regarded as the result of investments and useful for personal happiness, social effectiveness and the well-being of nations (cf. Coleman 1988; Putnam 2000; OECD 2001).

However, we should be careful not to look at entrepreneurship in empirical, anthropological or (strict) economic (and anti-social) terms, nor as kind of ideal-type (Bröckling 2001: 3). Instead, it refers to a kind of governable self-government in today's governmental regime. This means that within entrepreneurship three dimensions come together. First, on the level of the governmental rationality, entrepreneurship has an *epistemological* dimension; i.e. the domains to be governed and government itself can be thought of and problematized in terms of the presence or absence of entrepreneurship, in terms of investment in human capital and the presence of a 'will to learn'. The main characteristic of this governmental rationality is therefore a kind of 'economization of the social' (Lemke 1997: 253). Second, since entrepreneurship is part of a governmental rationality, it also has a *strategic* dimension. The state is thought of as an 'enabling' and 'facilitating' entity that should use governmental technologies and procedures (for example marketization and enabling choice) to stimulate, enforce or bring about entrepreneurship (cf. Rose 1996). However, this epistemo-strategic dimension of entrepreneurship also brings an ethical dimension to the fore.

Ethical refers to the particular form of self-government or a way to practice freedom that implies the formation of a particular subjectivity (and of a particular self as an object of thought). This self-government can be described by identifying four components (cf. Foucault 1984a: 33). The material or (moral) 'substance' of this form of self-government is human (and social) capital, and more particularly, knowledge or competencies. The 'mode of subjection' of the entrepreneurial practice of freedom is the permanent economic tribunal: people should develop a managerial attitude of calculation towards this material or substance and should for example find out which competencies are required or could be(come) functional, which competencies they want/should invest in, etc. This substance and mode of subjection, thus, brings us to the 'work upon the self' that is needed: one is asked to *invest* in human capital, to *learn* or to *add* value to the self and to *find ways* of productive inclusion. Finally, this work upon the self has a particular teleology: the aim is the production of satisfaction of one's own needs or the needs of others.

Due to the combination of these dimensions, entrepreneurship refers to the governable form of freedom in the present regime of government. Hence, government is not opposed to freedom, but operates through freedom.

The business ethics of self-mobilization

In the previous section, we explained that it is the entrepreneurial self, and its managerial, calculating and speculative attitude towards life, that conceives learning as a fundamental process. In this section, the implications of entrepreneurial self-government, and the learning involved, will be explored in order to understand the assemblage of a learning apparatus in advanced liberalism. We introduce 'the ethics of self-mobilization' and the 'capitalization of life' in order to understand this assemblage.

As argued, the horizon for (governmental) reflection today is that individuals move around in environments (and networks) rather than having a social, normalized position in society. For survival in an environment with limited resources, entrepreneurship is required to generate and employ a (human) capital that can deliver incomes. This means that environments or networks require people to mobilize skills, knowledge or competencies (Edwards 2002: 359). Mobilization can be understood as bringing something (a potentiality) into a condition whereby it becomes employable (Sloterdijk 1991: 42–3). Typical for the *movement* of the entrepreneurial self in environments is the self-mobilization of knowledge and skills. To live an entrepreneurial life is not about having a position in a normal, socialized structure but is about moving around in different environments or networks and to remain employed in the 'continuous business of living' (Gordon 1991: 44).

Thus self-mobilization refers not only to the responsibility of the entrepreneurial self to mobilize its human capital but also to the responsibility to capitalize one's life in such a way that it has economic value (Rose 1999: 162). For the entrepreneurial self economic value is not only expressed in financial terms (and what is valued in the environment of the labour market) but applies to everything that enables the production of satisfaction of whatever needs in whatever environment. Furthermore, self-mobilization and the ongoing capitalization of life require the fundamental disposition to renew one's human capital; in other words, a *willingness and preparedness to learn*. For the entrepreneurial self this decision to learn is similar to an act of investment – to be precise, an investment in human capital that is expected to offer an income or return. Learning as a well thought-out investment and as a responsible capitalization and mobilization of life is the main prerequisite for the ongoing business of life. In short, this business ethics is a kind of *adaptation* ethics based upon the following maxim: do what you want but take care that your human capital is adapted.

It is important to stress at this point that this business ethic (this responsibility towards a capitalization of the self, towards self-mobilization and learning as investment) is actually being shaped in specific procedures and instruments. An illustration is the portfolio. A portfolio is a kind of 'wallet' including all knowledge, skills and attitudes that can be employed or mobilized (Birembaum and Dochy 1996). To use a portfolio implies that one is reflecting upon the self in terms of economic value, i.e. identifying and classifying one's stock of human capital that could offer access to environments. More generally speaking, this wallet with its stock of human capital descriptors can function as a kind of passport to obtain access to the business of life itself. Exemplary at this point is the 'Europass-program' of the European Union and the proposal to develop a single framework for the transparency of qualifications and competencies (Vandenbroucke 2004: 11). This instrument (an electronic portfolio) requires of people an ongoing documentation and marketization of the self and a formalization of its learning. At the same time, these kinds of instruments offer strategic data allowing (educational) policy to govern learning processes and to assess the learning force of the population.

These illustrations help to explain how the learning, entrepreneurial self (and its ethics of adaptation) is at the same time a governable subject that is of strategic importance for advanced liberal government. For this kind of government, citizens who experience learning as a fundamental force of adaptation have a strategic meaning because they guarantee that human capital will be adapted. Within this governmental rationality, the policy of change and adaptation is delegated to each entrepreneurial individual (or community, or organization) separately. In addition, the role of the state is to offer the infrastructure for self-mobilization and the opportunities for investment in human capital. Thus, it is the entrepreneurial self who should herself have a 'policy of change and adaptation' and who is able to do so by managing in a responsible, calculating, proactive way her learning capacity. Hence, within the advanced liberal regime of government the strategic role of learning is to secure adaptation.

At this point, we can introduce the concept of the 'learning apparatus'.[5] With this concept, we do not refer to an apparatus that is created, implemented or imposed by the state in order to organize learning. What we notice however is that different and dispersed components become interconnected and are assembled in a kind of strategic complex. As a strategic complex, the learning apparatus embodies a kind of intention for it seeks to secure adaptation. The state has not invented this apparatus in order to secure adaptation. Instead, the 'power of the state' is an outcome of dispersed practices and discourses that seek to promote entrepreneurship and the capitalization of life through learning. What we see is therefore not the 'étatization' or domination of society and the learning potential of citizens by the state, but a kind of 'governmentalization of the state' in the name of learning. Drawing upon a multitude of locales and practices that stimulate entrepreneurship the state can 'translate' all types of policy challenges (e.g. unemployment, democratic participation, health care …) into learning problems and seek to utilize components of the learning apparatus to offer solutions (e.g. training, citizenship education, programmes of risk prevention …) (cf. Rose 1996: 43).

In a similar way, this apparatus to secure adaptation through learning should not be regarded as the logical outcome of an original 'will to learn'. Instead, this 'will' is part of this apparatus and its strategy. More precisely, this willingness to learn is both an effect and an instrument of the present governmental regime and its strategy to secure adaptation. It is an effect since the regime asks that entrepreneurial selves be prepared and able to learn, but at the same time an instrument because this 'will' is used to secure adaptation within society as a whole.

Learning to be free or freeing ourselves from learning?

The aim of this article was to answer the question: for whom i.e. for which kind of subject does learning appear as a fundamental force to position and reposition oneself in society? What we have tried to show is that it is the entrepreneurial self (i.e. *we*, as entrepreneurial selves) who experience it as such and that the historical condition for this experience of learning (as capital, as what should be managed and as what is our responsibility) to emerge is a particular space of thought and a particular governmental configuration. Moreover, throughout the chapter we have tried to give a voice to a critical concern that Foucault formulated as follows: 'People know what they do, they frequently know why they do what they do; but what they don't know is what what they do does' (Foucault, in Dreyfus and Rabinow 1982: 187). With regard to the latter, we have demonstrated that our present experience of learning cannot be disconnected from a governmentalization of learning; learning is both a force of adaptation for entrepreneurial self-government and an instrument to secure the adaptation or added value of capital within society. Therefore, looking at learning and the liberation of our learning (from the state, from institutions, from the dominance of the teacher, from the impact of the economy, etc.) as a condition for our freedom and autonomy implies that we forget that this learning and the way in which we conceive it are from the very beginning both effect and instrument of the current governmental regime.

As a conclusion therefore, we find it necessary to point out the irony of the learning apparatus within this governmental regime: it makes us believe that it is about our freedom (cf. Foucault 1976). Accordingly, we do not think that what is needed today is a liberation of learning (from the state, from the economy, from ideology ...), nor yet another distinction between learning with an emancipatory potential and learning with a disciplinary potential.[6] What we find necessary is that we free ourselves from learning, that is, from the experience of learning as a fundamental force that is necessary for our freedom and for collective well-being. In line with this, we hope our critical re-reading of 'what is being said and written' today brings about a kind of de-familiarization that is at the same time a kind of de-subjectification: pulling oneself free of oneself. Perhaps this act of 'liberation', that is, a transformation of the relation of the self to the self, points at another idea and practice of education (beyond learning or learning to learn).

Notes

1 This is a shortened and revised version of the article 'The governmentalization of learning and the assemblage of a learning apparatus' published in *Educational Theory*.
2 The order of names is arbitrary. Maarten Simons expresses his gratitude to the K.U. Leuven Research Council for the receipt of a postdoctoral research grant in order to conduct the research reported in this article.
3 There is a growing body of studies that focus in a similar way on these topics: Edwards 2002; Edwards and Nicoll 2004; Fejes 2005.
4 It was Foucault who first focused on this figure of 'entrepreneurship' and the 'entrepreneurial self' in his analysis of neo-liberalism at the level of governmentality (cf. Gordon 1991: 44; Foucault 2004a).
5 For the notion of apparatus or 'dispositif': Foucault 1976: 125. For the idea of assemblage or putting components together 'fabricated' in different (temporal, spatial) contexts: Burchell 1996: 26; Dean 1999: 29; Rose 1999: 53.
6 For this kind of distinction: Delanty 2003. For a similar discussion, see also: Biesta 2006.

References

Biesta, G. (2006) *Beyond Learning*, Boulder: Paradigm.
Birenbaum, M. and Dochy, F. (eds) (1996) *Alternatives in Assessment of Achievement, Learning Processes and Prior Knowledge*, Boston: Kluwer Academic.
Bomers, G. (1991) 'De lerende organisatie', *Gids voor de Opleidingspraktijk*, 8: 1–25.
Bröckling, U. (2001) 'Gendering the Enterprising self: Subjectification Programs and gendering Differences in Guides to Success', paper presented at the international symposium *Welcome to the Revolution*, Institut für Theorie der Kunst und Gestaltung, Zurich, November 2001.
Burchell, G. (1996) 'Liberal government and techniques of the self', in A. Barry, T. Osborne and N. Rose (eds), *Foucault and the Political Reason: Liberalism, Neo-Liberalism and Rationalities of Government*, London: UCL Press.
Coleman, J.S. (1988) 'Social capital in the creation of human capital', *American Journal of Sociology*, 94: 95–120.
Dean, M. (1999) *Governmentality. Power and Rule in Modern Society*, New Delhi: Sage.
Delanty, G. (2003) 'Citizenship as a learning process: disciplinary citizenship versus cultural citizenship', *International Journal of Lifelong Education*, 22: 597–605.
Dreyfus, H. and Rabinow, P. (1982) *Michel Foucault: Beyond Structuralism and Hermeneutics*, Brighton: Harvester.
Drucker, P. (1969) *The Age of Discontinuity. Guidelines to our Changing Society*, New York: Harper & Row.
Edwards, R. (2002) 'Mobilizing lifelong learning: governmentality in educational practices', *Journal of Education Policy*, 17: 353–65.
Edwards, R. and Nicoll, K. (2004) 'Mobilizing workplaces: actors, discipline and governmentality', *Studies in Continuing Education*, 26: 159–73.
European Commission (1995) *Teaching and Learning: Towards the Learning Society*, Brussels: European Commission.

Faure, E., Herrera, F., Kaddoura, A-R., Lopes, H., Petrovsky, A.V., Rahnema, M. and Champion Ward, F. (1972) *Learning to Be. The World of Education Today and Tomorrow*, Paris: Unesco.

Fejes, A. (2005) 'New wine in old skins: changing patterns in the governing of the adult learner in Sweden', *International Journal of Lifelong Education*, 24: 71–86.

Flavell, J. H. (1976) 'Metacognitive aspects of problem solving', in L.B. Resneck (ed.), *The Nature of Intelligence*, Hillsdale: Laurence Erlbaum.

Foucault, M. (1976) *Histoire de la Sexualité 1. La Volonté de Savoir*, Paris: Gallimard.

Foucault, M. (1984a) 'Qu'est-ce que les Lumières', in D. Defert, F. Ewald and J. Lagrange (eds), *Dits et Écrits IV 1980–1988*, Paris: Gallimard.

Foucault, M. (1984b) *Histoire de la Sexualité 2. L'usage des Plaisirs*, Paris: Gallimard.

Foucault, M. (2004a) *Naissance de la Biopolitique, Cours au Collège de France (1978–1979)*, Paris: Gallimard/Le seuil.

Foucault, M. (2004b) *Sécurité, Territoire, Population, Cours au Collège de France (1977–1978)*, Paris: Gallimard/Le seuil.

Gagné, R.M. (1970) *The Conditions of Learning*, London: Holt, Rinehart and Winston.

Giddens, A. (2000) *Paars: De Derde Weg. Over de vernieuwing van de sociaal-democratie*, Antwerpen: Houtekiet.

Glasersfeld, von E. (1995) *Radical Constructivism: A Way of Knowing and Learning*, London: Falmer.

Gordon, C. (1991) 'Governmental rationality: an introduction', in G. Burchell, C. Gordon and P. Miller (eds), *The Foucault Effect: Studies in Governmentality*, London: Harvester Wheatsheaf.

Husén, T. (1974) *The Learning Society*, London: Methuen.

Kirzner, I. (1973) *Competition and Entrepreneurship*, Chicago: The University of Chicago Press.

Knowles, M.S. (1970) *The Modern Practice of Adult Education: Andragogy Versus Pedagogy*, Chicago: Follett.

Lemke, T. (1997) *Eine Kritik der Politischen Vernunft. Foucault's Analyse der Moderne Gouvernementalität*, Berlin/Hamburg: Argument.

Lindeman, E.C. (1926) *The Meaning of Adult Education*, New York: New Republic. Online. Available www.infed.org/archives/e-texts/lindem1.html (accessed 17 January 2007).

Mayer, R.E. (1983) *Thinking, Problem Solving, Cognition*, New York: W.H. Freeman.

Ministry of Flemish Community (MFC) (1999) *Beroepsprofielen en Basiscompetenties van de Leraren. Decretale Tekst en Memorie van Toelichting*, Brussel: Departement Onderwijs.

OECD (2001) *The Well-Being of Nations. The Role of Human and Social Capital*, Paris: OECD.

Putnam, R. (2000) *Bowling Alone: The Collapse and Revival of American Community*, New York: Simon & Schuster.

Rose, N. (1996) 'Governing 'advanced' liberal Democracies', in A. Barry, T. Osborne and N. Rose (eds), *Foucault and the Political Reason: Liberalism, Neo-Liberalism and Rationalities of Government*, London: UCL Press.

Rose, N. (1999) *The Powers of Freedom. Reframing Political Thought*, Cambridge: Cambridge University Press.

Senge, P. (1990) 'The Leader's New Work: Building learning organizations', *Sloan Management Review*, 23: 7–23.

Shuell, T. J. (1988) 'The role of the student in learning from instruction', *Contemporary Educational Psychology*, 13: 276–95.

Sloterdijk, P. (1991) *Eurotaoïsme. Over de Kritiek van de Politieke Kinetiek*, trans. W. Hansen, Amsterdam: Uitgeverij De Arbeiderspers.

Tjepkema, S. (1996) 'Ondersteuning van de kenniswerker in een lerende organisatie', *Opleiders in Organisaties/Capita-Selecta*, 26: 83–98.

Vandenbroucke, F. (2004) *Onderwijs en vorming. Vandaag Kampioen in Wiskunde, Morgen ook in Gelijke Kansen. Beleidsnota 2004–2009*, Brussel: Ministerie van de Vlaamse Gemeenschap.

Westhoff, G.J. (1996) 'Naar een didaktiek van de studeerbekwaamheid', in J. Kaldeway, J. Haenen, S. Wils and G. Westhoff (eds), *Leren Leren in Didactisch Perspectief*, Groningen: Wolters-Noordhoff.

Chapter 5

The operation of knowledge and construction of the lifelong learning subject

Ulf Olsson and Kenneth Petersson

The purpose of this chapter is to problematize contemporary thought about knowledge and knowledge production by comparing discursive practices in the fields of teacher education, public health and criminal justice. Knowledge and knowledge organization cannot be thought of without considering the notion of governance. Governance takes place in relation to the ways in which we develop and organize knowledge about things and phenomena that are to be governed, and knowledge is not intelligible without an understanding of how it is situated in the present as embedded in historical conditions. The subject is continuously (re)constructed as an object that is known, through the discursive practices of education, public health and criminal justice systems. Thus, from this point of view, knowledge does not represent reality, but has instead a productive role in shaping and configuring reality. Knowledge can be regarded as a practice of governance taking place in various social areas, and thus a knowledge society is a governing society (cf. Olsson *et al.* 2006). With the increasing importance of knowledge in our actions there is good reason to explore and pay attention to the effects and power of the production of knowledge itself. It is said that we live in a *knowledge society* and that as subjects we are to be treated as *lifelong learning citizens.* And here the idea of the 'knowledge society' is characterized as a changing pattern in the governing of the Swedish welfare state, in which the school, education, public health and criminal justice are included.

Changing rationalities of government also means a changing view of ourselves. That is, changing forms of governmental reason are part of the ways in which we reconfigure ourselves as active subjects. The changing political and historical circumstances of government also implicate changing conditions and changing views of knowledge production and knowledge organization, especially when it comes to *learning, education* and *pedagogy.*

In this chapter, we seek to understand how narratives about knowledge operate in the contemporary practices of governmentalities to design and responsibilize learning communities and educable and lifelong learning subjects.

Our main interest is to explore the interior relationship between knowledge and governance.

Our concern is with the assemblies of rules and principles for knowledge production that design individuality across different institutional settings within a contemporary learning society. Contemporary policy programmes and scientific texts in the fields of education, criminal justice and public health are preoccupied with notions of learning and knowledge, as a response to a future that is conceived as constantly changing and fraught with ever-greater risks. The epistemological premise of contemporary governance is that it is possible to order and control the future in the present, by qualifying and preparing the individual citizen and inculcating a disposition for new commitments in a constantly changing, pluralistic and fragmented world (Olsson and Petersson 2005; Popkewitz *et al.* 2005). The governmental practice generates principles about subjects whose mode of living entails an autonomous, responsible and 'future-oriented' life. In this context, knowledge operates as a central regulatory notion in the fabrication of the subjects to be governed.

The empirical material for our study consists of a variety of contemporary Swedish texts: government reports, scientific texts, proposed reform programs, text books, project presentations and evaluations as well as periodicals from the three political fields and from the fields of democracy and lifelong learning. The Swedish case is an illustration of general global trends concerning the organization of knowledge in the fabrication of the lifelong learner (Nóvoa 2002; Hargreaves 2003; Popkewitz *et al.* 2005).

The governmentalities of the modern learning subject

Educational science has traditionally been concerned with the study of the institutions that provide formal education. In contemporary society, one important trend is the expansion and spread of the 'pedagogical paradigm' to areas not traditionally considered educational. Today, education anywhere in the world is not just a question of what is taught in school, but is, in the name of lifelong learning, something that permeates the governance of all social activities. An increasing number of institutions regard this paradigm as vital for their activities. This is evident in, for example, the national plans of the Swedish National Agency for Education (SNAE), where the main focus is on lifelong and life-wide learning. Here, the boundaries between political, social and cultural sectors are removed, giving them all 'a common responsibility for the life long and life wide learning' (SNAE 2000: 10).

This changing mode of government is obvious in, for example, the domain of criminal justice and the current system of criminal law. Compared to the classical and traditional penal regimes, the trend today seems to be that more and more pedagogical and empowerment-oriented features are regarded as useful. The example below is an illustration from New Zealand but the situation is the same in Sweden or in other European countries (cf. Petersson 2003). Today, the settings of the prisons should offer:

> [A]n opportunity for the offender to recognize (treatment goals) and to learn strategies to change his behaviour and beliefs ... The ways in which the offender overcame his own, the victim's, and other social restraints to offending, permit comprehensive planning for his future, through adopting a 'life long plan' for avoidance of further molestations.
>
> (Pratt 1997: 186)

The idea of the pragmatic and designing role of knowledge is linked to Michel Foucault's later intellectual works (cf. Foucault 1991). Here he, among other things, emphasized the way in which governance in modern societies has become increasingly oriented towards governing how individuals and collectives see themselves in terms of who they are and are supposed to be.

The inherent relationship between the governance of society, the production and organization of knowledge of human beings, social questions and the political aspects of the production of knowledge is summed up by Foucault (1991) in the notion of *Governmentalitè/Governmentality*. Governmentality directs attention to the principles of reason as inscriptions in which different cultural practices come together to govern, shape and fashion the conduct of conduct. According to Foucault, the governing of subjects – individuals as well as collectives – since the eighteenth century has rested on knowledge and knowledge production. The concept of knowledge in itself does not have any essential meaning, its meaning changes with historical and discursive contexts.

> The possibility of knowing, Foucault claimed, was neither in the inherent structures of the brain nor in Kant's transcendental categories but in the historical archives of knowledge. For example, we are used to thinking of the State, the Nation, and the subject as fixed entities with certain localization and as distributed in time. The concept of governmentality enables us to take another route. Instead of asking about the essential character of things and people, we might ask how such conceptions emerged, where and in which contexts, and what effects they have on ourselves and on other people.
>
> (Hultqvist 2004: 155)

Consequently, knowledge possesses a political dimension and in the light of this fact it is not far-fetched to think of this dimension as 'that kind of epistemology that is organizing the production of knowledge', that is, a *political epistemology* (Petersson 2003: 23).

We can specify this terminology further by looking at the way in which we consider the different empirical domains we have chosen to explore in this chapter. We regard teacher education as well as public health, criminal justice and criminology in the same way as the school, that is, as educating and disciplining practices that impact on the way we govern others and ourselves. In this way it is possible to designate them as *pedagogical technologies*. Pedagogical technologies are to be regarded 'as intellectual and practical tools for governing and shaping individuals according to the assumptions that are written into the technology itself' (Hultqvist *et al.* 2002: 4). It is these and similar assumptions we designate in terms of *political epistemology*.

Our point of departure is thus not just to try and investigate the mentalities of governing by exploring only figures of thought, ideas or knowledge as such. We also try to explore the ways in which these operate and are embedded in our institutionalized and pragmatic ways of making people and things up, and in the problems that are raised and solutions to be achieved.

The re-ordering of the educable subject

Today, Swedish crime policy and forms of correctional care, as for example they are expressed by the Swedish Prison and Probation Service (SPPS), are keen to emphasize and demonstrate their mission of *learning*, that is, they recognize themselves as *learning organizations* and the people involved as *learning subjects*:

> The inmate at Östragård discovers that there exists human dignity since he/she is met by knowledge and revenge. He/she feels that his resources (the human behind the crime) have a capacity to advance and develop the institutional activities, both when it is comes to himself as an individual and to Östragård as a whole – once again the learning organization.
>
> (SPPS 1994: 5)

It is more or less obvious that the field of crime policy is about moving towards a new governmental approach to pedagogy and that the penal institutions function more as schools than, as traditionally, as an apparatus of punishment and correction.

A different view of the governing of pedagogy and education also includes a different view of the subject, that is, the object of government. Current thoughts about the individual learning subject are supported by terms such as skills improvement, communication, reflectivity, flexibility, autonomy, responsibility, empowerment and so forth.

The reframing of political thinking goes hand in hand with thinking about how to prepare for the future, in this case, 'the future of correctional care': preparing for the future is the same as preparing for the organization of learning and knowledge, which is 'constructing a learning, experimental, inter-disciplinary (humanistic/scientific), knowledge-intensive and goal-directed organization, which has measurable tangible goals' (SPPS 1995: 8). With such a knowledge-oriented mode of governance, it is not the learning of basic standards of knowledge or subject-specific knowledge that is at the top of the agenda. Rather, the focus is on the kind of contemporary schemes of governance that we experience and are related to, locally and globally, in our considerations of the world and of ourselves. Lifelong learning, as we have stated earlier, appears as a self-regulatory scheme. Thus, 'active citizenship, entrepreneurial culture, lifelong learning or reflexive life are part of the same reconfiguration of the *self*' (Nóvoa 2002: 141–2).

Let us now turn to a closer exploration of contemporary thought about knowledge production and knowledge organization in connection with current teacher education. At the same time, let us introduce a perspective of the cross-fertilization between changes in current political epistemology and the repositioning and reconfigurations of the subject of lifelong learning within the discourses and practices of educational policy and other institutional settings at the beginning of the twenty-first century.

Knowledge production as a pedagogical technology

The focus of our exploration is not on education and knowledge as a means of preparing the individuals for the future. Instead, we argue that the future is constructed *by* education and knowledge, as a means of fabricating specific and 'future-oriented' subjects and to order and govern a set of heterogeneous elements, men, things, institutions and discourses to achieve useful ends. Knowledge thus has an important role in the current shaping of future-oriented subjects who are active in the governing of themselves and society (Hultqvist 2006). The knowledge produced by the subject becomes a means for her/his participation as a responsible agent in the governing of society, and the production of knowledge of the subject becomes a technology for the governing of the self.

Knowledge as subject construction

A precondition for the fabrication of this responsible and lifelong learning subject is, as we have argued in Petersson *et al.* (2007), a contemporary narrative about a constantly changing society. Thus, it becomes, according to the Commission on Teacher Education as expressed in their report published by the Ministry of Education (ME), important for teachers to support the pupils to find 'the best way in which to develop for him/herself the ability to understand and handle his/her future' (ME 1999: 58). Similar stories about the importance of knowledge in dealing with the future are told in most political contexts. In all these stories, the concept of knowledge operates as a productive tool in the creation and governing of responsible, lifelong learning, future-oriented and self-governing subjects. However, one difference between the field of teacher education and the fields of criminal justice/crime prevention and public health/health promotion is that the commission emphasizes that teacher education must be regarded as a 'knowledge-conquering project', as a knowledge practice (ME 1999: 63, 78). The texts from the other two fields do not stress this in the same way.

It is obvious that the narratives in the context of education emphasize that the world has become increasingly changeable and difficult to predict. One of the voices within these narratives asks how the school could prepare itself for a 'future we know less of but have to know more and more about' (Carlgren and Marton 2000: 25). The answer given is about developing talents to be able to manage new situations.

> We can nevertheless contribute to developing their (teachers, *our addition*) ability to learn from new situations, to be able to discern what is critical, important and subsequently take action. The best we can do is to contribute to developing the eyes that make them able to see new situations.
>
> (Carlgren and Marton 2000: 25)

The notion or the knowledge of the changing society becomes embedded in 'the eyes' of the subject and thus operates as a productive force in the fabrication of the pupils/students as subjects. The knowledge of the changing society becomes in a similar way embedded in the construction of the teacher. If the teacher is to be able to contribute to the development of the talents of the pupils/students, he/she must have the ability to diversify activities in school with respect to differences between situations as well as pupils/students.

> The object of the professional teachers is learning, that is, development of different abilities and approaches among the pupils … insight into the professional object is of crucial importance if the individual person practicing the profession is to be able to – on the basis of that sort of insight – manage situations never predicted before.
>
> (Carlgren and Marton 2000: 25)

All this presupposes a teacher subject equipped with the capability to act in new and constantly changing situations on the basis of insights into and understanding of the professional object of the teacher; that is, the quality of learning the teacher is supposed to bring about (Carlgren and Marton 2000: 25).

The knowledge of the constantly changing society thus operates as a constitutive part, not just in terms of fabricating the pupil/student subject, but also in the construction of the teacher. In Hultqvist's words: 'The formation of knowledge is therefore just as much about the formation of the teacher's person' (Hultqvist 2006: 46). The conception of knowledge configured in the narratives of teacher education, the local and self-governed forms of learning, thus operates as a technology in the responsibilization and construction of individual as well as collective local subjects.

Even though the field of public health is not emphasized in contemporary narratives as a 'knowledge project', it operates as such in terms of subject-construction: The search for knowledge is thus 'considered not just as a condition for responsibility, but also that a responsible person is characterized by an active attitude when he/she is searching continuously for knowledge concerning health and ill-health' (Kjellström 2005: 79). Searching for knowledge is thus one central disposition that characterizes a contemporary responsible subject, both in the case of questions of health and when it comes to the disposition of the subject itself. The subject is inscribed in the notion of future and the future is inscribed in the subject in a similar way as in teacher education. This means that the 'patient of tomorrow will be a demanding consumer and a conscious consumer. This development will create bigger opportunities for the individuals to take responsibility for the health of their own as well as for their intimates' (Ministry of Health and Social affairs 2000: 569) (MHSA). Knowledge is considered to be a tool for organizing and changing the conditions governing people's lives. It is thus a notion of knowledge that is homological with and supports the very fabrication of an active responsible subject. One could say that the conceptions of knowledge and thereby the imagination of the future will become inscribed in the subject and the subject will be inscribed in the notion of knowledge: one cannot exclude the other.

The responsible subject as knowledge producer

The subjects made responsible, the future teacher and the teacher, as well as teacher education and the school, are supposed to be able to develop the new knowledge needed to confront the future. The teacher must be 'able to develop new knowledge of the educational activity and thus exert an influence on the future' (ME 1999: 59). This future, according to the commission, is impossible to know anything about, except in that it is changing and impossible to foresee. According to the commission, teacher education should support the ability of students of teaching 'to create something new and not just take over and repeat already established knowledge or patterns of conduct' (ME 1999: 63). In this matter, neither the teacher of today nor the teacher of tomorrow is constructed as a subject whose learning, primarily, is based on knowledge 'created' by different kinds of scientific experts outside the context of the practice of the teacher. Instead, the subject constructed as an autonomous producer of knowledge, a creator of the necessary flow of knowledge for participating as a responsible subject in the governing of an ever-changing society. The most important task for the teacher will thus be to organize stimulating learning environments and learning settings which 'supports exploring processes' (ME 1999: 57) for the learning human being, that is, settings 'in which the individual in an active manner acquires knowledge and where knowledge is regarded as a process rather than as a product' (ME 1999: 70).

The teacher that is created in the texts is, as we have seen, also a knowledge-producing subject with the capacity to organize settings in which the pupil/student is an active knowledge producer. One of the dispositions inscribed in the learning subject is the ability to consider, practice and in a critical manner examine her/his practice and thus adopt a scientific view of the teaching profession and professional knowledge.

> The professional teacher of tomorrow would, among other things, be educated to be a reflecting – and critical – practitioner. Being critical means that one adopts a scientific perspective towards professional knowledge and the teaching profession ... But it also implies that the professional practice of the teacher could be the point of departure for theorizing and knowledge production.
>
> (ME 1999: 63)

The teacher's own professional practice should be the platform of knowledge production designed by the teacher her/himself. The teacher subject, engaged in local self-governed learning for knowledge development, and furnished with the ability to be active in influencing the future, becomes embedded in a scientific 'paradigm' by being constructed as a self-reflective knowledge-producing practitioner who adopts a scientific approach.

A similar but different story about citizens as knowledge-producing subjects is told with regard to practices of crime prevention, where citizens become crucial for the development of informal ways of influencing and controlling the local community. One example is from a Swedish suburb project 'The Future Hjällbo' in the Gothenburg region, reported by the Swedish National Council for Crime Prevention (BRÅ), the aim of which was to address 'a general sense of insecurity to be found among those living on the estate and [to] the high level of crime' (BRÅ 2000: 1). A security group was formed to promote collaboration between a number of different players in the local community. The principal activities of the group consisted of observing and patrolling the surroundings, and in this way 'acquires knowledge of different forms of illicit activities and speedily observes abnormalities and anomalies on the estate' (BRÅ 2000: 3).

The citizen in the local community was constructed as a knowledge-producer, producing knowledge indispensable for the governing of the local community. The so-called everyday crime in the local community required everyday knowledge, and this in part sidelined professional and expert knowledge (cf. Andersson 2002). Although there was collaboration between institutions, professionals and citizens, it was the estate residents who were empowered to be active and responsible as knowledge producers and problem-solvers. It is in this way that the knowledge-producing citizen and lifelong learner, at the same time as he/she is offered a kind of autonomy and freedom, is educated to govern her/himself, others and the local environment through crime prevention.

> The Estate Security Group's activities are based on a professional role that its members have developed themselves. This role is neither that of guard, field worker, leisure time leader or property maintenance worker. It lies somewhere in between these categories and can be seen as an emerging new profession.
>
> (BRÅ 2000: 4)

The results of the Hjällbo experiments are thus a fabrication of a new unique local 'private'/'public' profession that serves the individual, the local community as well as society/the country. The Estate Security project is an illustration of the way national concerns are expressed in the name of local governing through local knowledge development.

In the field of health promotion, the construction of the subject as knowledge producer is not emphasized as much as in the field of education. In this field, knowledge operates as a technology to help people to make 'informed decisions' about matters affecting their personal health and that of others. 'Health promoters should work to increase knowledge and understanding, and individual coping strategies' (Naidoo and Wills 2000: 86). The subjects in this field are, rather, constructed as 'knowledge searchers' who actively search, rather than, as in the field of teacher education, actively produce knowledge (MHSA 2000).

In line with Paulo Freire, Meredith and Wallerstein (2002) propose a dialogical problem-posing process, with equality and mutual respect between the health educator and the citizens in the community. Naidoo and Wills (2000), in a similar way, inscribe Freire's figures of thought in the health-promoting process, emphasizing that 'instead of experts and professionals diagnosing problems, the people themselves define health issues of relevance to them in their local community' (Naidoo and Wills 2000: 82). Further, they argue that it is about 'working with individuals and groups to enhance their knowledge and understanding of the factors affecting their health' (Naidoo and Wills 2000: 85). And in this process, it is important to acknowledge the knowledge that the people in the local community are supposed to have, because one key feature in the philosophy of empowerment of individuals and communities is 'an emphasis on lay knowledge and the valuing of people's own experience' (Naidoo and Wills 2000: 202). 'An important aspect of community development work is legitimizing people's knowledge about health and illness and giving this a voice' (Naidoo and Wills 2000: 206). Thus, although the subjects in the field of health promotion are principally constructed as searchers and not producers of knowledge, they are still constructed as subjects with knowledge of importance for the governance of the local environment and of themselves as subjects.

As the reorganization of teacher education, crime prevention and health promotion is more and more a question of governing at the local and personal level, it also tends to reconfigure or fabricate local knowledge-producing subjects into new forms of semi-professionals. Expert knowledge moves from the formal expert and professional subjects and becomes embedded in local citizens themselves. In this respect, both crime prevention and health promotion have created conditions for the dispositions of the local citizens that have some similarities with the creation of the new teacher.

Governing oneself through knowledge produced by oneself

The reflexive knowledge-producing subject in the field of education is expected to focus critical attention on the teaching profession, teaching activities and her/his school. Thus, it is about directing one's gaze towards all the processes that contribute to governing to achieve the educational or teaching mission. However, by focusing her/his attention inwards, on the subject, the teacher is also expected to produce knowledge, 'self-knowledge and personal development' is necessary for the governing of her- or himself (ME 1999).

> Reflections on experiences make it possible to develop a kind of knowledge, which can operate as a frame for the interpretation of the work of the teacher. This makes it possible to pay attention to underlying assumptions concerning the teachers' actions and values connected to the goals of the education.
>
> (ME 1999: 66)

The subject (the teacher) is thus constructed as a knowledge subject, where practice in schools produces knowledge indispensable for the governing of the school, the pupils and the subject itself. A crucial component in the process of learning is how to produce knowledge about ourselves and to understand how knowledge works in practice, that is, to design our 'own learning processes as a research object (a meta-perspective)' (ME 1999: 13) for the future. The government report on teacher education emphasizes that it is a knowledge project where one of 'the main tasks for the future' is to give future teachers insights 'into how knowledge is constituted' (ME 1999: 78).

> In teacher education, the student participates in his or her own knowledge production about how knowledge is constituted. This means that the students' way of reasoning, thinking and experiencing becomes a process parallel with their own way of teaching.
>
> (ME 1999: 82–3)

Thus, a central dimension of teacher education is the ability to develop knowledge about how knowledge is produced and constituted. In this context, the students' own knowledge and learning processes become a knowledge practice for the production and development of teachers' knowledge. The teacher's production of knowledge is considered to be a crucial component for governing her- or himself, as well as of the designing of learning settings and thus governing of the pupil as subject.

Also in the field of public health the subject and the life of the subject are designed as a practice of knowledge, producing knowledge as a technology for governing: 'Human beings' knowledge about themselves is an important and fundamental form of knowledge. Self-knowledge or self-awareness concerns, for instance, how your body works and about your needs and feelings' (Kjellström 2005: 79). According to Kjellström, self-knowledge is, like other forms of categories of knowledge, 'tools that individuals can use, to acquire more power over her or his life-situation and to expand the possibilities of improving health' (Kjellström 2005: 78). Thus, also in the field of health promotion the individual is constructed as a knowledge-producing subject, producing knowledge about her/his inner life, feelings, thoughts and goals that can be used as a technology for governing her/himself.

Self-knowledge also operates in a similar way in the field of crime prevention, where 'naturally-arising situations in the therapy groups are explored and utilized to help the men learn about themselves and develop more appropriate social behaviours and self-concepts' (Pratt 1997: 186).

Conclusion

In current political narratives, the teacher, classroom pupil, student teacher and health-promoting and crime-preventing citizen seem to be confronted with the mission to embody new dispositions of responsibility, future orientation and knowledge production.

Today, the future seems a term used to implicate a set of technologies that establish a horizon of intelligibility and makes the present situation possible to govern. In teacher education, health-promotion and crime-prevention, the future is the name of *the present* in which knowledge-producing subjects are constructed and inscribed with responsibility as subjects through the notion of lifelong learning. Although knowledge in these contexts is supposed to be a concept of the collective, it also operates as a technique for personality development, or as it is emphasized in the report of the teacher education: knowledge should 'create a personal context for each individual' (ME 1999: 57). It should also be noted that since knowledge is viewed on the one hand as a contingent process based on local semi-professional everyday activity and on the other as a technique of personality development, the concepts of knowledge become more or less synonymous with the notion of lifelong learning.

Without any doubt, 'learning' in contemporary narratives means something different compared with those of other historical periods. Today it is stressed more than ever before that we are living in a risky, uncertain and ever-changing society. In this context, political epistemological turn-inscribing lifelong learning and constant re-education and knowledge production in everyday practice as a key to a manageable future becomes comprehensible. To plan for the future is to plan the inner dispositions and sensitivities that order the ways in which people solve problems as future-oriented citizens. The making of the future thus becomes an individual lifelong learning project (Petersson *et al.* 2007).

So today, the subject is thought of as the prime organizer of her/his own destiny and the task of education is to empower subjects to put life into order by themselves. The tendency to regard society as a school and the prevalence of the individual assignment, expressed in terms of lifelong and life-wide learning, self-regulation, empowerment and so forth, make these appear as conditions of possibility for governance in the early twenty-first century.

There are, of course, differences in the circumstances of the individual subjects in the contexts of health education, criminal justice and teacher education referred to in our study. There are obvious differences, for example, between the circumstances of teachers and criminals. However, as we have seen above, they all have to become knowledge-producing or knowledge-searching subjects in a space called the future.

References

Andersson, R. (2002) *Kriminalpolitikens Väsen*, Stockholm: Kriminologiska institutionen, Stockholms universitet.

Carlgren, I. and Marton, F. (2000) *Lärare av Imorgon*, Stockholm: Lärarförbundet.

Foucault, M. (1991) 'Governmentality', in G. Burchell, C. Gordon and P. Miller (eds), *The Foucault Effect. Studies in Governmentality*, London: Harvester Wheatsheaf.

Hargreaves, A. (2003) *Teaching in the Knowledge Society: Education in the Age of Security*, Maidenhad: Open University Press.

Hultqvist, K., Popkewitz, T.S., Petersson, K., Olsson, U. and Andersson, D. (2002) *The State, the Subject, and Pedagogical Technology. A Genealogy of the Present of Political Epistemologies and Governmentalities at the Beginning of the Twenty-First Century*, Proposal to The Swedish Research Council, Stockholm: Swedish Research Council.

Hultqvist, K. (2004) 'The traveling state, the nation, and the subject of education', in B.M. Baker and K.E. Heyning (eds), *Dangerous Coagulations. The Uses of Foucault in the Study of Education*, New York: Peter Lang.

Hultqvist, K. (2006) 'The future's already here – as it always has been. The new teacher's subject, the pupil and the technologies of the soul', in T.S. Popkewitz, K. Petersson, U. Olsson and J. Kowalczyk (eds), *The Future Is Not What It Appears To Be. Pedagogy, Genealogy and Political Epistemology*, Stockholm: HLS Förlag.

Kjellström, S. (2005) *Ansvar, Hälsa och Människa. En Studie av Idéer om Individens Ansvar för sin Hälsa*, Linköping: Studies in Arts and Science.

Meredith, M. and Wallerstein, N.B. (2002) 'Improving health trough community organization and community building', in K. Glanz, B.K. Rimner and

F.M. Lewis (eds), *Health Behaviour and Health Education: Theory, Research and Practice*, San Francisco: Jossey-Bass.

Ministry of Education (ME) (1999) *SOU 1999: 63, Att Lära och Leda: En Lärarutbildning för Samverkan och Utveckling*, Stockholm: Utbildningsdepartementet.

Ministry of Health and Social affairs (MIISA) (2000) *SOU 2000: 91, Hälsa på Lika Villkor, Nationella Mål for Hälsa*, Stockholm: Socialdepartementet.

Naidoo, J. and Wills, J. (2000) *Health Promotion Foundation for Practice*, Toronto: Balliére Tinda.

Nóvoa, A. (2002) 'Ways of thinking about education in Europe', in A. Nóvoa and M. Lawn (eds), *Fabricating Europe. The Formation of a European Space*, Dortrecht: Kluwer Academc Press.

Olsson, U. and Petersson, K. (2005) 'Dewey as an epistemic figure in the Swedish discourse on governing the self', in T.S. Popkewitz (ed.), *Inventing the Modern Self and John Dewey: Modernities and the Traveling of Pragmatism in Education*, New York: MacMillanPalgrave.

Olsson, U., Petersson, K. and Popkewitz, T.S. (2006) 'The future is not what it appears to be. An introduction', in T.S. Popkewitz, K. Petersson, U. Olsson and J. Kowalczyk (eds), *The Future Is Not What It Appears To Be. Pedagogy, Genealogy and Political Epistemology*, Stockholm: HLS Förlag.

Petersson, K. (2003) *Fängelset och den Liberala Fantasin*, Norrköping: Kriminalvårdsstyrelsen.

Petersson, K., Olsson, U. and Popkewitz, T.S. (2007) 'Nostalgia, future and the past as pedagogical technologies', *Discourse*, 28: 49–67.

Popkewitz, T.S., Olsson, U. and Petersson, K. (2005) 'The learning society, the unfinished cosmopolitan, and governing education, public health and crime prevention at the beginning of the twenty first century', *Educational Philosophy and Theory*, 38: 431–49.

Pratt, J. (1997) *Governing the Dangerous. Dangerousness, Law and Social Change*, Sydney: The Federation Press.

Swedish National Agency for Education (SNAE) (2000) *Det Livslånga och Livsvida Lärandet*, Stockholm: Skolverket.

Swedish National Council for Crime Prevention (BRÅ) (2000) *The Hjällbo Estate Security Group*. Online Available: www.bra.se/extra/publication (accessed 4 December 2006).

Swedish Prison and Probation Service (SPPS) (1994) *Måldokument*, KVA Östragård.

Swedish Prison and Probation Service (SPPS) (1995) *Projekt Trestad*, Kriminalvården.

Chapter 6

The reason of reason

Cosmopolitanism, social exclusion and lifelong learning

Thomas S. Popkewitz

This chapter focuses historically on the lifelong learner and the learning society as the cultural thesis of cosmopolitanism and its double gestures that both include and exclude. The hope of contemporary reforms embodied mutations of the hope of the Enlightenment's cosmopolitan citizen whose reason and rationality produced an emancipated humanity that included hospitality to 'Others'. That hope of the universal was never universal but brought to bear a particular system of reason that differentiated and divided the cosmopolitan from those who were not as 'civilized'. Today's notions of the lifelong learner reassembles the cosmopolitan hope to unify the whole through universal values of reason that simultaneously express fears of the dangers and dangerous population to that cosmopolitan future.

The chapter begins with the overlapping of the 'reason' of the lifelong learner and cosmopolitanism. I examine notions of problem solving and community in producing a cultural thesis about who the child is and should be. I speak of cosmopolitanism as a cultural thesis to consider how different historical trajectories overlap about a mode of living. The second section explores lifelong learners as the cultural thesis that links individuality with norms of collective belonging. The universality of that collective 'home' signifies the unity of the whole – the learning society – but ironically is bound to the particularity of a nation – an Americanness or the scaling of Europeanness. The third section considers the given unity as embodying double gestures. The double gestures are the hopes of the enlightened child and fears of the dangers and the dangerous individuals who threaten that cosmopolitanism – the child 'disadvantaged', 'urban', 'at-risk' and 'left behind'. The hope and fear are embodied in the same phenomenon and are not oppositions. The fourth and final section places the 'reason' of cosmopolitanism in relation to school subjects. I proceed in this manner to consider the overlapping and connections of pedagogical theories of the child with the translation tools through which school subjects are ordered and classified.

This chapter draws from a broader historical project concerned with the cosmopolitan fears of difference and schooling (Popkewitz 2008). The historicizing is to explore how givenness of the objects of the present have been ordered, connected and disconnected over time and space. The focus here is primarily on the present school reforms. My method is a history of the present. To borrow from Foucault, research is the '… matter of shaking this false self-evidence, of demonstrating its precariousness, of making visible not its arbitrariness, but its complex interconnection with a multiplicity of historical processes, many of them of recent data' (Foucault 1991: 75).

The hope: lifelong learner and community

This book illustrates the lifelong learner as cultural theses that move among a vast array of institutional sites in Europe and the US. The seduction of the lifelong learner is the enunciation of a particular Enlightenment attitude about a life guided by reason and compassion for the other (Popkewitz 2005). Today's cosmopolitanism is different, what I will call unfinished, the continual search for innovation and change in which the only thing that is not a choice is making choices.[1]

For some, the learning society and the lifelong learner are a cultural thesis about life as a continual process that defines the individual's agency as choice. Maeroff (2003), for example, embraces the notion of neoliberalism as maximizing choices in the instructional programs of online learning. Online learning is to enable the learning society where all children and adults live a life as a continual process of learning through the computer and the internet. Maeroff views the new education as making possible the highest development of cosmopolitan reason through a democratization of instruction that enables choice and diversity.

From a different ideological perspective, Hargreaves (2003) speaks of lifelong learners as a cosmopolitanism that rejects neoliberalism's free market approach, to prepare the child for the future that is not only about self-actualization but commitments to social goals of equity and justice. The child of the learning society has 'a cosmopolitan identity which shows tolerance of race and gender differences, genuine curiosity toward and willingness to learn from other cultures, and responsibility toward excluded groups within and beyond one's society' (Hargreaves 2003: xix).

The different ideological positions overlap in producing a cultural thesis about life as a continuous process of problem solving and innovation that has no end point. The lifelong learner is one who problem solves to deal with constant changes through an agency spoken about in political registers as 'voice' and empowerment in a life of continuous decision making. This particular individuality is one that I call an unfinished cosmopolitan. The qualities are not only about individual, but about collective belonging in communities.

The cultural thesis of the cosmopolitan mode of life is assembled and connected with discourses about choice and problem solving. Problem solving is not something natural to the mind. The child as the problem solver is calculated and mapped through theories about who the child is and should be.

This calculation is evident in mathematics education. The problem-solving tasks are to order and classify what a problem is and the strategies that count for finding solutions. These tasks are not merely about learning school subjects. Brousseau (1997), a French pedagogical researcher, argues that effective instruction is about the order of conduct, that is, to have children 'want to' as well as 'be able to' (Brousseau 1997: 12). The autonomy assigned to the problem solver is generated through social and cultural narratives through which individuality is assigned. Sutherland and Balacheff (1999) argue that mathematics education is the:

> 'modern' social answer to the need to enable children to become citizens – that is, members of a society who have access to both a shared culture and who are empowered with intellectual and emotional tools to face problems within the workplace and everyday life.
>
> (Sutherland and Balacheff 1999: 2)

Teacher education reforms carry the redemptive theme of the cosmopolitan lifelong learner as a problem solver. The 'new' teacher, as the child is perceived as an 'empowered' problem-solver capable of responding flexibly to problems that have no clear set of boundaries or singular answers. The professional teacher assesses the child through life histories or portfolios, and makes and remakes biography through personal assessment of self-development and self-management.

Problem solving entails a particular populism. The problem solving of the lifelong learner is one that actively participates and collaborates in an ongoing self-development that contributes to the common good. Choice and problem solving are salvation themes to promote a new unity that promises economic progress with social equity and justice.

The problem solving of the child is not only about individuality. It is continually connected with participation in communities as part of the same phenomenon that produced the cultural thesis of the lifelong learner. Community is where the processes of lifelong learning are effected. Although the notion of community appears in the Reformation and in the writing of John Dewey at the turn of the twentieth century, for example, the principles of conduct in community today are formulated in communication and constructivist psychologies. The choice and problem solving occur in 'learning communities' or 'communities of discourse'. The empowered individual lives in a pluralism of multiple communities to continually construct life.

The problem solving and collaboration in community do not locate responsibility in the range of social practices directed towards a single public sphere. Responsibility traverses diverse and plural communities to constitute the common good. If I look at the cultural thesis of the new teacher, it is an individual who goes into the community to better know their pupils and their families, and to become trusted partners who bring 'community knowledge' into their classrooms. The reformed teacher coaches and facilitates. Children construct knowledge and teachers work as partners and collaborators through principles seemingly governed only through communication systems and networks (discourse communities).

Whatever the merits of problem solving and community, they are not merely the natural reasoning of the child or the collective gathering of people from which personal and social values and commitments are articulated. The rules and standards of participation of the unfinished cosmopolitan operate through particular principles of reflection and action. The problem-solving child, the citizen and the worker are tourists and/or consumers in the world that seem to beckon as so many enticing paths. The location of responsibility seems no longer traversed through the range of social practices directed towards a single public sphere. The self-management of one's personal ethics is different from that in the early part of the twentieth century. The social, collective identities and universal norms embodied in the nation building of the previous century are replaced with images of multiple identities, collaboration, the local community and an individuality that embodies a flexible problem-solving. But the diversity and plurality is not without norms of collective belonging. Whereas problem solving was to validate external social norms and obligations, the lifelong learner is responsible to diverse, autonomous and plural communities that constitute the common good. However, there is no individuality without the social! That individuality is scaled in a hierarchy that includes nationness.

Cosmopolitanism and collective belonging

The new cosmopolitanism of the lifelong learner does not vacate the relation of individuality to collective belonging. They are reconstituted. Lifelong learning in European Union discourses, for example, project the unity of the whole scaled in hierarchy of nation, suprastate of the Union and individuality. The lifelong learner can be read in the US as providing a stability and harmony through the discourses of difference and flexibility, expressed in the phrase 'all children should learn', which directs attention to a unity that differentiates those who do not achieve in school.

The redesigning and scaling of the social through the narratives of lifelong learning is exemplified in US school reforms. The child as a lifelong learner is pedagogically described as inscribing universal values of the democratic citizen who promotes human rights, respects diversity and contributes to the global economy. But the global rhetoric is continually inserted into the vision of the nation in that global world. The teacher in the US reforms, for example in documents from the American Council on Education (ACE), is to create a new 'energized' leadership to 'work with others' and 'ensure that America and its children will have the schools they require and deserve' (ACE 1999: ii), to provide 'a down payment to renewal and reform' that the 'American public' demands in the promoting of democracy (ACE 1999: 1). The reform appears as a response to the inevitable processes of globalization. 'With each passing decade, education has become more critical to economic and social survival' (ACE 1999: 1).

The theme of reforming teacher preparation entails a cultural thesis of the unfinished cosmopolitan lifelong learner. The ordering of the teaching practices are not merely about individual choice and problem solving. The reform of teacher education is for 'reclaiming the soul of America' as expressed by the National commission on teaching and America's future (NCTAF).

> We must reclaim the soul of America. And to do so, we need an education system that helps people forge shared values, to understand and respect other perspectives, to learn and work at high levels of competence, to take risks and persevere against the odds, to work comfortably with people from diverse backgrounds, and *to continue to learn throughout life*.
>
> (NCTAF 1996: 12, my italics)

The soul of the nation inscribes a mode of living collectively and individually. The statement inscribes different qualities of the child to assemble a particular cultural thesis about the cosmopolitan mode of living. This entails 'forging values', 'respecting others', 'taking risks', working with 'diverse people' and an individuality that 'continues to learn throughout life'.

The struggle for the soul is now in the autonomous learners who are continuously involved in self-improvement and ready for the uncertainties through working actively in 'communities of learning' (cf. The National Council of Teachers of Mathematics, NCTM, 2000). Reason is no longer for the perfection of the ideal of the Republic through making multiple communities into the collective embodiment of the social good.

Fears of who is not the unfinished cosmopolitan

The lifelong learner travels as a comparative instantiation that simultaneously constructs what is not that individuality. The lifelong learner functions as an imaginary whole from which differences are understood. The comparative reason is not only of education. Modern philosophy and sociology, Rancière (1983/2004: 205) argues, makes the arbitrary of differences into the necessary and inevitable. The new discourses of the Enlightenment and the positivist sciences of August Comte posed differences in a comparative system that divided people into potential states of rehabilitation that were no longer a product of an arbitrary order. The social and individual were seen and acted on as the movement towards a universal norm of 'the good society' and differences disclosed about groups of the excluded – workers, artisans and racial groups. Rancière argues that social theory needs difference to substantiate it. Once the excluded were disclosed, the differences can be recognized for inclusion. But the recognition of difference was ironic. The recognition of difference stabilizes groups as outside of normality and 'incapable of ever acquiring a taste for the philosophers' goods – and even of understanding the language in which their enjoyment is expounded' (Rancière 1983/2004: 204).

The comparative system of recognition and difference is embedded in the founding of the modern Republic. There was an optimism of an inclusive society formed around notions of participation and democratization. Yet that inclusion simultaneously contained fears of difference. The fears were of the masses who could not acquire enlightened reason. Education for the founding figures of the American nation was to create a culture of sensibility to cosmopolitan ideals that would simultaneously form a national identity and prevent the savages, barbarians and 'others' from entering and destroying the nation.

The comparative instantiation that includes and casts out appears today through the invocation that '*all* children are to learn'. The name of 2001 US federal legislation, *No Child Left Behind* enunciates this phrase as the social commitment of schools contributing to an equal society in which there are no academic differences among children from all racial, ethnic and economic groups. The juxtaposition of the phrases 'all children' and *No Child Left Behind*, however, gives recognition to an inclusionary practice and establishes difference from the *unity of the social whole.* The unspoken cultural thesis about the 'all' needs no enunciation as everyone 'knows' who that child is and therefore there is no need for further explanation. That child embodies the qualities and characteristics of the lifelong learner.

The anthropological 'other' child left behind is a child recognized in need of rescue because the child does not belong in the space of 'all children'; yet that child left behind is recognized for inclusions and as different. The cosmopolitan hope and its fears of the dangers to, and dangerous, populations are expressed in the National Commission on Teaching and America's Future (NCTAF 2003), second major report of reforming teacher education. The title *No Dream Denied, A Pledge to America's Children* is, at one layer, the hope for an inclusive society built on universal cosmopolitan values. The fears have a double quality that is neither binary nor dialectical. They are fears that the school might not be able to create inclusion unless specific teacher education reforms are carried out. Schooling is 'to provide every child with what should be his or her educational birthright', and it is argued, 'requires that the child has access to competent, caring, qualified teaching in schools organized for success ...' (NCTAF 2003: 6). The achieving of the child's birthright is a phrase that locates the report in a more cosmopolitan attitude of universal human rights that now is relocated in childhood. The human rights are spoken about through conceptualizations of lifelong learning in which the successful school creates 'a culture of continuous learning' for teachers.

The fears are both inside and outside of parameters of normality. Teachers worry about providing adequate learning for the child who is academically and socially 'at-risk' (Brown 2006). The fear of not succeeding with particular children, however, establishes difference. The differences are the qualities and characteristics of the dangerous populations – the at-risk child, dysfunctional families, divorced and single parents, juvenile delinquency, drug abuse and sexual promiscuity, among others. The US congressional legislation *No Child Left Behind*, and professional reforms bear this double sense of recognition and difference – the fear of not being able to achieve the hope of schooling in making a more equitable society and the fear of the dangers and dangerous populations for the future.

The unspoken distinctions about the child left behind exist in overlapping territories of social and psychological membership. The child left behind is inscribed in a space of social disintegration (the loss of 'civilization') and moral degeneration that coexists with the hope of rescue and redemption through proper planning. Psychological dangers of low self-esteem and a poor self-concept overlap with social categories about, for example, dysfunctional families, single-parent households, juvenile delinquency and homes without books to read. A determinate category is formed as children:

> who live in poverty, students who are not native speakers of English, students with disabilities, females, and many nonwhite students [who] have traditionally been far more likely than their counterparts in other demographic groups to be victims of low expectations.
>
> (NCTM 2000: 13)

The inscription of distinctions and divisions is illustrated in a study of urban and rural teacher education (Popkewitz 1998). In the US the category that describes the child to be rescued and disadvantaged is signified as the 'urban child'. The same categories and differentiations classify the child who is left behind and the 'urban child'. What emerges as also important in this study is that the same system of ordering, differentiating and dividing children occurred in urban and rural schools. In a practical sense, then, the geographical location of urban and rural folded into one another as a single cultural space whose distinctions were about the disadvantaged, the at-risk and low achievement child that was the focus of the 'no child left behind' reforms. This is easy enough to consider when it is recognized that children who live in a city's high rent apartments and brownstones of the American cities are not classified as belonging to the space of urban education. The children of the brownstone appear as 'urbane' and cosmopolitan, and not 'urban'. And the urban child is not only of the city but assigned to particular children in suburban and rural schools who occupy that cultural space (Popkewitz 1998).

The child left behind is one whose mode of living is different from that of the unfinished cosmopolitanism and can never be 'of the average'. The urban child, in the study of urban and rural teacher education, is classified as having 'street-wise' intelligence. The word 'street-wise intelligence' signified the child as different from an unspoken mode of acting with intelligence. The deployment of street-wise intelligence recognizes and gives equal value to the teachers' hope and faith that the innate potential of the child can be drawn out by school reforms to rectify past inequalities and to rescue the child for success in schooling. The recognition of street-wise intelligence inscribed comparative distinctions that recognizes the child for inclusion and differentiates the urban child as different, one who learns by doing from the learning of 'others' who manipulate abstract ideas.

The distinctions and divisions circulate in policy, research, school pro-grammes, patterns of classroom communication, as well as international reporting about the conditions of education. I say this not as a form of pessimism or a fatalism, but to consider how historically particular patterns of governing mutate to the present as the 'natural' and commonsense. It is the limits of this commonsense and its causality that are in question.

Democratization, alchemies of school subjects and naturalizing the world

The cultural theses that produce the unfinished cosmopolitan and its 'others' take-for-granted the rules of selecting and organizing school subjects. What are selected and organized as school subjects are related to the principles generated about the child made into objects of intervention and administration. This relation can be understood as 'an alchemy'. While the labels and symbols of the curriculum content perform as a rhetorical device to signify that the academic disciplines and school subjects are one and the same thing, they are not. There are magical changes that occur in the disciplinary knowledge of music, mathematics or history in the school curriculum. Like the sorcerers of the Middle Ages, concern with transformations from one space to another, pedagogy magically transforms sciences, social science and humanities into 'things' taught in schools (Popkewitz 2004).

Academic fields of knowledge production need filtration processes and models of translation for teachers and children to work on and within schooling. Children are neither scientists nor concert musicians. My interest is with the particular inscription devices or intellectual tools that translate and order school subjects. When examined, the selection of the curriculum has little to do with the norms of participation, truth and recognition of academic fields associated with school subjects, whether that is mathematics, physics and linguistics. Nor are they about the network and relations that order the norms of participation, truth and recognition in the academic fields associated with school subjects. The selection and organization of school subjects are ordered through the cultural theses of cosmopolitanism and its double gestures of including and casting out. The school subjects are examined here to ask about the relation of the representations brought into the school and assembled in the cultural theses of modes of living. School subjects are assembled and connected to the psychologies and sociologies related to the unfinished cosmopolitanism discussed above.

Reforms in teacher education in the US, for example, assert that teachers should possess deep knowledge of the subjects they teach. The assumption is that students in school are to learn, for example, the cultural norms of the discipline of mathematics in classroom instruction. The path to becoming a lifelong learner is through learning how to argue and use evidence related to the discourses of the communities of scholars in the disciplines themselves. The language of reforms of school subjects re-inscribes the principles of the cultural thesis of the lifelong learner through discussions of problem solving, engaging children in greater participation and collaboration and notions that draw from particular psychologies about children making meaning and constructing their own knowledge. Children's involvement and agency in this calculation of reason is spoken as finding relevance and individual interests.

The populist and democratic impulse in children's 'constructing' knowledge, ironically, is not about constructing knowledge but about constructing paths to identify the already known structures of a given content. The rules of conduct relate to particular contemporary cosmopolitan notions about participation and action through which democracy is watched over. Children's construction of knowledge involves finding multiple ways of making apparent the presupposed logical and analytical foundations of mathematical properties. The stability of the knowledge of schooling is connected to the selection of the 'conventional ideas' as the core of mathematical education. The notion of 'conventional' is used in mathematical education as the foundational rules of the 'nature' and logical 'structure' of knowledge taught to children (cf. Simon 1995: 20). School subjects are classified as 'bodies of knowledge' – systems of concepts, proofs, generalizations and procedures – that children must learn. The linguistic quality of the curriculum words – bodies, content, content coverage, conceptual knowledge – treats disciplines as inert, unchanging and unambiguous 'things' (concepts or proofs) whose structures are the base of children's learning.

Taking 'conventional' knowledge of physics or mathematics 'makes sense' if pedagogy is understood as cultural theses about modes of living. To fix and stabilize the content knowledge of disciplinary knowledge brought into the school curriculum enables a focus on the psychological principles that order the cultural theses in pedagogy. The notions of community, negotiations of meanings and problem solving are concepts of pedagogy shaped and fashioned by the governing practices of pedagogy rather than by the governing practices of disciplinary communities. The alchemy in which the selection of conventional mathematical ideas (its language and symbols) occurs provides a consensus and harmony in the a priori structures that enable a focus on the principles that order conduct. The function of pedagogy is normalizing that which is put into a populist democratic language about enhancing learning, negotiation and the autonomy that comes with making one's own meaning.

Yet the classroom focus on students' learning the rules of argument is not only a process of modelling truth. It is also a process of normalizing the inner characteristics of the students. When contemporary curriculum is examined internationally, there are dramatic pedagogical changes in the narratives and images of classroom textbooks over the past decades (McEneaney 2003). Curriculum has been rewritten to produce greater student involvement and participation, personal relevance and emotional accessibility – values that can be associated with the unfinished cosmopolitan. But the increase of student participation in classrooms gave wider latitude to scientific authority over what was given as true and therefore unproblematic about the management of the natural world. Children's participation and problem solving in the classroom are to function to learn the majesty of the procedures, styles of argument and symbolic systems asserted as the expertise of science. The conclusions of academic expertise are located as outside the bounds of children's questioning and problem solving. The latter serve as mere procedures through which to ascertain the givenness of reality. The irony of the inscriptions of participation in the curriculum is to narrow the range of what is questioned and the authority of the knowledge by which children are to determine the truth and falseness of statements.

If we place children's involvement in curriculum in relation to the increased authority of science in defining the truth of the world, the child-as-future lifelong citizen is more and less of an active participant. The child is more active in the sense of modelling a particular argument and questioning in school subjects. But the child is less active in defining the terms and extending the possibilities and boundaries of that engagement. The child is a tourist and/or a consumer in the world of propositions and generalizations presented in school subjects as fixed and unchanging. Participation, problem solving and collaboration give children flexibility in learning how to appreciate the majesty of that already given reality. On the other hand and equally important, the pedagogy fixes the cultural relations (community) in which the images and narratives of school subjects are sought and disowns the fragility or conditionality of the world by assembling a particularly programmed agency for the child in its stead.

The unfinished cosmopolitanism, power and resistance

Contemporary curriculum consistently places the reforms of schooling within salvation themes about emancipation, agency, freedom and democracy. The easy flows of these words are not merely normative ideals that will be reached if only the right mixtures are found for policy and research in planning. The words are embedded in systems of reason that order, differentiate and divide through the principles generated for conduct. The problem of school study is to continually interrogate how the objects of reflection and action enclose and intern who the child is, and should be. The analytic of the chapter directs attention to the 'reason' of schooling and its research about the lifelong learner as not an epiphenomenon of social interests and 'forces' in society. The knowledge of schooling is a historical practice that construes and constrains the possibilities of reflection and action. The diagnosis of the cultural thesis of the lifelong learner and its 'others' is to make fragile the causality of 'the subject' of schooling. The approach recognizes that such inscriptions are always dangerous, if not always 'bad', to draw of Michel Foucault.

Ironically, the focus on the principles generated in the making of 'the self' is a theory of change. Change lies problematizing what seems nature in the present, thus opening up the possibilities of other alternatives. My use of cosmopolitanism in examining the lifelong learner considered the limits of the cultural theses through which freedom and agency, central themes that mutated from the Enlightenment, are linked to a comparative reason whose universality is also particular and dividing. The principles of agency, science, problem solving and community assembled in the cosmopolitanism embody cultural theses that intern and enclose the possibilities for action and reflection.

The conditions of the present require a rethinking of the foundational tools and 'commonsense' of the practices of policy and research. I say this as there is no question that inequities exist and, to use a phrase appearing in US teacher education reforms, there is a continual need to express outrage to the sufferings encountered. To declare further that the world is socially constructed and therefore can be changed through human efforts does not help, however. The problem still exists in finding intellectual tools to examine the concrete practices that order and differentiate. The inclusionary practices to mark the unity of 'all children' naturalize divisions and stand as a comparative principle from which 'the children left behind' are differentiated and divided so that the latter 'can never be of the average'. The uses of democracy and collaboration in pedagogical reform literatures do not escape the terrains of generating division and difference even when in seemingly oppositional ideological registers. The words of democracy and collaboration are politically seductive in mobilizing groups, but their deployment should not be confused with the necessary historical and analytic work to consider the assemblies and connections through which the governing of the self is produced.

The historicizing of cosmopolitanism is a strategy that places the particular system of reason of pedagogical reforms within a broader historical trajectory of the epistemological ordering and comparing which that qualify and disqualify people for participation. The focus on cosmopolitanism is 'to learn to what extent the effort to think one's own history can free thought from what it silently thinks, and so enable it to think differently' (Foucault 1978: 9). This historicizing of knowledge is to unthink the distinction between the nominalist (discourse, text) and realist (contexts) in policy and the education sciences.

The bifurcated world distances, divides, erases and hides how expert knowledge works dialectically in the forming of social relations.

Notes

1 I appreciate my conversations with Ruth Gustafson from which this phrase, unfinished cosmopolitan, emerged.

References

American Council on Education (ACE) (1999) *To Touch the Future: Transforming the way Teachers are Taught: An Action Agenda for College and University Presidents*, Washington, DC: American Council on Education.

Brousseau, G. (1997) *Theory of Didactical Situations in Mathematics. Didactique des Mathematiques, 1970–1990*, Dordrecht: Kluwer Academic Publishers.

Brown, A. (2006) *Mapping Risks in Education: Conceptions, Contexts & Complexities*. Unpublished Dissertation, Madison, WI: University of Wisconsin-Madison.

Foucault, M. (1978) *The History of Sexuality: The Use of Pleasure*, New York: Pantheon Books.

Foucault, M. (1991) Governmentality. In G. Burchell, C. Gordon and P. Miller (eds), *The Foucault Effect: Studies in Governmentality*, Chicago: University of Chicago Press, 87–104.

Hargreaves, A. (2003) *Teaching in the Knowledge Society: Education in the Age of Insecurity*, Maindenhead: Open University Press.

Maeroff, G. (2003) *A Classroom of One: How Online Learning is Changing Our Schools and Colleges*, New York: Palgrave Macmillan.

McEneaney, E. (2003) 'Elements of a contemporary primary school science', in G.S. Drori, J.W. Meyer, F.O. Ramirez and E. Schofer (eds), *Science in the Modern World Polity: Institutionalization and Globalization*, Stanford, CA: Stanford University Press.

National Commission on Teaching and America's Future (NCTAF) (2003) *No Dream Denied: A Pledge to America's Children*, Washington, DC: National Commission on Teaching and America's Future.

National Commission on Teaching and America's Future (NCTAF) (1996) *What Matters Most: Teaching for America's future*, Washington, DC: National Commission on Teaching and America's Future.

National Council of Teachers of Mathematics (NCTM) (2000) *Principles and Standards for School Mathematics*, Reston, VA: National Council of Teachers of Mathematics.

Popkewitz, T.S. (1998) *Struggling for the Soul: The Politics of Education and the Construction of the Teacher*, New York: Teachers College Press.

Popkewitz, T.S. (2004) 'The alchemy of the mathematics curriculum: inscriptions and the fabrication of the child', *American Educational Research Journal*, 41: 3–34.

Popkewitz, T.S. (ed.) (2005) *Inventing the Modern Self and John Dewey: Modernities and the Traveling of Pragmatism in Education*, New York: PalgraveMacmillan.

Popkewitz, T.S. (2008) *Cosmopolitanism and the Age of School Reform: Science, Education and Making Society by Making the Child*, New York: Routledge.

Rancière, J. (1983/2004) *The Philosopher and His Poor,* Durham: Duke University Press.

Simon, M. (1995) 'Reconstructing mathematics pedagogy from a constructivist perspective', *Journal for Research in Mathematics Education*, 26: 114–45.

Sutherland, R. and Balacheff, N. (1999) 'Didactical complexity of computational environments for the learning of mathematics', *International Journal of Computers for Mathematical Learning*, 4: 1–26.

Chapter 7

Historicizing the lifelong learner

Governmentality and neoliberal rule[1]

Andreas Fejes

In contemporary Western policy narratives of the welfare/post-welfare state lifelong learning is put forward as a way to keep individual nations and the European Union at the forefront of education, research and the economy. In Sweden, much as elsewhere, adult education, learning at work and learning during leisure time are narrated as contexts where the vision of lifelong learning is able to be realized (ME 1998). Within such narratives there is a promise of betterment for all; everyone is to be included in lifelong learning as a way of achieving their desires in life. Learning is constructed as a way of reaching 'paradise' (Popkewitz 2003) at the same time as it constructs sites for governing.

In this chapter I want to question such increasingly taken-for-granted ideas about lifelong learning and problematize them as being historically related to a problem of governing within the changing contours of the present. By historicizing the present, inspired by Foucault's (1977, 2003a) concepts of governmentality and genealogy I will focus on questions such as: What visions of the future are constructed in Swedish policy documents? What subjects are constructed and what are they to become? With the help of these Foucauldian concepts I will analyse official policy documents concerning education and liberal education for adults produced during the twentieth century and at the beginning of the twenty-first century in Sweden. Thus, I am able to problematize ideas – mentalities – of how the adult subject 'should' be governed during the twentieth century, to consider how these have been formulated at different times and emerged in new linguistic forms. This analysis will make visible how power operates to exclude as it includes. Through this I create a space for reflection on what policy making does to our subjectivities.

I will argue that lifelong learning is constructed by and is constructing a neoliberal governmentality. Within this mentality the future is constantly changing, as so 'must' the citizen. Thus, everyone is educable and needs to become a lifelong learner. But the 'other', the one who is not a learner, is excluded. The state constructed in this is an enabling state, as it is through each citizen's active choices that the state is to be inscribed. I will show how in the mid-twentieth century a quite different mentality was promoted within Swedish policy texts. Here it was a conditional educableness that was constructed, where only talented adults were to study. The 'other' was therefore also quite different from that of contemporary times, as they were the ones not following their talent as an inherited potential. The state constructed at this time differed also and was distant from practices of governing. Going back even further, during the early twentieth century, the educable adult was constructed as the politically responsible citizen. Threats to the nation came from within, and citizens 'needed' to become politically responsible as a way to keep a stable society. The 'other' was therefore, at this time, the one not making politically responsible choices. The state was constructed as a social state which planned the future.

Inventing the educable lifelong learner and its 'other'

Today it is argued within Swedish policy documents that not everyone is a part of lifelong learning. Study opportunities for excluded groups have to be created, otherwise people risk being marginalized. They must be given the opportunity to gain the skills necessary for employment through lifelong learning. The groups at risk are the long-term unemployed, immigrants and people dependent on social security. The goal is to make the educable subject employable (ME 1998). The adult subject normalized within contemporary Swedish policy documents is one who has basic social skills. Basic skills are to be acquired through an adult education that aims to 'guarantee access to relevant education for individuals, who, because of insufficient basic skills, risk being marginalized in society and being excluded from the labour market' (ME 1998: 22). The skills that are to be developed 'include the capacity to communicate, think critically and creatively and to develop self-criticism and social competencies' (ME 1998: 18). Adult education should also, just as the elementary school in Sweden, 'provide opportunities for continuing education and personal development, both in the role as a citizen and in the role as a worker. It should include knowledge and creativity, and aptitude to learn new things and handle change' (ME 1998: 8). The implication is that with such qualities it should be possible to acquire a job. Those who are not part of lifelong learning lack these basic social skills and cannot handle change; therefore they should participate in adult education.

We can see how the existing power relations in society assign a specific meaning to the lifelong learner and lifelong learning. Through participation in adult education everyone will acquire the prerequisites to participate in lifelong learning. Thus, everyone is constructed as educable. Such construction is based on the knowledge production performed by social scientists and other experts. One of the most central ways of collecting knowledge is through statistics, both in a quantitative and qualitative way (ME 1998). Based on such information, governing measures can be taken to create the subjects presented as desirable, thus the lifelong learner is being fabricated. There is a desire for truth which has always been present in different discourses; it is one of its productive elements. It acts as a closure system that is renewed and strengthened by institutional support, e.g. pedagogy, science (Fejes 2006a, b). In this case, different scientific disciplines – pedagogy, education, sociology, psychology, statistics, etc. – are used to create knowledge about the adult subject.

Today, and even more than previously, reasoning about the educable subject includes an idea of the 'environment'. According to the texts, everyone can be part of lifelong learning if they are supported by the environment, as society. In other words, the educable subject is combined with the idea of learning as a norm; the will to learn is constructed as a mentality. We are constantly learning (should learn) and are encouraged to do so. Thus, we can see how inclusion is at the forefront of educational policy today. Policy texts argue that everyone can be included. What is not mentioned are the effects of this in terms of exclusion. By creating a normalized adult, an exclusionary practice is created where the 'other' is constructed (Fejes 2006a, b). We can see how lifelong learning is presented as something that everybody should be a part of, but that this is not the case. It is presented as a possibility and a natural goal for all individuals. The idea that we learn our entire lives, at all stages and in all contexts, formally, non-formally and informally, is put forward. At the same time some people are constructed as not having the prerequisites to participate. Such a use of language is an expression of the current power relations within policy discourse, were 'all' is defined as certain groups.

> Lifelong learning for all has become an increasingly important feature of long-term policy in Sweden. This idea is best understood as a process of individual learning and development throughout a person's entire life, from the cradle to the grave – from learning in early childhood to learning during retirement. It is an all-embracing concept that refers not only to education in formal settings, such as schools, universities and adult educational institutions, but also to the 'lifewide' learning in informal environments, both at home and at work.
>
> (ME 1999: 10)

At the same time as learning is put forth as something we do our entire lives, some people are constructed as not having the prerequisites to participate. Such a use of language is an expression of the current power relations within policy discourse, where 'all' is defined as certain groups. First, there is a speech about all being included in lifelong learning. Second, only certain groups are included. Thus, all is redefined as meaning specific groups; all is not all in a strict sense. All are those who have the prerequisites to participate in lifelong learning. What happens to those who choose not to participate in lifelong learning or those who do not have the prerequisites to participate? Through the texts these people become constructed as the others who are in need of normalization through social policy, something which is not acknowledged in educational policy and practices. This way of creating subjectivity is what Foucault (2003b) called dividing practice. It is a procedure that objectifies subjects; they are made objects that can be known. At the same time, it contributes to a subjectification wherein the normal and abnormal are created and divided. Such a practice, related to the political ambition to govern, was made possible by pedagogy, education, sociology, psychology and statistics. These disciplines produce knowledge that operates within the discourse and defines who is and who is not a lifelong learner.

The enabling state

The subject does not stand by itself within the discursive practices of policy. It is overlapped by different discourses through which knowledge of the subject is placed in relation to visions of the future. For example, it is expressed that: 'Lifelong learning for all has become an increasingly important part of long-term policy in Sweden' (ME 1998: 10). The educable subject is part of the future; it is something to be realized in future terms. Indeed, every rationality of government has a vision of the future. Governing is seen as necessary and possible as a means of reaching this future, the teleos of government (Dean 1999). Through these visions of the future techniques of governing are inscribed. This can be seen in the discourse of lifelong learning where there is talk about the need for a highly educated population, as a means to create a knowledge-based society that can compete with the rest of the world (ME 1998). This has to be done to 'increase growth and maintain welfare and employment' (ME 1999: 90). And this implies a threat, for if we do not have a highly educated population Sweden will lag behind. This kind of talk is not local in character. It can be seen at the European level; where, for example, Swedish texts say that Europe needs to become 'the most competitive and dynamic knowledge-based economy in the world', and where the European citizens' 'established patterns of behaviour have to change' (ME 2001: 44) in a constantly changing world.

To avoid this future threat it is argued there is a need to invest money in adult education, so that everyone can be a part of lifelong learning (ME 1998). This ambition is combined with the prospect of improved living standards in Sweden and the scenario of a better future. You could say that what we see is governing in the name of the future. By painting scenarios of the threat of what can happen if certain measures are not taken, we are governed along a path presented as desirable. We are fabricated as wanting to live in a democratic and highly productive society; no one wants to come in second place. The future in these texts is a projection that does not exist – someone writes about a future, as if it were natural and real. Threat is written as a fact, and some measures will have to be taken to avoid it.

In these narratives we can also see how discourses of the future, society and the subject overlap and merge. Society and the future are constantly changing and so are subjects since they have to adapt. This is a vision of the future; something that will be. Such a future cannot be planned. Here, we can see how there is an emphasis placed on the subjects themselves. We all have to adapt to changes, and established patterns of behaviour have to be changed, which implies that subjects are their own actors in their own local welfare. As stated in one of the documents: 'This not only implies that the individuals have to adapt to changes, but also that established patterns of behaviour have to change' (ME 2001: 44). There is no one to strictly guide you in the world of changes; it is up to you to become flexible and adaptable to them. However, if you fail, you will be categorized as the 'other' in need of correction through participation in adult education.

This seems to imply a state absent in the practice of governing. However, instead what we see is a neoliberal rationality of government. The state is constructed as the enabling state, which makes it possible for subjects to make their own choices. It is in the choices and actions of the subjects themselves that the state is inscribed (Rose 1999a). By enabling subjects to become autonomous, self-regulated actors, responsible for their own futures, the future can be controlled, but not planned. What is invented is the educable individual as a lifelong learner, constantly learning to handle the ever-changing future and by so doing he and she are co-creators of the future.

As we will see, this construction of the state differs from earlier ones. During the twentieth century the state became distanced from direct practices of governing. However, the contemporary state is not now governing less than it did before; instead it is a new form of governing. In texts from the early- and mid-twentieth century the future was seen as open to planning by the state, through different interventions.

Inventing the educable subject as gifted and its 'other'

In the texts of the 1950s the focus was on a gifted or talented subject:

> The individual, who finds a place in life where he best can use his talent and other resources, will achieve a sense of satisfaction. This is also in the interest of society since the individual can then be expected to make a greater effort in his work.
>
> (ME 1952: 14)

The subject was constructed as having an inner potential that could be developed with support from society. Everyone therefore was seen to end up in a place in society that corresponded to their inner potential. Those who 'should' study at that time were the people with an inner potential that corresponded to the aptitude to study. There was, therefore, a conditional educableness constructed, where only some people were seen as having the aptitude to study in adult education. Others did not, and they should do what their inner potential foresaw.

Such narratives were made possible by the idea of heredity. Citizens were seen as divided by birth into those either able or not able to study, based on techniques for measuring this potential. This could be argued to be the mentality of eugenics being inscribed into the practice of adult education – the desirable subject could be created by manipulating heredity traits (Selden 2000). But the idea of heredity ran at this time parallel with recognition of the environment as a 'force' constructing educableness which is illustrated in this quotation: 'Such qualities as ambition, interest in knowledge and ability to adapt to studying and the study environment cannot be evaluated by the test result' (ME 1952: 23–4). Therefore, characteristics of the subject together with aspects of the environment could also induce some changes in the subject.

If you were categorized as gifted you had the opportunity to study no matter what social background you came from (ME 1952). If you were not gifted you would still find satisfaction if you chose according to your inner potential. However, even so a practice of exclusion was created. Those adults not gifted enough were excluded from education. This was a distinct categorization, not visible today. It seems to have been possible to combine the ambition to include with a clear categorization related to adult education in the mid-twentieth century. There were the gifted and non-gifted ones. Such dividing practice was created based on knowledge from psychological and statistical research conducted from the mid-1940s to the beginning of the 1960s. During this time, extensive research was carried out on conscripts' abilities and aptitude to study. The results were generalized to apply to the entire population (cf. Husén 1956). The starting point for this research was the notion that all people have a certain intelligence that can be measured. This combined with extensive tests and evaluations of grades provided information on how many people in a population should be able to study up to a certain level of education. In this example, research divided humans into the gifted and not gifted, and created an idea of the inner potential according to which the subject should choose their path in life. The 'others' were those who did not choose according to this potential.

The distanced state – planning the future

In this practice of the construction of the subject and the other, the state was in one sense a very visible actor. Those who should study were the gifted ones, and it was a Board of Exemption (in which the state was inscribed) who decided who was gifted or not (ME 1952). This implicates a two-sided role for experts (teachers, counsellors, etc.) at this time: one to gather knowledge of who should study and who not, the other to give advice to subjects based on this knowledge.

We can also say that the idea of the gifted individual was part of a discourse of the future. In the policy texts from the 1950s, a scenario of the need for a highly educated population to satisfy the labour market was drawn up. Sweden was argued to need more educated people so as to be able to maintain good living standards. Especially argued was a need for qualified teachers (ME 1952). The scenario was one of the threat of the future to the nation. If something were not done, there would be a risk of the positive economic trend stagnating. By drawing up a threatening scenario the desirable future was legitimized, and this acted as a technique for creating the desirable subject. At the same time, the future became possible to plan. By planning for an adult education provision according to the number of gifted persons that were predicted, the future could be controlled.

Parallel with the practice of this visible state, there was a discourse focusing on the adult making his or her own choices and thus constructing the subject as active. By referring to inner potential and maturity, subjects were made responsible for governing themselves.

> The value for the individual to be able to, as far as possible, freely choose the path of education is a central point of view. Finally, you should be able to count on persons with the experience and maturity mentioned here will not choose an area for which he/she does not have the aptitude.
>
> (ME 1952:60)

But at the same time the subject had limits. He or she could only choose within the framework of an inner potential. What this example illustrates more generally, is that there are no unified discourses within policy discourses. Instead, there are constantly parallel discourses that are assigned different positions by the discursive power relations of the time. These discourses suggest that the state was constructing itself increasingly as distant from practices of governing. Instead of a narrative of politically irresponsible citizens, as illustrated in the next section, there is an idea of citizens making good choices on their own. Through the psychological and statistical research on talent and ability, and its ways of speaking, linguistic possibilities were being created to govern subjects at a distance (Rose 1999b), in which the citizens were encouraged to make their own choices – a positioning that is prominent in contemporary discourses of neoliberal rationality, as illustrated previously.

Inventing the educable subject as citizen and its 'other'

The policy narratives of the 1920s also refer to an educable subject, but this subject was not conditional on being gifted in the way that it became in the 1950s. In the 1920s everyone could learn something. The entire population was the target of education: 'The term liberal education means that it targets everyone, irrespective of their previous education and what social class they belong to' (ME 1924: 9). This began to point to an idea about the environment.

Since you could participate in learning no matter what your background was, it was possible that the environment (as, for example, liberal adult education) could produce a change in the subject.

What was to be constructed for the future were subjects aware of the different social issues present in society. Liberal adult education was said to create opportunities to 'freely and without constraint gather the broad mass of the people around general civic and cultural interests. The goal is thus a general public feeling of spiritual alertness to the present time's social and cultural mission' (ME 1924: 197). These social issues were accentuated in relation to a new general right to vote which had been introduced in 1919. It was said that now 'ever larger groups of citizens need more knowledge of economic and social issues and a more far-reaching social education' (ME 1924: 6). It was argued that citizens needed to learn about these issues to be able to handle the new future that lay ahead. They had to be able to make good political decisions to become responsible democratic citizens. This was the invention of the generally educable subject as a political citizen.

The idea of lifelong learning – that you learn all the time – seems at first glance to be present in these narratives of the 1920s. Even during leisure time, education 'should' have its place. It was said that study circles and lectures had

> been of great value in that they have contributed to the creation of sound and improved leisure time ... Indisputably, these modest entertainment evenings have been of great value, not least in the countryside, as a counterbalance to the uncultivated and dull/vapid leisure life that, sadly often, has been the only entertainment offered to the public.
>
> (ME 1924: 128)

However, learning was not constructed as a norm where people were construed as learning all the time. Instead, lectures and study circles were constructed as non-formalized activities, part of an institutionalized governing through liberal adult education in which learning *could* take place. Furthermore, there was a construction of a subject that should be improved; it was construed as immature and thus as possible to foster to maturity. It was an uncultivated subject with a dull/vapid leisure time. Through liberal adult education, the subject could be changed and educated. This was a question of civic education, cultivation of the intellect and the creation of good habits during leisure life. We could say that the population was constructed as an entity that was to be governed and improved; lifelong learning was a question of the fitness of the population.

Even though everyone was identified as educable in the 1920s policy texts, and even though liberal adult education was defined as including everyone, there was still a definition of special groups; those who had not reached the 'correct' cultural level. These groups were identified as needing to be properly educated, and through this saved from their passions and uncivilized lives.

Otherwise, they would not be able to handle their rights as citizens. What was proper was decided by the state, and a close relationship with science and the university was seen as important. It was stated that liberal adult education had to be in 'contact with modern scientific knowledge' (ME 1924: 7). Lecturers should elaborate on the issue at hand in an objective way, as part of the development of a citizen engaged in self-study. Scientists were construed as experts who were taking part in the governing of adult subjects so that they might become democratic and politically responsible citizens.

This division into the normal, responsible citizen and the irresponsible one merged with the idea of the future. Domestic threats were presented. Society would be threatened if the common people did not get educated about their civic rights in a correct way. There was a risk of them only becoming superficially educated, which was dangerous for society: 'An educational activity that only results in invoking interest for a certain subject matter, without the opportunity for a deeper study of this subject, will lead to shallowness and superficial education' (ME 1924: 79). As the quotation illustrates, superficial education would happen if the adult student only scratched the surface of the subject matter. So that the student could continue to educate him- or herself, a lecture had to include literature references, otherwise there would be no funding for lectures (ME 1924). This regulation of literature acted as a technique for governing the lecturers; their actions were a result of a governing practice and were a governing practice in themselves. By suggesting 'good' books for the lectures, the adult was given the opportunity to study in greater depth and thus acquire the correct education. A shallow education was dangerous for the individual and society because the consequence could be irresponsible political action; the other was constructed as the one not able to make responsible political decisions. In other words, the idea of superficial education acted as a technique for governing subjects so that they could become educated people who could make responsible political decisions.

The social state – planning the future

The texts of the early twentieth century construct a social state planning the future. For example, there is a focus on attaining official 'hygiene' (ME 1924), a word made possible through the emergence of the social sciences. One practice where this took place was in the library with its task of judging how a book influences the person reading it:

> Socially detrimental and unethical sexual relationships of a sort that from an ethical point of view could be bad, if they are placed in the hands of young and immature readers, should not, either by lending or in other ways, be accessible to persons who are not regarded as having reached the required maturity.

> (ME 1924: 25)

Here, there was someone bringing up someone else. In this case the state, which, by regulating what literature is to be available, sees to it that no 'wrong' book falls into the hands of the immature. The person responsible for this was the librarian. This person had to make judgements about who was not mature enough to read certain books. In this way, the librarian was a co-creator of the immature, educable subject; she or he was the expert who collected information on what was being read and contributed to the governing of the subject. This idea of the state as a mode of governing through the social can also be seen in the following quotation where liberal adult education is construed as part of a national organization (together with the state), which will foster desirable citizens:

> It is, of course, also of great significance that a really comprehensive and thorough investigation is made with the aim of determining what the state can and should do to further develop the liberal adult education intended for adult citizens, so that it truly takes its place in the national fostering organization.
>
> (ME 1924: 6)

By means of the institutional support offered by the state for liberal adult education, a framework of governing was created; governing was in the process of being institutionalized. We could say that society was constructed as being possible to plan and that this made it possible for a visible state to emerge. The state was constructed as the one planning the future. This idea of the planned future was accentuated in the 1930s when the welfare state began to emerge with its ideas of social engineering (Hirdman 2000). As Olsson and Petersson (2005) suggest, there was no distinction in Sweden between the state and society during the early 1900s. Shaping the future was a collective affair and the individual 'should' conform to the common standards of welfare.

However, related to the lectures discussed in the former section, there was also an idea about the adult subject becoming self-governed. According to one of the documents 'One of the founding principles of the free educational efforts should be that it leads to self-activity' (ME 1924: 120). Subjects should be inspired by lectures and then start to study by themselves and together with friends in study circles. This idea points to a governing practice where the self-responsibility and self-governing of the individual were combined with specific measures taken by experts (with support of the knowledge of the social sciences). For example, the knowledge which defined good books was combined with the idea that people could freely choose to start study circles. The social administration of the population was to be carried out by creating active, self-responsible citizens involved in liberal adult education.

In conclusion, life was according to the texts of the early 1900s seen as being possible to plan and this would be done by the state and civil society, its representatives and the individuals themselves as a means of attaining a stable society, governing through society.

The lifelong learner in a 'changing' society

In this chapter, I have argued that new ways of governing the adult subject have taken shape over the last eighty years in Sweden. There has been a shift from governing through society to governing through the action of individuals. In this shift, the idea of the adult educable subject has travelled and been constituted in different ways. Today, the educable subject is a lifelong learner created through a neoliberal governmentality that governs through the choices of each citizen.

The discourse of lifelong learning has been inscribed in Sweden as a 'truth' and a remedy to keep Sweden as a welfare state and at the forefront of the world in economic terms. It is not possible to question this idea as those who might are of the 'other' who are in need of remedy. As has been argued, the spread of the discourse of lifelong learning in Sweden and its normalizing practice of learning are not only tied to practices of schooling. As Olsson and Petersson (2005) identify, this discourse can be seen as inscribing itself within society as a whole; society is construed as a learning society. The notion of 'school as society' as expressed in Sweden based on ideas from Dewey has turned into 'society as a school'. In this society, the educable subject is a necessary construct; if you are to learn, you have to be educable. Adult education is positioned as crucial in making this society a reality. Those who do not have the competencies to be part of lifelong learning will acquire them in adult education. If everyone is constantly learning, the teleos of government can be achieved in Sweden, a vision of the 'good' future – the welfare state. This vision acts as a technique for creating this future and the lifelong learner. Such a discourse on the welfare state is local in character. In, for example, the US, the welfare state is also used as a technique for creating a good future, but in an opposite way. It is presented as a negative vision of the future, a risk that has to be avoided if the good future is to be reached (Canella 2003).

What is similar in all these narratives during the twentieth century is that they create practices of exclusion. As the educable subject is constructed, so is the 'other'. Both are the focus of different techniques of governing so that they may be normalized. The ambition has always been to include everyone. In the 1920s everyone was to be included in society so as to make good political choices. In the 1950s, everyone was to choose according to their potential and so social class did not stand in the way of education. Today everyone should be part of lifelong learning. This chapter has argued that the political ambition for inclusion has exclusion as one of its effects, something which is not acknowledged in the policy documents analysed. Not all people will make good political decisions, not all people will choose according to their potential, not all people will participate in lifelong learning.

Therefore, one needs to take a critical attitude towards the narratives of lifelong learning, to try to understand what kinds of subjects are their effects and what kinds of exclusionary practices this creates. How can lifelong learning be rephrased as a way of avoiding exclusionary practices? Is such a narrative possible?

Notes

1   This article is a revised version of the article 'The planetspeak discourse of lifelong learning in Sweden: What is an educable adult?' published 2006 in the *Journal of Education Policy*, 21: 687–716.

References

Cannella, G.S. (2003) 'Child welfare in the United States: the construction of gendered oppositional discourse(s)', in M. Bloch, K. Holmlund, I. Moqvist and T.S. Popkewitz (eds), *Governing Children, Families and Education: Restructuring the Welfare State*, New York: Palgrave Macmillan.

Dean, M. (1999) *Governmentality: Power and Rule in Modern Society*, London: Sage.

Fejes, A. (2006a) 'The planetspeak discourse of lifelong learning in Sweden: what is an educable adult?' *Journal of Education Policy*, 21: 697–716.

Fejes, A. (2006b) *Constructing the Adult Learner: A Governmentality Analysis*, Linköping: LiU-tryck.

Foucault, M. (1977) 'Nietzsche, genealogy, history', in F.F. Bouchard (ed.), *Michel Foucault: Language, Counter-Memory, Practice: Selected Essays and Interviews*, Oxford: Blackwell.

Foucault, M. (2003a) 'Governmentality', in P. Rainbow and N. Rose (eds), *The Essential Foucault: Selections from the Essential Works of Foucault 1954–1984*, New York: The New Press.

Foucault, M. (2003b) 'The subject and power', in P. Rainbow and N. Rose (eds), *The Essential Foucault: Selections from the Essential Works of Foucault 1954–1984*, New York: The New Press.

Hirdman, Y. (2000) *Att Lägga Livet till Rätta: Studier i Svensk Folkhemspolitik*, Stockholm: Carlssons.

Husén, T. (1956) 'En försummad begåvningsreserv', *Tiden*, 5.

Ministry of Education (ME) (1924) *SOU 1924:5, Betänkande med Utredning och Förslag Angående det Fria och Frivilliga Folkbildningsarbetet*, Stockholm: Ecklesiastikdepartementet.

Ministry of Education (ME) (1952) *SOU 1952:2, Vidgat Tillträde till Högre Studier*, Stockholm: Ecklesiastikdepartementet.

Ministry of Education (ME) (1998) *SOU 1998:51, Vuxenutbildning och Livslångt Lärande. Situationen Inför och Under Första Året med Kunskapslyftet*, Stockholm: Utbildningsdepartementet.

Ministry of Education (ME) (1999) *SOU 1999:14, Från Kunskapslyft till en Strategi för Livslångt Lärande*, Stockholm: Utbildningsdepartementet.

Ministry of Education (ME) (2001) *SOU 2001:78, Validering av Vuxnas Kunskap och Kompetens*, Stockholm: Utbildningsdepartementet.

Olsson, U. and Petersson, K. (2005) 'Dewey as an epistemic figure in the Swedish discourse on governing the self', in T.S. Popkewitz (ed.), *Inventing the Modern Self and John Dewey: Modernities and the Traveling of Pragmatism in Education*, New York: Palgrave Macmillan.

Popkewitz, T.S. (2003) 'Governing the child and pedagogicalization of the parent: A historical excursus into the present', in M. Bloch, K. Holmlund, I. Moqvist and T.S. Popkewitz (eds), *Governing Children, Families and Education: Restructuring the Welfare State*, New York: Palgrave Macmillan.

Rose, N. (1999a) *Powers of Freedom: Reframing Political Thought*, Cambridge: Cambridge University Press.

Rose, N. (1999b) *Governing the Soul: The Shaping of the Private Self*, London: Free association books.

Selden, S. (2000) 'Eugenics and the social construction of merit, race and disability', *Journal of Curriculum Studies*, 32: 235–52.

Governing pedagogical subjects

Chapter 8

Self-governance in the job search

Regulative guidelines in job seeking

Marinette Fogde

In contemporary working life, training and guidance on how to write curriculum vitae or succeed at an interview are fundamental features of job seeking. Increasingly what counts is to become an *entrepreneur of the self* – to use Rose's (1998) phrase – in the labour market. Such skills and capacities are taken-for-granted in advice about job seeking, with the implication that where they are not already held learning is crucial. Training for job seeking is an example of learning for work in a flexible and global labour market, where lifelong learning involves education and training during working life as well as creating demands that go beyond the workplace (Payne 2001). The analysis offered here focuses on how a Swedish trade union for white-collar workers, Sif,[1] within different periods of time, and through its brochures for job seekers, has constructed the 'job seeker' through advice and guidance on the knowledge and skills that are important. This chapter aims to examine techniques of governing and the construction of subjects in the job search.

Here then, the constitution of a contemporary normative-regulatory ideal is problematized through a genealogical approach. In drawing the ethical contours of different periods of time a Foucauldian genealogy emphasizes that there can be different technologies and means of constituting the self (Besley 2005). By identifying and discussing within this chapter some illustrations from a more detailed genealogical study of brochures from the 1950s until today,[2] history is used as a tool to understand contemporary discourses of job seeking.

A new agenda for workers/learners

The kind of work-related learning that is examined in this chapter must be understood against a background of social and economic change. Today working life as well as society is characterized by rapid change, and 'flexibility' is a word signifying this within the framework of global capitalism. 'Employability' is another term that is increasingly deployed at a state or supranational level such as in the European Union when talking about education or working life. Within welfare states, employment was previously considered to be the responsibility of the state and government, and the goal was to achieve full employment (Finn 2000; Stråth 2000; Garsten and Jacobsson 2004). An emphasis on employability today can be seen therefore as a change in ideas regarding responsibility for employment and learning, as well in those of the appropriate distribution of risk between the state, enterprise and individuals. A general consequence is a shift from a view of state responsibility to emphasize the responsibility of the worker (Garsten and Jacobsson 2004). The idea of employability is connected to an ideal whereby individuals 'should' take responsibility for being employable, for example, by having the right education and skills for the demands of the labour market (Salomonsson 2003). For working life, soft skills and personal characteristics such as social competence and enjoying working in teams are part of being an employable individual.

This ideal of employability is related to discourses of lifelong learning and competence development, where the individual takes responsibility for competence development to maintain employability. A new business logic with 'learning and knowledge as the only true sources of competitive advantage for firms and ... [as] thereby the key to individual survival in the labour market' (Huzzard 2004: 109–110) is set out. Gustavsson (2002) portrays this shift within discourses of education as an ideological turn in the 1980s, when knowledge and learning became more and more coloured by economic vocabulary and transformed into commodities within the market. With this context of transformation for the worker/learner, the advice and guidance on working life is interesting to study empirically. It is one endeavour amongst others within wider techniques of governing in the shaping of the conduct of individuals for the labour market.

The emphasis on lifelong learning, competence development and on an autonomous and self-steering individual within education and working life has been illuminated by a number of researchers. Fejes (2005) shows how the learner is constructed to 'conduct its own conduct' in official documents on adult education. Responsibility for learning is promoted through schoolwork by teachers and students (Bergqvist 2001; Gustavsson 2003). Edwards and Nicoll (2004) discuss the workplace as a key site for learning, where certain subjects and subjectivities are mobilized in contemporary practices of workplace learning. They suggest, on the one hand that the emphasis on an active, enterprising and flexible learning subject needs to be regarded in relation to the wider social formation, and on the other that how the identification with these discourses is expressed within workplaces and in terms of subjectivities is an empirical question. In studies of workplaces, Iedema and Scheeres (2003) and du Gay (1996) distinguish between those who are favoured by the changes in work identity and those who have problems adjusting to new worker ideals. Taking into account the possibility of different subjectivities, Walkerdine (2005) asserts that some groups more easily embody dominating discourses, while others, especially working class men, have difficulties with this. In her empirical work she concludes that a major change in contemporary work identity has been in its focus on the personal characteristics of the worker, and the ability to 'sell' oneself, which are regulated in practices of self-management. For many researchers, the dimensions of choice and freedom come up frequently in relation to new work identities. The subject of liberalism and neoliberalism is a free and choosing individual (Giddens 1991; Bauman 1998; Rose 1998; Walkerdine 2005). A divide between 'freedom' as an obligation and as a 'new freedom' is noticeable. As Walkerdine (2005) argues, the latter position, represented by Gidden's 'new freedom', means greater reflexivity and possibilities. Another perspective, however, is to look upon new freedom as a new form of government, which implies regulation of the self, where choice is not liberating but instead a responsibility and obligation (Rose 1999). This is the perspective taken in this chapter.

Empirical analysis concerning employment has focused on training for work. Dean (1998) illuminates the regulative practices in the making of an active job seeker, through the provision of job-search assistance for people who then get access to benefits. Job training, or the learning of relevant skills for working life, is exemplified in Persson Thunqvist's (2003) study of simulated job interviews within temporary projects for young unemployed people. In his micro-analysis of speech, he focuses on resistance to dominant discourses of preferred competence. Gee *et al.* (1996) are important contributors in relating the changes in the labour market to changes within discourses, and in particular the impact of 'management language'. They describe the language of management as a language of new capitalism, and focus on the consequences of this for workers, educators and learners in the new work order. Cameron (2000), in her empirical studies of call centres, examines how communication skills and regulative training guidelines have become an important part of education and working life.

The Swedish model in labour market relations

Historically, labour market relations in Sweden have been characterized in terms of a 'Swedish model'. The Saltsjöbaden agreement in 1938 between the blue-collar trade union confederation (LO) and the employer organization (SAF) was an important event. It defined the model as a bargained arrangement between employers and unions that became legally binding for a fixed period of time. Consensus and co-operation between the employer organizations and the trade unions was thus important. A relevant feature was and is still today the 'non-desirability of direct government intervention in collective bargaining' for both sides (Huzzard 2000: 156) and even though the state has an important role in the wider socio-economic development of the country (Forsberg 2000; Huzzard 2000; Lundh 2002). The model has also been influenced by the Social Democratic Party (a leading force in post-war Swedish politics), which has put pressure on employers to take social responsibility within the context of a capitalist economy (Pontusson 1988). During the 1990s, Sweden, among other countries, suffered from an economic crisis and high unemployment rates. The political landscape changed, and as a consequence there was a weaker role for the unions (Bruhn 1999). From an international perspective, many countries experienced a decline in union activity at this time. In the Swedish context, the unions still have a great deal of influence and approximately 80 per cent of the labour force is unionized. The trade union movement in Sweden still has a key role in regulating the labour process, in contrast to other countries such as the UK or US (Bruhn 1999; Huzzard 2000, 2004). A relevant feature of the labour market in Sweden is the clear distinction between and organization of white- and blue-collar workers into separate trade unions. The union, Sif, chosen for this study is a vertically organized trade union, organizing white-collar workers at all levels from office workers to leadership in industry (Kjellberg 1997).

The uptake of Foucault

Taking inspiration from Foucault, discourses are here viewed as productive of knowledge within 'ways of thinking' that classify and justify what is normal or deviant (Foucault 1977). Rose (1998) has used the Foucauldian concept 'governmentality' (Foucault 1991) in discussing how political power is related to the subject. Political power is not divided between the state and private life, but is instead intertwined, and positions the subject as the target of and as regulated by normative practices. The governing of subjects can in a broad sense be understood as 'techniques and procedures to direct human behaviour' (Foucault 1994a: 80).

Doing a genealogical analysis is to alert the reader to the fact that things have been and can be done otherwise (cf. Besley 2005). The empirical material chosen here shows the governing and discursive shaping of subjects in the job market today, and this is contrasted with examples from the 1950s and 1970s. The analysis focuses on the attitudes, behaviours and practices that are put forward within job-seeking advice and guidance, as a means to help regulate and shape the job seeker and worker. There are specific conventions for job seeking today and the aim is to illuminate these in relation to those of previous times. A contemporary normative-regulatory ideal is thus illustrated and then problematized.

But this is not to suggest that subjectivities are determined through training, advice or guidance. There are limitations to this kind of study and I am cautious about drawing any conclusions about the constitutive effects of discourse in relation to subjectivity and the negotiating dimension of discourse in social contexts (cf. Fairclough 1992). As Foucault (1994b: 87) stresses in discussing techniques of the self, they are: '... suggested or prescribed to individuals in order to determine their identity, maintain it, or transform it in terms of a certain number of ends, through relations of self-mastery or self-knowledge'. As Edwards and Nicoll (2004) emphasize, discourses may not have the consequences that we expect.

Techniques of governing in contemporary job seeking

There are a number of pieces of advice and guidance that are emphasized today as important for the job seeker to adopt when entering working life. Today's brochures are written as more or less explicit prescriptions of what is 'good' or 'desirable'. They are written in a style that implies authoritative knowledge on how to act in order to get work. This is expressed in normative ways, with verbs such as 'ought to' (Sif 2002: 9). The trade union describes itself as expert and coach in prescriptions of what should be done, and as helping the job seeker with 'tools' (Sif 2005: 9–11) for the job search. It positions itself as 'giving professional counselling and feedback' (Sif 2005: 2) and personal services for its members.

The trade union's guidance in job seeking aims to improve one's knowledge and skills in order that one can make a good impression. It offers statistics about salaries, and to review curricula vitae and simulate job interviews, so that job seekers can be informed and improve and practice their communication skills. There are also feelings to overcome and manage. The trade union suggests that job seekers can have feelings of stress and insecurity in the job-search process, but that the union can help them overcome these through its training.

There are things to learn about how to engage with prospective employers so as to give a good impression both within initial engagements and the interview itself. A job seeker's self-presentation at the point of initial contact, within the curriculum vitae and job interview is considered important. In advice given for initial contact, the personality is something that can be allowed to show, but expression of the self is constrained by specific rules: 'Letting your personality shine through is never wrong. But there are a number of unwritten rules on how to express yourself in your initial contacts with employers. All to increase your chances of getting an interview' (Sif 2005: 2). The curriculum vitae should be structured in terms of key words and headings, and 'personal goals', 'interests' and 'hobbies' are all suggested to be important: 'Describe interests and hobbies, or something you like to do in your free time. Be aware that sedentary, inactive free time can raise doubt about your go and ambition' (Sif 2002: 10). The self that is expressed should be one that is both active and ambitious.

Within an interview, certain possible characteristics of interaction, person-ality and the body need to be controlled, channelled and managed, whilst still being oneself. Recommendations are made with quite some normative force; as both statements of fact and normative value claims:

> Exaggerated politeness or being pushy seldom pays – in interviews it is best to be yourself ... Become aware of your body language! More than

> 50% of what we communicate is through body language – not speech. Eye
> contact with everyone interviewing you is important, for example.
>
> (Sif 2002: 16)

Training then is useful in learning how to make the right impression, in
learning how to manage the self and body and in learning to give a good and
relaxed impression: 'In simulated interviews you can prepare in advance for
how it feels to be posed these types of questions. This increases your chances of
making a good and relaxed impression during the interview' (Sif 2005: 3).
Through practice, the job seeker can improve on the impression that is
ultimately made.

The job seeker is advised to be prepared for typical questions in interview
situations: 'How would you describe yourself with regards to: Efficiency,
Ability to cooperate, Stress tolerance, Initiative, Capacity to lead, Flexibility'
(Sif 2002: 19). The implicit prescription is to examine oneself in terms of
characteristics that act to shape a particular job-seeking subjectivity. This
dimension of self-presentation includes showing one's positive sides, but also
avoiding clichés: 'Describe yourself in positive terms. Avoid empty phrases and
stiff expressions' (Sif 2002: 7).

The overall message is that both planning and training are central for the
job seeker. These can be understood as forms of self-regulation that presuppose
that the individual takes responsibility for his or her learning. There is a moral
quality involved, in that the individual 'should' take such responsibility, so
that they can express their personality and present themselves as active and
ambitious. In this context, where the individual should market themselves
in competition with others – both 'sell yourself' and 'be yourself' – this
involves a dilemma. On the one hand the instructions strictly standardize
the self that is to be expressed. On the other, the self is to *be* itself. There is
an emphasis on performance *and* authenticity and an element of insecurity
for the individual in negotiating between these. At the same time job-search
discourses are productive and constraining of the identity position of a job
seeker – productive in their prescription of skills to learn and how to perform,
and constraining through this prescription.

The normative ideals – such as flexibility, the ability to co-operate and personal qualities – are elements of a typical management discourse (cf. Gee *et al.*
1996). These regulate the subject by presupposing reflexivity. Job seekers are
encouraged to present themselves as having 'strategies to develop those parts of
your personality that you are less satisfied with' (Sif 2002: 15). There are clearly
references to self-improvement through taking individual responsibility and
learning who you are as a person. In order to succeed, the reflexive ability of
evaluating and constructing oneself is needed. It implies introspection about
personal skills and bears a resemblance with discourses of self-help with their
questions of 'who am I' and 'how can I better myself'? (Rimke 2000). In this
context, the discourse is not about becoming a better mother or lover. It is

advice from experts on becoming more employable in the labour market, with an expressive style of communication that resonates with that of the 'how to' genre within discourses of self-help.

On a general level of discourse, two intertwined tendencies are significant for understanding contemporary job-search discourses. They are those towards *employability* on the one hand and towards *self-governance* on the other. The former must be understood in relation to the wider ideological change regarding the dimension of risk and responsibility for the worker/learner. The employability of the worker is thus constructed as the responsibility of the individual. The latter is a neoliberal rationality that emphasizes entrepreneurial capacities in constructing the entrepreneur of self (cf. Rose 1998) that was mentioned earlier. Central to this rationality is both the taking of individual responsibility and the taking of support from experts such as, in this context, the trade union, thus reducing the risk of being replaced or not fitting into a flexible labour market. The implication is that, by displaying employability, by performing and acting according to normative ideals, the individual can get into the labour market. The trade union acts as an authority in shaping the conduct of the white-collar worker, it functions as an expert in trying to shape conduct, and it does so by positioning the subject as a self-steering individual who takes responsibility for their own learning.

Learning for employment – a retrospective tracking

Discourses of planning and learning for entering working life were also evident within the brochures of the 1950s and the 1970s. The difference is *what* was communicated as being important to learn and prepare for. Here I track the construction of subjects in the job seeking during previous times and illustrate some similarities and distinctions with examples.

In both the 1950s and 1970s, to have knowledge about terms and conditions of employment and the rights of the employee *before* entering the labour market and *before* signing a contract for work was emphasized as important. This was made explicit in the following example from the 1950s: 'In no case should one take employment without assessing the conditions of employment' (Sif 1955: 5). Implicitly, terms of employment were central aspects of what the trade union communicated as important to learn. In the 1970s, one should be prepared by knowing about tasks, vacation, hours and salary:

> If you apply for work in the industrial sector you can get information from SIF about normal starting salaries for the position, general employment conditions, that is vacation, period of notice, sick pay, overtime, retirement etc. This information strengthens your position and gives you greater security with regards to your employer.
>
> (Sif 1970: 18)

In the 1970s, employment rights and empowerment through knowledge were underlined: 'Get information about the company ... (But be critical!) If you are seeking work in the industrial sector SIF will gladly help you when you apply for your first job. Among other things you can make use of our information about working conditions in companies' (Sif 1970: 12).

Especially in the 1970s, Sif emphasized the need to be critical. There was an implied undercurrent of suspicion between Sif and employing bodies, with a message from Sif to prospective workers that there were risks in working life if one was not careful. This is seen within descriptions of that time: 'Don't be fooled by an impressive ad or fancy words. We advise against answering anonymous ads' (Sif 1974: 8–9). Being careful as a strategy for managing entry into working life is not found in contemporary discourses about applying for work. But, just as they do now, the trade unions of previous times portrayed themselves as having expert knowledge and communicated through that knowledge the norms of the worker.

The trade union's representations of employers within the contemporary discourse emphasize how they evaluate job seekers in their capacities to communicate and act in the job-search process. As we have seen, the focal point today is on the performativity of the job seeker and on guidance for job seekers in how to act and communicate in order to display employability. The union is positioned as providing 'personal services' for their members and the utility of the union for the individual worker is emphasized. In the brochures from the 1950s we find the question: 'How can the individual member make use of SIF?' (1955: 12). In the 1950s and 1970s, the responsibility of the worker was to make use of Sif by gaining knowledge with the help of the union. This was, again, to presuppose individual action, as is the case today, but was quite a different kind of activity. Here one 'should' take responsibility for gaining knowledge about the conditions of the labour market and employment rights, as the moral quality.

In brochures from the 1970s there were guidelines for how to act in the job search and in front of prospective employers much as there are today. However, here the importance of the white-collar worker and his or her value as manpower was emphasized as well as having a critical stance towards the employer:

> Remember your value as manpower and do not let yourself be impressed too easily. Pay attention to the interviewer. Give sincere answers to the questions and don't be afraid to open up. Ask! There is a lot you don't know about the possible position. It gives an alert impression if you ask questions.
>
> (Sif 1970: 18–19)

This focus on the white-collar worker as valuable manpower implied a more collective stance than the one that is found today. The trade unions focused on worker education and status *as* white-collar workers – the advice was primarily directed to the white-collar worker, rather than to his or her position as a job seeker. Guidelines emphasized that knowledge of terms of employment was important when entering working life.

My argument is that the 1970s discourse had similarities to contemporary ones in terms of instructions about job seeking as knowledge about where to apply for work, what to include in applications and the job interview. A difference is that the skills to be learned are now generally more those of a 'job seeker', as identity position. Contemporary job seeking is now more of a social practice, based on social and communicative skills that must be learned for the individual to get work. In earlier times the white-collar worker was encouraged to learn about his or her rights. Of course, employment rights are still an important question for trade unions in general and within workplaces. But, today, the white-collar worker should show their personal qualifications, and who they are and what they can contribute as a person, instead of showing an understanding of rights. The important thing for the contemporary job seeker is to market oneself as an individual. This is a commodification of the self, which could be seen in relation to the wider discourses of flexibility and employability in the labour market (Garsten and Jacobsson 2004).

Concluding remarks

This chapter has illustrated how contemporary advice and guidance on job-search practices regulate the subject through a shaping and presentation of the body and self. It presupposes a self-steering subject and focuses upon individual action in constructing the employable individual for a flexible and global labour market. This governing of a learning subject is part of wider neoliberal practices for self-management.

This advice for contemporary job seeking emphasizes planning; it encourages introspection and knowing who you are as an individual. The performance of the job seeker is stressed, and there are normative regulations around ways of acting, performing and even simulating job interviews to learn how to present oneself in the 'right way'. These specific ideas are in contrast with those governing in earlier times. 'Applying for work' seems to be what Fairclough (1992: 132) calls a process of *semantic engineering* of the self and its moral qualities, associated with skills in knowing how to write a winning curriculum vitae and perform in an interview situation. These are skills in marketing oneself and in social and communicative skills in the job search. As researchers have argued (cf. Cameron 2000; Walkerdine 2005), communicative skills and personal characteristics are significant ideals in the governing of contemporary workers.

Notes

1 (Sif) The Swedish white-collar union of Industrial and Technical Workers in Industry. They have 3,46,000 members and are the third largest union in Sweden. Members are mostly employed in the private sector. For more information see www.sif.se (also in English).
2 Twenty-two brochures from the 1950s until 2005 have been chosen for the study. The analysis does not intend to provide a thorough picture of important questions for the trade union over time. The study is one part in a thesis about contemporary job seeking.

References

Bauman, Z. (1998) *Arbete, Konsumtion och den Nya Fattigdomen*, Göteborg: Daidalos.
Bergqvist, K. (2001) 'Discourse and classroom practices – reflectivity and responsibility in learning and instruction', *Nordisk Pedagogik*, 21: 82–91.
Besley, A.C. (2005) 'Self-denial or self-mastery? Foucault's genealogy of the confessional self', *British Journal of Guidance and Councelling*, 33: 365–82.
Bruhn, A. (1999) *Individualiseringen och det Fackliga Kollektivet, en Studie av Industritjänstemäns förhållningssätt till Facket*, Örebro: Örebro University.
Cameron, D. (2000) *Good to Talk? Living and Working in a Communication Culture*, London: Sage.
Dean, M. (1998) 'Administrating asceticism: reworking the ethical life of the unemployed citizen', in M. Dean and B. Hindess (eds), *Governing Australia, Studies in Contemporary Rationalities of Government*, Cambridge: Cambridge University Press.
Du, Gay, P. (1996) *Consumption and Identity at Work*, London: Sage.
Edwards, R. and Nicoll, K. (2004) 'Mobilizing workplaces: actors, discipline and governmentality', *Studies in Continuing Education*, 26: 159–73.
Fairclough, N. (1992) *Discourse and Social Change*, Cambridge: Polity.
Fejes, A. (2005) 'New wine in old skins: changing patterns in the governing of the adult learner in Sweden', *International Journal of Lifelong Education*, 24: 71–86.
Finn, D. (2000) 'From full employment to employability, a new deal for Britain's unemployed?', *International Journal of Manpower*, 21: 384–99.
Forsberg, P. (2000) 'Nya former för institutionaliserat samarbete mellan stat, arbete och kapital', in A. Neergaard and Y. Stubbergaard (eds), *Politiskt Inflytande*, Lund: Studentlitteratur.
Foucault, M. (1977) *Discipline and Punish*, Harmonsworth: Penguin.
Foucault, M. (1991) 'Governmentality', in G. Burchell, C. Gordon and P. Miller (eds), *The Foucault Effect: Studies of Governmentality*, Chicago: University of Chicago Press.
Foucault, M. (1994a) 'On the government of living', in P. Rabinow (ed.), *Ethics, Subjectivity and Truth*, New York: The New Press.
Foucault, M. (1994b) 'Subjectivity and truth', in P. Rabinow (ed.), *Ethics, Subjectivity and Truth*, New York: The New Press.
Garsten, C. and Jacobsson, K. (eds) (2004) *Learning to be Employable, New Agendas on Work, Responsibility and Learning in a Globalizing World*, Basingstoke: Palgrave McMillan.
Gee, J., Hull, G. and Lankshear, C. (1996) *The New Work Order, Behind the Language of New Capitalism*, St. Leonards, N.S.W.: Allen & Unwin.

Giddens, A. (1991) *Modernity and Self-Identity, Self and Society in the Late Modern Age*, Cambridge: Polity.

Gustavsson, B. (2002) 'What do we mean by lifelong learning and knowledge?', *International Journal of Lifelong Education*, 21: 13–23.

Gustavsson, K. (2003) 'Fostran till humankapital i 2000-talets grundskola', in M. Idvall and F. Schoug (eds), *Kunskapssamhällets Marknad*, Lund: Studentlitteratur.

Huzzard, T. (2000) *Labouring to Learn*, Umeå: Boréa.

Huzzard, T. (2004) 'Constructing the competent individual, trade union roles, responses and rhetoric', in C. Garsten and K. Jacobsson (eds), *Learning to be Employable, New Agendas on Work, Responsibility and Learning*, Basingstoke: Palgrave McMillan.

Iedema, R. and Scheeres, H. (2003) 'From doing work to talking work: renegotiating knowing, doing, and identity', *Applied Linguistics*, 24: 316–37.

Kjellberg, A. (1997) 'Hur formades de svenska tjänstemännens organisationsmönster?', in A. Johansson (ed.), *Fackliga Organisationsstrategier*, Stockhom: Arbetslivsinstitutet.

Lundh, C. (2002) *Spelets Regler: Institutioner och Lönebildning på den Svenska Arbetsmarknaden 1850–2000*, Stockholm: SNS förlag.

Payne, J. (2001) 'Lifelong learning: a national trade union strategy in a global economy', *International Journal of Lifelong Education*, 26: 378–92.

Persson Thunqvist, D. (2003) *Samtal för Arbete, Kommunikativa Verksamheter i Kommunala Ungdomsprojekt*, Linköping: Tema Kommunikation.

Pontusson, J. (1988) *Swedish Social Democracy and British Labor: Essays on the Nature and Condition of Social Democratic Hegemony*, Ithaca: Cornell University Press.

Rimke, H. (2000) 'Governing citizens through self-help literature', *Cultural Studies*, 14: 61–78.

Rose, N. (1998) 'Governing enterprising individuals', in *Inventing our selves, Psychology, Power and Personhood*, Cambridge: University Press.

Rose, N. (1999) *Governing the soul*, London: Free Association Books.

Salomonsson, K. (2003) 'Kompetensindustrin, rekrytering, personalutveckling och karriärplanering', in M. Idvall and F. Schoug (eds), *Kunskapssamhällets Marknad*, Lund: Studentlitteratur.

Sif (1955) *Med Betyget i hand och .....SIF i Bakfickan*, Stockholm: SIF.

Sif (1970) *Hur Gör man ...för att Få ett Bra Jobb?*, Stockholm: SIF.

Sif (1974) *Ett Jobb Får man inte hur Lätt som Helst! Några Råd i Tid*, Stockholm: SIF.

Sif (2002) *Att Söka Jobb. Sifs Guide till Ditt nya Arbete*, Stockholm: Sif.

Sif (2005) *Coaching för en Tuff Karriär*, Stockholm: Sif.

Stråth, B. (2000) *After Full Employment, European Discourses of Work and Flexibility*, Bruxelles: Peter Lang.

Walkerdine, V. (2005) 'Freedom, psychology and the neoliberal worker', *Soundings, A Journal of Politics and Culture*, 29: 47–61.

Chapter 9

Adult learner identities under construction

Katarina Sipos Zackrisson and Liselott Assarsson

With the emergence of lifelong learning within the Swedish policy agenda, an Adult Education Initiative (AEI) was launched in the years 1997–2002 as the largest investment in formal adult education ever made, and this despite the fact that Sweden, as other Nordic countries, has a strong and established tradition of liberal adult education. The policy purpose of the AEI was to reduce unemployment, do groundwork for future adult education services, decrease the differences in educational attainment between groups and lay foundations for individual personal growth. Policies of lifelong learning in Sweden, as elsewhere, are emphasizing the importance of post-compulsory education, extending its limits, reconfiguring institutional boundaries and emphasizing formal and informal learning (Edwards 1997; Edwards and Usher 2001; Edwards and Nicoll 2004). Through ideas of lifelong learning, Swedish citizens are now being positioned as 'needing' to learn all the time and everywhere, during their entire life.

Within this chapter we tell the story, from our exploration of the Swedish AEI project, of the subject positions that are constructed for learner identities by educational institutions and of those articulated by learners themselves. We have been interested in examining the relationships between the identities articulated – for discourses construct identity positions and norms for acting, and it is in part through these that power is exercised in practices of governing (Foucault 1991, 1994). The text draws upon data from ethnographic fieldwork of formal learning situations in different institutions of adult education (Assarsson and Sipos Zackrisson 2005). The intrigue of the story is that the exercise of power is partially effective but not always in ways that appear intended through the identities and norms constructed by institutions. Dominant identities emerge as important within our story, and these are discussed within two sections. Within the first, an identity emerges at the level of the education institution through a discourse of the organization of adult education within a consumer-oriented market. This is one of the applicant dominantly as the 'chooser'. Here there appears regularity between the various identity options constructed for the applicant as chooser and those articulated by applicants as they make their choice in becoming learners. Within the second section, a second characteristic learner identity emerges from data of teaching and learning processes, as articulated by the teacher. This identity is quite different from that generated at the level of the educational institution. Within the third section, the various identity positions are discussed in terms of how they operate in a relational way to bring adult learners into education and attempt to 'produce' them within the teaching and learning setting. These activities of power lead us to consider what is at work in and through identity construction.

Over the five years of the AEI, the number of adult students in upper secondary education in Sweden increased by 4,40,000. The project was financed to the tune of 16.5 billion SEK (Swedish Kronor) and organized by the municipalities. These latter were supported financially by the government until the end of 2006, with a mission to provide education for those unemployed or with disabilities and all adults who had not previously earned upper secondary qualifications. Within Swedish policies produced by, for example, the Ministry of Education (ME), education is represented as a tool to handle a diverse society with different dilemmas, as well as supporting humanistic and democratic values (ME 2000, 2001). Adult education is stated to be able to solve such dilemmas and include everyone – no one will ever finally graduate as there will always be knowledge to gain. The lifelong learning agenda positions individuals so they are unable to go through life without taking part in education in one way or another. The enormity of the merits portrayed for adult education within policy texts makes it difficult for citizens to be critical about what it actually offers. In other words, who can say 'no thank you' to participating in lifelong learning?

Subject positioning

In drawing on the Foucauldian notion of governmentality attention is directed towards power relations (Foucault 1991). Governing takes place in part through figures of thought, or ideas, within modern society, and power is decentralized. The exercise of power is spread through different channels but creates similar norms. Within advanced liberalism, inhabitants are positioned as 'independent' and 'responsible' for making choices in all areas of life (Rose 1996). People are incited to act as well-oriented 'consumers', making choices about, for instance, the form of education that they take up and pursue. This exercise of power is successful when people reproduce these ideas in their ways of thinking whilst believing that their thoughts are 'natural' – have sprung out of their own initiative. Thus, there is a question over whether human action within advanced democracies should be thought of as determined and not free? However, it is in the unpredictability of the relation between the exercise of power within different forms of governing and the subject that our freedom can be found (Dreyfus and Rabinow 1982; Hörnqvist 1996; Rose 1996). Hence, governmentality is an idea that offers a dynamic way to explore issues of identity. Identities are considered as discursive constructions. They position subjects and are drawn upon as resources within discourse. 'People' emerge through the various discursive practices in which they participate (Foucault 1988, 1994). Identities are thus versatile, plural and contradictorily negotiated and established through social interaction and specific patterns of activity. They are relational phenomena, where people are positioned and take up positions.

In the context of adult education and formal learning settings some questions of identity emerge: What identities do the educational organizers target? What identities do participants in adult education take up as they engage in learning? What learner identities do teachers support?

A 'chooser' within a market

Our data were collected as a part of the previously mentioned study that focused on teaching and learning processes within the AEI and wider benefits of learning (Assarsson and Sipos Zackrisson 2001, 2005). It was collected from sites of liberal, municipal and distance learning adult education through observations of learning situations, staff meetings and so forth, and 155 interviews with politicians, school heads, AEI project group participants, teachers and adult learners. Although the study involved different actors, the subject positions constructed by them for adult learners were studied extensively.

What identities do the educational organizers target? There were various ways in which the theme of adult education within a consumer-oriented market emerged within our study. A variety of institutions drew upon this theme within their practices and were seen, through the evidence of our study, to attract different people in part as an effect of this. The AEI was organized by the municipalities all over Sweden. In our case study of the municipality of Nystad, a project group was formed for local organization. The group members had experience from student counselling, administration of education, politics and labour organizations, local trade and industry, different educational associations, unemployment agencies and social security programmes. They were considered well-experienced ambassadors for lifelong learning, with knowledge of arenas connected in the project.

The project group members were well informed of the political goals of the AEI, talked about their own work in adult learning provision in these terms, and articulated the ways in which adults interested in education within the municipality would reason about learning. The project leader described the way education, in his view, was generally perceived in Nystad, and his own responsibility in relation to this:

> When you talk to an individual the individual's needs will be affected by the experiences they have and they know there are limits within themselves.

Everything will be a result of that. If there were no limits, what would you like to do? I for one would want to be an author in a sunny paradise like Hawaii and do my writing. But then, when considering this ... first, I am really not good at writing and second I can't stand the heat, so welder is what it is going to be. The challenge is having the adults entering the centre. Once they step inside these doors we won't let them go. Like spiders we catch them in our net [smiles] ... Since the adults' view on education is formed by everyday life I have the responsibility to offer relevant education in relation to different needs; the individuals, the labour market and the society as a whole.

(Curt, interview 2:10)

The AEI project leader Curt describes peoples' choices and participation in adult education as closely related to their everyday life. Work is articulated as central to this identity. This way of reasoning guided Curt and his colleagues when organizing adult education. The conditions for adult education were being shaped at the intersection of discourses of the supply of adult education and the participants' patterns of life.

In terms of the formal learning settings that we studied within the municipality of Nystad, adult education appeared to be dominantly organized around the idea that people were in need of 'qualification', 'rehabilitation' and 'socialization'. In other words, education was a tool to enable adults to become employable, healthy and responsible as democratic citizens. These figures of thought, or 'technologies' of power, emerged within data transcripts of interviews held with politicians, school heads and study and vocational guides. Adult education was primarily positioned for those with lower qualifications and schooling who were categorized as 'unqualified', 'ill' or 'marginalized'. These citizens' lives and strategies for living were seen to need to be 'corrected'. Lifelong learning was represented as being offered to meet different kinds of demands within a varied market, with several actors organizing education aimed for active citizenship.

Within the AEI there had been shift from a situation where the municipality had been the only provider of adult education, to one where different providers were brought together and funded by the AEI project group. The study and vocational guide, Susanna, describes the logic in this reasoning:

The purpose of the purchase is to create a market of different adult organizers. We find it fundamental to operate with a variety of teaching and learning strategies. A broad spectra of multiple and different organizers could recruit different adults in Nystad.

(Susanna, interview 1:12)

The identity of a prospective student was talked about in terms of a market within a variety of discourses. However, within those institutions that positioned themselves within a market, 'citizens' taking an interest in education were positioned as 'consumers'. As Margaret, a local politician, said: 'It's like a kind of the Swedish "smorgasbord", we offer the whole range of appetizers so everyone will find something tasty. As you know, no one usually resists this great variety, it appears just irresistible!' (Margaret, interview 1:5). As within market discourses of consumption more generally, the consumer was expected to inform him- or herself of the possibilities offered, and this acted to 'require' preference by the subject for a certain educational setting (Biesta 2004).

The data showed that this 'technology' of recruiting was successful. People differed in what they chose to study, and how and with whom this would be done. In interviews with adult learners it did indeed become visible that people articulated their use of education in terms of getting a job, and who ended up in which educational institution did not appear coincidental, but the result of well-considered choices. Adults seemed to want to take part in studies where the identities promoted were those related to everyday life. The variety of providers that were available created possibilities for different identity positions to be taken up by individuals selecting their studies. Institutional differences appeared needed for the adults to take part in the project, in other words to become students.

The institutions in Nystad appeared to have attracted different kinds of individuals. A pattern evolved that showed that participants were aligned through their discourses of identity to those of the educational institution that they selected. People presented themselves as distinct identities in relation to their chosen courses. They were not only interested in participating, but also articulated which educational institution was appropriate and in what way. Institutions appeared to work as markers of the identities that individuals' choosing that institution had taken up. By creating specific identities, organizers told a story of who their prospective students were or ought to be within institutionally organized education as well as outside within community education settings. Adults who constructed their identities similarly in relation to education, appeared prone to choose the educational organizer that marked their identity. Within the research, the municipal adult educators represented their courses as 'demanding' in terms of studies, grades and merits, and as a way into higher education. As the adult learner Pete said, 'This is a normal school, but for adults'. Liberal adult educators represented their courses as to do with personal growth, bildung, teacher support and work in groups. The adult learner Zarah said, 'They are not only teachers, I think it's about life, you can't learn without socializing'. The distance learning adult educators represented their courses as the lonely highway to higher education, with efficient studies offering flexibility in time and space, and as attractive for the adult education elite. The adult learner Paula said, 'If you really want to learn you don't want to waste your time on endless discussions with your classmates, I have plans for the future and need higher education as soon as possible'. These voices indicate the kind of relational pattern that we found between each educational provider and their student group.

If education is described as a possibility without limits, then the consequence appears to be that choices concerning education are active ones. Participation is viewed as an individual project where subjects make use of the whole range of possibilities that education provides. The individual is constructed as an independent subject, with the power to control and be responsible for their own life (Assarsson and Sipos Zackrisson 2007). However, such normalizing techniques of power do not only produce obedience, but 'defiance' and the choice of not taking part in lifelong learning is able to be constructed as the problem of the individual (Rose 1996, 1999).

A learner within teaching and learning processes

On entering education the student is required to confront certain expectations of themselves as learners within teaching and learning processes. The study showed that these expectations were similar, whatever the course, teacher or educational institution. We characterized this subject position, constructed within the discursive practices of teaching and learning processes, as the 'interested', the 'prone to change', the 'independent' and the 'well-behaved' student (Assarsson and Sipos Zackrisson 2005, 2006). Illustrating this, we turn to a lesson in Social Science within a municipal adult education class. The teacher, Boel, explained to her class that the curriculum was about reading, watching and discussing the news. A recurring task for her class was to critically analyse the news, a task that she introduced within this particular lesson. She argued that everyone, as a member of society, must learn to be critical, analysing the newspapers, the television and other media. In a powerpoint presentation she presented some criteria to use when working with this task. Then she turned to the adult learners and asked if they knew what they were supposed to do. Here, one of the participants, called Frida, posed a question:

FRIDA (ADULT LEARNER): But, those programmes you talked about ... and read everything, when am I supposed to do such things?
BOEL (TEACHER): Well, everything is not scheduled. You have to use your spare time and do this outside the lessons. But you don't have to just sit in front of the TV or radio, or buy every newspaper. You find a lot of newspapers in the library and you can do your laundry when watching telly! Or listen to the radio when driving your car...
FRIDA: But those kinds of programs, I never watch them!
BOEL: Well, you know you can learn from such things too. We are all in the powerful hands of the media, and as a former journalist I know that you don't problematize you just go for it to keep up to the deadline.
FRIDA: I watch other channels and other programmes and will continue doing that! Not these boring documentaries...

BOEL: Well it's your own choice, but it's a main part of this course. To pass you have to do all these tasks. But, but ... social sciences is about knowing and understanding. That's how you as a member of society can have some influence. We are just overwhelmed by information and sometimes it affects us directly. Then the first step is always to find out if the information is <u>true</u>.

(Fieldnotes school M, 1:2)

The excerpt shows how the adult learners were told what counts as knowledge and were to engage with it. First, they were to show *interest* in something that was sketched out as valuable. Second, the teacher argued that all members of the society must be active, knowing their rights and obligations. This produced the idea that those who do not take part in society in a certain way have to *change*. Third, the scheduled lessons didn't allow enough time to solve these tasks. The constructed adult learner was *independent* of the teacher and able to take responsibility for the task provided, that is, in doing the tasks outside the educational framing. Fourth, the adult learner was *well behaved*. One of the ground rules seemed to be to adapt to the patterns of communication established by the teacher. In this excerpt, the teacher reminded the student of the coming assignment task – their examination. The differential positions, afforded the teacher and student, were emphasized. Thus, a quite specific active learning subject was produced as that which is appropriate, engaging with knowledge of particular form in a particular way and with specific responsibilities and ways of behaving. This learning identity was quite similarly constructed within the teaching and learning processes of the study. In other words, a characteristic subject emerged as normalized within teacher discourses within the data of this and other teaching and learning settings (Hargreaves 2003).

Presented within the descriptions of the AEI and spoken about within discussions at the national level are ideas of a 'new didactics' and of 'self-directed learning' (Sohlman 1997; ME 1998). Discourses of the AEI and lifelong learning reject the use of traditional lectures and emphasize ways of working: problem-based learning, project-oriented and thematic studies as well as working in groups. And, even though participants' differences come forward when looking at interview data about their stated interests and ways of learning, these new views of learning appear to be normalized within student discourse. Knowledge is identified by students as developed through processes of self-directed learning, which take place in the classroom, at the library or at home. Adults are portrayed by them as active, responsible and independent. Learning as an activity is represented as something that is fun and naturally rewarding. The adult, contrary to the child, is taken to be free – and this is why education must be organized on principles of independence and influence. When learning is described, as in this case, in terms of one overriding discourse theme or figure of thought, it becomes difficult to escape. These norms of acting as learners that the AEI students articulate are not specific to adult education, but can be found at different levels in the education system. One might say that inexperienced students, like those within the AEI, are being positioned through the same expectations as experienced students at the university.

Dynamics of power within the classroom

Adult education appears to become reconfigured through wider discourses of lifelong learning within this case study of the AEI project. It is presented as offering possibilities to individuals in their qualification, rehabilitation and socialization. It is presented as an opportunity for anyone. Discourses of lifelong learning imply that adult education 'should' vary in order that there is a choice.

The analysis of discourses of education as market in this study shows that learners' identities may well be construed differently in relation to a range of institutional positionings within a market discourse. That is, different identities are available for individuals to align themselves with – different 'people' can be involved in education. However, as has been shown here, within the classroom, participant identities are restricted and only one learner identity becomes possible (Nesbit 1998). If participants do not accept this challenge and adopt this position, the teacher will work in the direction of changing behaviour (Ball 1990). The logic within the interaction that takes place within the classroom is based on intentional learning regulated by teachers, at least in formal education.

But that does not mean that adult learners actually meet these demands. Let us return to the excerpt with the teacher Boel and the adult learner Frida. Most of the adult learners in this situation acted as 'compliant' subjects, adapting to Boels' demands. The 'defiant' subject, illustrated by the adult learner Frida, opposed the demands and challenges of the implicit rules of participation in education. When negotiation is an activity within the classroom, participants become actors in the dynamics that are created. Teachers are not in total control of the situation as participants have a crucial role in the interplay. However, those who strive for identities other than those constructed and allocated to them by the teacher are likely to be positioned as failures and as unwilling to undertake necessary change. This specific situation illustrates how the dynamics of power works. As a participant, Frida used specific strategies to handle the teachers' discourse of the appropriate learner. Frida did never watch the news, nor did the intended analysis work. Instead her sister-in-law wrote those tasks so that Frida could pass the exam. To sum up, Frida got her grades and became employable, that is, she has been included in society as an adult. But, she did not learn what was intended of her – to become a well-informed and critically analysing citizen – at least not in the way in which the teacher had expected. Thus, education is a tool for disciplinary action, but it can be handled through a variety of learner strategies.

Societies' investments and the system of financing in Sweden makes studying more economically fruitful for adults than being unemployed and creates and legitimates a variety of participant identities. Adults are therefore not always interested in learning or prone to change and challenge educational demands. The opportunity to negotiate and act in different ways is always present in social settings. One could suggest that adult education is an important arena for negotiation for those marginalized from other adult public spheres, such as working life. If recruitment is successful in attracting those with low formal qualifications, the system has to deal with different ways of negotiating the use of education, and interpreting knowledge and learning. Simultaneously, the discourse of lifelong learning prescribes self-directed learning and the offer of flexibility of choice in the time and place of learning. From the professionals' perspective these processes appear quite contradictory and difficult to manage. Negotiations in educational settings create dilemmas and teachers may well tell of having to neglect teaching the skills that they believe in; a teacher within our study said: 'Am I supposed to give up the project of teaching people who actually need to learn?' If intentional learning is about changing people in prescribed directions but at the same time participants are varied, there appears to be a tension and challenge for the maintenance of the professional role.

On governing through identity construction

In the previous sections we described the teaching and learning processes as characterized by a specific subject position or learner identity for the student. It is easy to picture wider institutions in society making the same kinds of demands in their encounters with employees, clients and patients. Being interested, willing to change, independent and well behaved are characteristics required of the flexible and adaptive worker within civil society (Wilson 1999). When considering the binaries constructed – an interest in study versus no interest, willingness to change versus unwillingness and stability, being well behaved or not behaving and being independent rather than dependent – it appears to be a question of which kind of citizens the society approve. However, the idea of governmentality suggests power as intrinsic to social relations (Foucault 1980, 1991). Power is taken to be a dynamic and relational phenomena, it is about its exertion – its exercise – but also about the agency that permits alternative action. One might call this defiance. The idea of governmentality is thus based on the notion of people as subjects, actively involved in different processes of the exercise of power. Put in another way, relations of power can be confirmed and consolidated, where norms are taken up by the subject, but they can also be diverted. These power relations do not seize the subject and can be channelled in different ways. In this chapter we have told a story of participants' strategies as those of compliance and defiance so as to describe the dynamics of power. Drawing on the conception of governmentality we have identified that there is both a price and possibilities for defiance.

The mobilization of education in Nystad turned it into something many citizens encountered in their everyday lives. Participants in adult education approached a market of education in different ways. Those entering adult education acted as consumers; they talked about considering the alternatives and making choices. Participants talked about education as the highway to get a job or change career. They talked about using studies to interrupt a long period of sick leave from work, or to get away from drug abuse or criminal activity. The intrigue of the story is that they had been part of marginalized groups in society and through education were hoping to find a fruitful way of handling their lives. Whether they finished or dropped out study seemed, for them, to have changed their lives. The exercise of power appeared productive because change was attributed to study by the participants themselves. In the follow-up study, one and a half years after participating in education, participants categorize themselves as respectful, responsible, able to take initiative and as worthy. For example, as the adult learner Roger tells us in the final interview (in which his wife Lisa also participates):

> I dropped out and I don't work with web design as I planned, but my wife tells me you're not a pain in the ass anymore. I think that my study mates have something to do with this. I learned to listen and be respectful in relation to others. I don't just watch telly now a days, I think I am a more caring husband and parent than before.
>
> (Roger, adult learner, interview 4:51)

In other words, subjects seemed to have been reconfigured in certain ways even though not necessarily in the ways that were intended.

People do comply by taking part in education. This does not necessarily mean that they become interested, prone to change, independent and well behaved. They use adult education within their own stories of their own patterns of life. In the group of participants within the study, only one third finished their studies and graduated from upper secondary level. From this viewpoint normalizing techniques of power not only produce obedient and predictable people but also those whom we might label disobedient and unpredictable. However, defiance does not create 'losers' who are forced to give up their own life projects. Power relations are always productive (Foucault 1980) and it is possible to act defiantly – a defiance that creates alternative possibilities.

The ideal implicit within discourses of lifelong learning will not be met. The formation of an ideal society will always be incomplete, counteracted and contradicted. Rather than adapt, citizens make discourses work for them even when they take part in education. Like the adult learner Rajiv, who said:

I tried different adult organizers and finally got my driving license as a chauffeur. But I'd rather be unemployed than driving the local bus in Nystad, since I'm waiting for the vacation tours in Europe. To the vocational guide I always say I want to qualify further, for example joining some more security courses.

(Rajiv, adult learner, interview 3:37)

Those participants in the study who qualified for the labour market often found strategies to work discourse to their own ends. And, this highlights the dynamics of power, where there are always possibilities.

References

Assarsson, L. and Sipos Zackrisson, K. (2001) What did you learn in school today...? Everyday patterns of classroom interaction in adult education – who learns what?, in *ESREA Wider Benefits of Learning. Understanding and Monitoring the Consequences of Adult Learning*. Lisbon: Edicoes Universitárias Lusófonas.

Assarsson, L. and Sipos Zackrisson, K. (2005) *Iscensättande av Identiteter I Vuxenstudier*, [*Staging identities in adult education*]. Linköping: Linköping University.

Assarsson, L. and Sipos Zackrisson, K. (2006) 'Möten i vuxenstudier – om undervisning och deltagaridentiteter' [Encounters in adult education], in S. Larsson and L.-E. Olsson (eds), *Om Vuxnas Studier*, Lund: Studentlitteratur.

Assarsson, L. and Sipos Zackrisson, K. (2007) *Med Förstoringsglas på Flexibelt Lärande* [*Highlightening flexible learning*], Härnösand: Nationellt centrum för flexibelt lärande, Informationsavdelningen.

Ball, S.J. (ed.) (1990) *Foucault and Education: Disciplines and Knowledge*, London: Routledge.

Biesta, G.J.J. (2004) 'Against learning: reclaiming a language for education in an age of learning', *Nordisk Pedagogik*, 24: 70–82.

Dreyfus, H.L. and Rabinow, P. (1982) *Michel Foucault. Beyond Structuralism and Hermeneutics*, Chicago: The University of Chicago Press.

Edwards, R. (1997) *Changing Places? Flexibility, Lifelong Learning and a Learning Society*, London: Routledge.

Edwards, R. and Usher, R. (2001) 'Lifelong learning: a postmodern condition of education? *Adult Education Quarterly*, 51: 273–87.

Edwards, R. and Nicoll, K. (2004) 'Mobilizing workplaces: actors, discipline and governmentality', *Studies in Continuing Education*, 26: 159–73.

Foucault, M. (1980) *Power/Knowledge: Selected Interviews & Other Writings 1972–1977 by Michel Foucault*, New York: Pantheon Books.

Foucault, M. (1988) 'The ethic of care for the self as a practice of freedom', in J. Bernauer and D. Rasmussen (eds), *The Final Foucault*, Cambridge, MA: MIT Press.

Foucault, M. (1991) 'Governmentality', in G. Burchell, C. Gordon and P. Miller (eds), *The Foucault Effect. Studies in Governmentality with Two Lectures and an Interview with Michel Foucault*, London: HarvesterWheatsheaf.

Foucault, M. (1994) 'Technologies of the self', in P. Rabinow and N. Rose (eds), *The Essential Foucault. Selections from Essential Works of Foucault, 1954–1984*, New York: The New Press.

Hargreaves, A. (2003) *Teaching in the Knowledge Society: Education in the Age of Insecurity*, New York: Teachers College Press.

Hörnqvist, M. (1996) *Foucaults Maktanalys*, Stockholm: Carlsson Bokförlag.

Ministry of Education (ME) (1998) SOU 1998:51, *Vuxenutbildning och Livslångt Lärande – Situationen inför och under Första året med Kunskapslyftet*, Stockholm: Utbildningsdepartementet.

Ministry of Education (ME) (2000) SOU 2000:28, *Kunskapsbygget 2000 – det Livslånga Lärandet*, Stockholm: Utbildningsdepartementet.

Ministry of Education (ME) (2001) Proposition 2000/01:72, *Vuxnas Lärande och Utvecklingen av Vuxenutbildningen*, Stockholm: Regeringskansliet.

Nesbit, T. (1998) 'Teaching in adult education: opening the black box', *Adult Education Quarterly*, 48: 157–70.

Rose, N. (1996) 'Governing "advanced" liberal democracies', in A. Barry, T. Osborne and N. Rose (eds), *Foucault and Political Reason: Liberalism, Neo-liberalism and Rationalities of Government*, Chicago: The University of Chicago Press.

Rose, N. (1999) *Governing the Soul: The Shaping of the Private Self*, London: Free Association Books.

Sohlman, Å. (1997) 'Kunskapslyft och livslångt lärande', in S. Dahl (ed.), *Kunskap så det Räcker? 18 Debattinlägg om Utbildning och Forskning*, Stockholm: SACO, SULF.

Wilson, A.L. (1999) 'Creating identities of dependency: adult education as a knowledge-power regime', *International Journal of Lifelong Education*, 18: 85–93.

Chapter 10

Recognition of prior learning as a technique of governing

Per Andersson

The recognition of prior learning (RPL) is an idea, a figure of thought, which has been part of the policy and practice of adult education and lifelong learning for a long time, but in different ways in different times and places. It is an idea for 'making learning visible' (Bjørnåvold 2000) that is promoted with arguments of gain for the individual and society. Most initiatives in RPL have had one or more of the following aims: *social justice* (individual opportunities, widening access to education, etc.), *economic development* (making it possible to use existing competence more effectively in the labour market) or *social change* (making the real competence of the population visible creates better conditions for changing society) (Andersson *et al.* 2003, 2004). The idea of RPL is related to the somewhat similar concepts of accreditation, validation, assessment of prior learning that have been used in different countries.

> Although its origins are commonly traced to post-World War Two USA (Weil and McGill 1989), when returning veterans wanted their skills recognised by universities, RPL is not a totally new phenomenon ... Rather, it is the formalisation and (re)naming of pre-existing practices concerning alternative access and admissions, mature age entry, and so on.
>
> (Harris 2006: 3)

In Sweden, for example, the idea of recognizing prior learning was in a sense already present in the seventeenth century, when the priests checked in the catechetical meetings that the population could read (reading religious texts was part of being a good Christian and Lutheran). This ability to read was developed without any formal schooling. In the twentieth century, the idea of identifying a 'reserve of ability' and the construction of a scholastic aptitude test (SweSAT) are examples of how the idea of RPL or actual competence has been expressed in Sweden (Fejes and Andersson 2007). Nevertheless, it was not until 1996 that the French concept *validation* ('validering' in Swedish) was introduced in Sweden. Today, 'validation' is also used in English, particularly in the European Union context, and to some extent synonymously with those related concepts of recognition, accreditation and assessment of prior learning.

In this chapter, I discuss how RPL, or validation, acts as a technique of governing not only the lifelong learner but also lifelong learning and adult education. The official Swedish adult education discourse of validation is used to make this argument. It is a discourse that is expressed within policy texts that are produced to govern adult education in the municipalities, including a report from the Swedish Ministry of Education (ME 2003). When this report was presented, the topic of validation had already been investigated thoroughly and two previous official reports (ME 1998, 2001) published. A government bill was expected to be laid before the Swedish Parliament for decision, but instead the new report encouraged further developmental work. These and other official texts are used in the analysis here as they have been within previous such work (Andersson and Fejes 2005; Fejes and Andersson 2007). In this chapter I also use two official reports about admission to higher education in Sweden, where validation is one aspect that is covered (ME 1995, 2004).

In Sweden, formal adult education is a municipal responsibility, and municipalities are obliged to provide adult education on the level equivalent to that of the compulsory school (primary and lower secondary levels). The state has the role of governing the provision of adult education and validation at upper secondary level, but not through rules and regulations that tell what and how this should be provided. A national curriculum, course plans and grading criteria for the upper secondary school are used as a framework for such regulation of adult education provision, and validation is organized in this context. This framework supports practices of governing through the provision of validation, at least now until a formal national policy decision is made.

When validation was introduced in Sweden it was part of the preparatory work for the Adult Education Initiative (AEI) (1997–2002), an initiative to expand and restructure adult education. The main incentive was that new state subsidies, providing resources for 1,00,000 new study places in adult education, would be based on examination rather than participation; a course would be 'validated' and an adult assigned a grade without having necessarily participated in the class. Whether participation was based on validation and examination or on participation in the class did not matter, it resulted in the same amount of money per participant being paid to the municipality. This emphasis on student examination, independent of participation in the class, was part of a wider discourse of adult education and lifelong learning in Sweden and in other countries at that time, where economic development and competitiveness became important arguments for education and learning. This can be compared to the 1970s, when humanistic ideas and social justice were important within discourses of the recognition of prior learning and wider associated discourses of adult education and lifelong learning.

The analysis in this chapter takes up Foucault's concept of governmentality (Foucault 1991). One technique of government is that of a more or less permanent state of surveillance, which is an exercise of power that takes its effect on the subject in that it is not ever possible for the individual to know whether they are currently being observed. Foucault (1977) illustrates this always possible but invisible surveillance through Bentham's idea of the Panopticon, a prison where a central observer is always able to observe the prisoners, but where the prisoners themselves are unable to tell whether they are observed or not. The fact that they might be observed is enough to exercise normalizing power – for them to behave in the way in which they are expected. The possibility that they might be being watched and could be punished for bad behaviour is enough to instill in them power effects.

Governmentality, however, also operates through rationalities and figures of thought. Validation is therefore explored in this chapter not only through its expression within and as techniques of government, but also as just such a figure of thought within wider rationalities. Figures of thought are ideas that are part of a discourse, they are not identical to, but are present 'under' and make up, the discourse (Asplund 1979). Thus, validation is in part a figure of thought that contributes to wider discourses of adult education and lifelong learning.

As will be shown, validation is partly a matter of governing through a technique of surveillance that then makes it possible for the intensification and extension of disciplinary power, through measurement according to specific norms and through examination. Practices of validation and the figure of thought, or idea, of validation act together to normalize, fabricating the lifelong learner as desirable, constantly mobile and mobilized. Validation acts to encourage learning and to encourage the subject to be brought forth for disciplining and normalization. The very possibility that the subject might have their learning validated in the future acts to normalize that which is learned within the present. The subject is incited to learn to develop knowledge that might have a future value in a coming validation process. Validation at the same time supports the fabrication of a reconfigured adult education provision within municipalities. According to the ideas of validation that are normalized and govern in Sweden at this time, adult education 'should' be organized in a way that makes prior learning visible – as a gain for society and the individual, in terms of the economy, learning and self-esteem.

A salvation narrative of validation

Validation is couched in terms of salvation in Swedish adult education – it is a 'salvation narrative'. Key to this is the idea that validation is a means for the economic gain of the individual and society. Education or training based on the validation of prior learning is said to be shorter and cheaper. It is presented as a way of making competence visible, and thus useable in the labour market. People will thus be saved from unemployment and from studying more than necessary to reach the required qualifications. There are also individual gains to be had, such as the strengthening of the self-esteem (cf. Fejes and Andersson 2007).

> Validating, that is, utilizing all the knowledge and competence a person has acquired through lifelong and lifewide learning, results, of course, in a variety of different gains ... They do not have to study in areas where they already have knowledge and skills. They enter the labour market faster, can earn their living and contribute to the welfare system. Validation also means that people in lifelong learning can complete formal education programmes in less time. Their real competence is made good use of. They can take on more advanced work tasks or, alternatively, study at higher levels than their previous formal level of knowledge would allow for. They contribute to higher economic growth and are paid higher wages.
>
> (ME 2001: 146)

In the report from the Ministry of Education (2003), validation is further inscribed through a discourse of lifelong learning and economic competitiveness, wherein the possibilities afforded by lifelong learning are necessary for the competence and quality of the workforce that is necessary for global economic competitiveness.

> The knowledge society is signified by a high pace of change and a constantly increasing flow of information. Organizations and activities with a high level in the use of knowledge have a demand on broad as well as specialized competence. Sweden shall be a competitive and successful economy in a European and global perspective. The competitiveness of the nation shall build upon competence and quality and not on salaries lower than in the world around us. This requires that the state, the municipalities and the social partners cooperate in providing opportunities for all adults to participate in lifelong learning.
>
> (ME 2003: 13)

Thus, the salvation narrative contributes to the normalization of validation *per se*, as an important and necessary part of lifelong learning and adult education, and for the economic development of the society.

Validation governing the lifelong learner

Validation is a technique for governing the lifelong learner that is promoted through adult education discourse. It fabricates the lifelong learner as the subject of an ever more inclusive discipline through practices of observation, normalization and examination. Educational assessments are, and have been, techniques for creating knowledge about the subject, particularly knowledge about what has (or has not) been learnt in terms of formal education – at school, in adult education, at the university etc. These assessments or examinations are a way of intensifying control and producing more effectively active subjects. They are objectified through different types of documentation of competence and through knowledge of how well each individual has achieved (Andersson and Fejes 2005). The basis of governance is knowledge about the subject (Foucault 1977) and assessments of the subject are a starting point for this. Through validation, '[e]verything you do, lifelong and lifewide, constitutes experiences that are part of the construction of the competent adult' (Andersson and Fejes 2005: 610). The introduction of validation within such a discourse of lifelong learning means a turn within these, in that informal and non-formal knowledge/competence 'should' now be transformed into formal competence through assessment and documentation, thus extending the basis of governing, effective production and control.

Validation as a figure of thought in Swedish policy on adult education is not new, even if the concept of 'validating' has only been used since 1996. In a general sense it has been part of a Swedish adult education discourse since the 1950s, but there have been differences in how the ideas of competence and knowledge were stressed. In the last ten years the focus in validation has been on the subject's specific experience and competence – the subject is constructed as an adult with specific experiences that have specific content and that are to be examined and validated as specific competencies. This idea of validation creates the desired subject as the competent subject. During the 1960s and 1970s, the focus was on the subject's general experience and competence. To a large extent this was valued independently of the contents of that experience and, for example, was used as a mechanism for admission to higher education. The following quotation illustrates how the current focus on specific experience has emerged, and how it is contrasted to a more general valuing of competence as measured in average grades from upper secondary school and in the Swedish scholastic aptitude test (SweSAT):

> There is a great risk that applicants with good aptitude for the education programme in question, but with more unusual merits, will not do themselves justice if you only use grades and SweSAT in the selection process. In addition to this, there are in many cases other qualifications that are important for the education programme applied for than those measured by grades or SweSAT. The most obvious example is art education, where you traditionally make the selection based on entrance tests or samples submitted by the applicant.
>
> (ME 1995: 84)

During the 1950s, it was not a focus on specific or general experience or competence that dominated. Rather, there was a focus on *ability*, a reserve of ability or reserve of talent was to be identified (Andersson and Fejes 2005), and those with the ability to study were to be accepted for adult and higher education. There was an intense discussion of ability, particularly among a number of researchers and politicians at this time. This notion of ability has since not been dominant, even though it is still to some extent present within policy discourses.

Of course, in a broader sense, the idea of validation has been present for much longer in catechetical meetings (as was mentioned within the introduction to the chapter), in the guilds and in relation to correspondence courses. Guilds assessed prior informal or non-formal learning within the vocations; learning was examined through apprenticeship tests and within masterpieces. In correspondence courses the adult learner used prior learning in the examination tasks that were to be completed and sent to a teacher/assessor (Fejes and Andersson 2007). Of course any prior learning could be used in any examination, but in the early form of correspondence courses it was not necessary for students to participate in a 'class' and thus they learned in different ways and contexts that were beyond the control of the teacher.

In these cases, the varying practices of validation fabricated somewhat different subjects. But common to this were techniques of the observation and normalization of the subject as they were made productive through the examination. Thus, validation is a practice and figure of thought of disciplinary power that functions through the examination. When prior learning is validated, new knowledge about both subject and population is created; as in, for example, knowledge about an individuals' (subject) knowledge, the prior experiences through which they learned this knowledge, the location of these experiences, and the many ways in which individuals such as these within a population might have had their learning supported in advance through the organization of flexible learning opportunities. The extension of knowledge of the individual and population thus go hand in hand. And when the idea of validation is present within policy and wider discourses of adult and lifelong learning, disciplinary practices are able to be extended from those of formal learning, and the previously invisible subject is now able to be governed as a part of a population about which then knowledge can be 'newly' created. That is, discourses of validation normalize the idea that not only learning in formal education should be formally assessed, but also informal and non-formal learning. This affects the extension of disciplinary practices across populations and the construction of new knowledge about the subject whereby both population and individual can be made more active and productive. The panoptic gaze becomes ever more all encompassing.

Validation governing lifelong learning

Validation methods do not only measure what has been learnt in the past (one could call this reactive measurement), nor do they only provide a mechanism of power for the extension of the panoptic gaze, they are also potential techniques for governing learning in the future. Assessments proactively govern learning, they are part of a 'hidden curriculum' (Snyder 1970) the message system of which implicitly tells those who may be active in their self-positioning as lifelong workers and learners, what knowledge actually counts. When the possibility of validation is introduced, there is a new 'message' concerning what learning is valuable, and when and how valuable learning can take place. Validation could be promoted as a possibility for the all-inclusive examination of learning, promoting learning always and everywhere within possible future assessments, and as an always present invisible surveillance. Or, rather it could be promoted towards the 'cue-seeking' subject (Miller and Parlett 1974) as a specific range of validation regarding specific knowledge areas to be covered. The following quotation represents a break in the dominant contemporary discourse on validation in Sweden with its idea of the broad and reactive possibility of the measurement of prior learning. It suggests the awareness that a strategy for the cue seeker might be a productive adaptation:

> Let us start by stating the following: all social systems and rules result in adaptive behaviour and optimizing strategies! This is true of social insurance and taxes as well as rules for admission to higher education. We should not believe anything else.
>
> (ME 2004: 71)

Validation promotes certain forms and contents of learning, similar to but at the same time perhaps quite different from those of formal education. In this way, validation becomes a 'new' and differentiated dividing practice and process of normalization. It is a way of making visible and promoting certain learning – seen as good in economic terms – while other learning is still de-valued or not valued. Thus, in a general sense, this is a question of shifts in knowledge organization within our societies. And, especially a matter of shifts in the previous boundary between on the one hand formal learning, and on the other hand informal and non-formal learning. However, validation is also a technique for the intensification of the techniques governing formal learning. It promotes flexible and individualized learning – adult education 'should' be a matter of new learning, not of studying things you already know, as we will see.

Validation governing adult education

The idea of validation was introduced to adult education during the AEI (1997–2002), the previously mentioned process for the restructuring of adult education in Sweden. A new structure was constructed through a discourse that decentralized the previous system of governance (Lumsden Wass 2004). This was narrated through discourses of 'marketization' and co-operation. However, there were also discourses of individualization and learning at play, and 'flexibility' and 'validation' were emphasized within these.

The report on validation from the Swedish Ministry of Education (2003) expressed the ambition of the government to place validation in a central position. One explicit purpose of the report was that of the general control of local planning in the municipalities (ME 2003: 15). As part of this, regions, municipalities, adult education institutions and other actors are expected to make use of validation, both as a structured process and as part of the teaching process. This is argued to encourage more flexible and individualized forms of adult education, within the 'salvation narrative' identified previously, and with the suggestion of gains for the individual and society in promoting validation. There are also organizational dimensions discussed within the text, regarding how to relate validation to adult education and labour market, and to payment.

Validation is represented within this text to be in line with one of the ideals of adult education and andragogy, whereby the learner's perspective is taken as a starting point. But here it is constructed as a *technique* for starting from and making use of the background of the learner for lifelong learning, rather than as a means to focus on the learner within pedagogy.

Validation is positioned as part of a structured process where guidance results in validation of prior learning, and in the following step results in flexible and individualized formal learning. It is argued as an important part of the infrastructure of adult learning *for* lifelong learning, which makes flexible learning possible. There is said to be a need for an infrastructure of adult learning that creates opportunities for flexible learning, and this is described as a 'chain' of guidance, validation and support for flexible learning (ME 2003: 14). Validation is not described as a *possible* link in this chain, but rather as a *necessary part* that the municipalities should organize. In a normalizing statement, it is postulated as a problem both for the individual and for society if competence from outside formal education is not documented: 'It is a problem from the perspective of the individual as well as of the society if competence acquired outside the formal educational system, through foreign vocational training, work-life experience and e.g. military service is not documented' (ME 2003: 18). Central to its positioning as a potential governing mechanism within adult education is the way of defining what validation is: '... a process including structured assessment, valuing, documentation and recognition of knowledge and competence that a person has, irrespective of how they have been acquired' (ME 2003: 19).

Three main areas of validation practice are defined within this document. First, it is stated to be a part of an educational process to identify the level of the individual's knowledge, adapt the level of the education and/or make the period of time of study shorter. That validation is part of an educational process and is described as an 'obvious part of every individualized, educational activity' (ME 2003: 22). In relating teaching to the student's knowledge and experience, validation becomes part of a process whereby assessments of curriculum knowledge could be credited to the student. This is referred to as an idea and attitude that has traditionally been promoted in adult education

(ME 2003). Second, validation is positioned as a part of a guiding process that defines the start of further education. Validation here is described as a 'natural' part of a guiding process. Third, it is a practice of documenting actual knowledge and skills before applying for a job, or in relation to learning and competence development in the workplace.

Here, it is possible to discern two, or perhaps three, figures of thought operating at the same time within the document. Validation as a part of every educational process may be conceived as a process of structured assessment, valuing and documentation, but it could also be a more informal process where the teacher, together with the learner, identifies, recognizes and builds on prior learning. These different figures of thought – the idea of validation as a formal and structured process, and the idea of a more informal presence of recognition of prior learning in an educational process – turn up at the same time more than once in the report. However, it is the idea of the formal process that dominates: 'It is important to emphasize that validation solely should be directed towards the process which aims at identifying and describing the knowledge and competence that the individual already has' (ME 2003: 23). Consequently, it is stated that validation should be kept separate from what is being prepared for, for example, supplementary education to reach a certain eligibility or formal competence (ME 2003: 23). Thus, in this idea of keeping validation and further learning separate, a delimitation of validation is made – validation as RPL (recognition of prior learning taking place before/outside the educational process) rather than rpl (recognition of prior learning within the educational process) (see Breier 2005).

Finally, validation is articulated as having an exploratory function (ME 2003). Exploring means finding out what knowledge and skills the individual has, without the prerequisite of goals or criteria to fulfill. This is another example of parallel and different ideas in the policy text: Even if the technique of recognizing prior learning is exploratory, the goal is still represented as one that 'should' be to document knowledge and skills in a way that is accepted within the educational system and labour market, and which might make control in relation to goals and criteria necessary.

The report (ME 2003) does not prescribe how validation should be provided. Instead, the report from the Ministry of Education (2003) encouraged further local and regional development. Thus, government (in its common usage of the term) is to be arranged at a distance, without a central decision on how validation should be organized. The role of the state could be described as encouraging and supporting the development of validation, and the responsibility is placed on state, municipal and private actors.

Validation is placed within the framework of the 'infrastructure'. This could and should not be the same in all municipalities, but has to be adapted to local needs and conditions (ME 2003). However, it is not only the responsibility of the local municipality. On the contrary, validation should be arranged in regional co-operation between educational organizations, employers (trade organizations) and trade unions, and as a responsibility of both the educational system and those enjoying working life. When it comes to financing, the Ministry of Education suggests that validation measures should be paid for by the responsible authorities or employers, depending on the purpose of the validation. Municipal adult education should pay when validation is part of the 'chain' of adult education. An individual could be validated on his or her own initiative within the framework of an 'orienting course' in municipal adult education (but this is only mentioned as a possibility, not as a legal right). Employers should pay when it is a matter of the validation of the vocational competence of their employees. The public employment office should pay for validation intended to help an unemployed person get a new job.

Finally, the role of the State is defined in the report. It should encourage and support the development of legitimacy, quality and methods in validation. More precisely, this encouragement and support should be realized through the establishment of a national commission on validation with a four-year mandate.

Final reflections

Validation is a technique of governing that connects the past of learning with its present and future. Formally, the idea of validation gives present recognition to the past, the prior learning of the subject. The subject is construed as having valuable experiences that should be examined in terms of learning, knowledge and competence. However, as has been shown in this chapter, validation also acts as a technique for governing present and future learning. A possible future validation process acts as a 'hidden curriculum'. Thus, this possibility of a future examination acts as a technique of invisible surveillance for lifelong learners of the present. This is the extension of the exercise of disciplinary power within contemporary life that indicates a disciplining of an extension of governing over all types of learning, or only certain more restricted kinds.

In the past, the exercise of disciplinary power through forms of the recognition of prior learning were to be found in the catechetical meetings, in the apprenticeship tests and pieces of work produced for these, and in correspondence learning. Now, the recognition of prior learning is exercised as power through and within discourses and as reconfigured techniques that govern the practices of lifelong and adult learning. And of course it was always likely – in the catechetical meeting, in apprenticeship tests or in correspondence courses – that the 'learner' asked her- or himself, what readings, mastery or competence he or she might in the future be asked to have already learned so as to be identified God's child, master of the trade, or competent worker or learner. None of this is particularly new. What is different is that the practices of the exercise of power within contemporary discourses of adult education and lifelong learning have been adjusted so that individuals who would not previously have identified themselves as learners or as learned become so identified. And, this is powerful, for once they have learned they know of themselves as learners in the past, present and as a potential for the future. Knowledge of them as individuals is able to be combined with knowledge of them as a population on the margins of those within formal learning or as individualized learners within formal learning. And this then permits the intensification of technologies of power, through the emergence of new tactics for their effective work on the body.

References

Andersson, P. and Fejes, A. (2005) 'Recognition of prior learning as a technique for fabricating the adult learner: a genealogical analysis on Swedish adult education policy', *Journal of Education Policy*, 20: 595–613.

Andersson, P., Fejes, A. and Ahn, S.-e. (2004) 'Recognition of prior vocational learning in Sweden', *Studies in the Education of Adults*, 36: 57–71.

Andersson, P., Sjösten, N.-Å. and Ahn, S.-e. (2003) *Att Värdera Kunskap, Erfarenhet och Kompetens. Perspektiv på Validering*, Stockholm: Myndigheten för Skolutveckling, Forskning i fokus nr. 9.

Asplund, J. (1979) *Teorier om Framtiden*, Stockholm: LiberFörlag.

Bjørnåvold, J. (2000) *Making Learning Visible. Identification, Assessment and Recognition of Non-formal Learning in Europe*, Tessaloniki, Cedefop – European Centre for the Development of Vocational Training.

Breier, M. (2005) 'A disciplinary-specific approach to the recognition of prior informal experience in adult pedagogy: "rpl" as opposed to "RPL"', *Studies in Continuing Education*, 27: 51–65.

Fejes, A. and Andersson, P. (2007) 'Historicising validation: the 'new' idea of validation in Sweden and its promise of economic growth', in R. Rinne, A. Heikkinen and P. Salo (eds), *Adult education – Liberty, Fraternity, Equality? Nordic Views o Lifelong Learning*, Turku: Finnish Educational Research Association.

Foucault, M. (1977) *Discipline and Punish: The Birth of the Prison*, London, Penguin Books.

Foucault, M. (1991) 'Governmentality', in G. Burchell, C. Gordon and P. Miller (eds), *The Foucault Effect: Studies in Governmentality with Two Lectures and an Interview with Michel Foucault*, Chicago: The University of Chicago Press.

Harris, J. (2006) 'Introduction and overview of chapters', in P. Andersson and J. Harris (eds), *Re-theorising the Recognition of Prior Learning*, Leicester: NIACE.

Lumsden Wass, K. (2004) *Vuxenutbildning i Omvanding. Kunskapslyftet Som ett Sätt att Organisera Förnyelse*, Göteborg: Acta Universitatis Gothoburgensis, Göteborg Studies in Educational Sciences, 219.

Miller, C. M. L. and Parlett, M. (1974) *Up to the Mark: A Study of the Examination Game*, London: Society for Research into Higher Education.

Ministry of Education (ME) (1995) SOU 1995:71, *Behörighet och Urval. Förslag till Nya Regler för Antagning till Universitet och Högskolor*, Stockholm: Utbildningsdepartementet.

Ministry of Education (ME) (1998) SOU 1998:165, *Validering av Utländsk Yrkeskompetens*, Stockholm: Utbildningsdepartementet.

Ministry of Education (ME) (2001) SOU 2001:78, *Validering av Vuxnas Kunskap och Kompetens*, Stockholm: Utbildningsdepartementet.

Ministry of Education (ME) (2003) *Validering m.m. – Fortsatt Utveckling av Vuxnas Lärande*, Stockholm: Utbildningsdepartementet, Ds 2003: 23.

Ministry of Education (ME) (2004) SOU 2004:29, *Tre Vägar till den öppna Högskolan*, Stockholm: Utbildningsdepartementet.

Snyder, B. R. (1970) *The Hidden Curriculum*, Cambridge, Massachusetts and London, England: The MIT Press.

Chapter 11

Pathologizing and medicalizing lifelong learning

A deconstruction

Gun Berglund

Education, often in the name of lifelong learning, is given a major significance in contemporary Western societies. Policy rhetoric stresses the importance of lifelong learning as an economic means to achieve prosperity, growth and development for nations and enterprises. It points out individuals' personal development as a matter of policy concern. Lifelong learning is thus supposed to accomplish a whole range of public as well as private goods, or to cite Donald Dewar (1999), Secretary of State for Scotland 'Learning is a vital element of a successful, healthy, vibrant and democratic society'. Given such prominence lifelong learning seems to be regarded as something of a miracle cure to whatever disease society might suffer, a kind of educational Viagra to create potent citizens for the so-called learning society.

One of the prominent features of lifelong learning policy rhetoric is its focus on health – not only on physical, but social and economic health. Policies often claim that education and lifelong learning promote healthy societies in terms of social and financial well-being. Health is thus discursively construed as something more than the physical or psychological health of the individual. This chapter argues that the construction of the healthy society where lifelong learners are healthy and desired individuals simultaneously produces that which it excludes – an unhealthy society and unhealthy individuals. This is 'how we ... indirectly constitute ... ourselves through the exclusion of some others: criminals, mad people and so on' (Foucault 1988: 146). When health is the norm, illness becomes a deviation, something that ought to be cured and restored to a normal and healthy condition. This is not to argue that people become 'really' sick. The argument is not to be confused with the naturalist conception where 'disease differs from a state of health, the pathological from the normal, as one quality from another' (Canguilhem 1991: 41). Rather, it shows how power/knowledge within discourse constitutes what is held as the true, normal and healthy way of speaking of lifelong learning, i.e. produces what is legitimate and thereby also illegitimate knowledge within the discourse.

What is considered normal and abnormal is construed differently in different discourses in different times in history (Foucault 1977/1991). Rhetoric promoting healthy societies, in its widest meaning, pathologizes as it targets those who are not identified as lifelong learners (i.e. held as normal, healthy and desired) and puts them under medical attention in order to normalize and cure them. The medical system, with its use of hospitals and clinics, and the educational system, using schools, universities etc., are sites where bodies are remodelled in order to become normalized and considered natural and healthy. Thus, both these institutional systems deal with the government of others, through which the bodies and souls of individuals become objects of the legitimate power/knowledge held by experts. A central assumption within the increasingly dominant position held by, for example, experts in education embracing social constructionist theories is that 'bodies are not born, they are made' (Lupton 2006: 23). 'The human body can no longer be considered a given reality, but as the product of certain kinds of knowledge and discourses which are subject to change' (Lupton 2006: 23). The body is thus treated as an unfinished project, something that can be disciplined and changed. This is evident in the discourses of lifelong learning which regard individuals as 'docile bodies' (Foucault 1977/1991), with the potential of becoming lifelong learners.

This chapter uses the Foucauldian concept of *governmentality* to consider the discursively produced mentalities surrounding the government of others and the government of the self (Martin *et al.* 1988; Dean 1999; Rose 1999) through lifelong learning. This analysis shows how knowledge and power relations are construed between policy makers, professionals and individuals. For Foucault *the body* is 'the ultimate site of political and ideological control, surveillance and regulation' (Lupton 2006: 25). The chapter shows how discourses of lifelong learning take the body as their target. It shows how lifelong learning policy rhetoric with its aspiration of creating a healthy society simultaneously construes a pathologizing and medicalizing discourse in which medical subjectivities – doctors, nurses and patients – are at play. The construct of such subjectivities and their relationships are analysed and discussed using an inventory methodology as will be described below.

What is here called policy discourse or policy rhetoric not only refers to that of governmental policy documents but also to the wider public debate and practices surrounding the policy-writing processes. Texts are treated as discursive artefacts that express taken-for-granted and normalized truths arising from the contexts of which they are part. Foucault (1972: 6–7) has suggested that such artefacts be taken not as historical monuments but as evidence of discontinuities. The documents selected for this analysis can therefore be studied as boundary documents, marking the transition from one era to the next. They can be read as efforts by the policy community to reconfigure the dominant discourses of an era. Truth is thus always on the move.

The discussion in this chapter draws upon a previous analysis of Swedish, Australian and American documents referring to lifelong learning. The texts selected were published on internet sites which had lifelong learning as a prominent theme. They were taken from four sectors: political government, education, the labour market and civil society. As discourses of lifelong learning operate in a variety of contexts such as schools, universities, adult education, liberal education, workplaces, libraries and community centres, there are different meanings and usages of 'life', 'long' and 'learning' (Berglund 2004). Although the documents display national and sectorial differences concerning these three aspects, they share a common meta-language pursuing the same urge to be proactive. To a large extent they also share a common analysis of contemporary problems and how these should be dealt with. The focus on health, and the role of lifelong learning as a key instrument to produce a healthy society, is part of this meta-discourse.

Health and illness in lifelong learning

Although not always obvious in dictionary or policy definitions, the meanings given to health have changed over time and place. Olsson (1997) discovered in his study of how public health is construed in political discourse in Sweden that while it used to refer to the absence of illness, it now has a wider definition that includes a state of physical or emotional well-being and quality of life. In 1946 the World Health Organization (WHO) adopted a definition of health which is still used: 'a state of complete physical, mental, and social well-being and not merely the absence of disease, or infirmity' (WHO 2006). Another dictionary definition is: 'the condition of the body and the degree to which it is free from illness, or the state of being well' (Cambridge Advanced Learners Dictionary 2006). Health has moved from being conceived of as a purely medical term, to becoming more closely linked to society as a whole and where physical, psychological and social aspects interact. Health is thought of as the well-being not only of individuals but of the whole population. Lupton (2006) refers to the cultural and political dimensions of health and illness and how the meaning of these conditions is discursively shaped through a number of technologies of power/knowledge. Dealing with illness as something excluded from what is considered as the healthy conditions of a society is thus a political act governed by the dominant mentalities of each society.

Currently, health is an almost taken-for-granted condition in highly developed societies since illness is perceived as, to a large extent, curable within the scientific and professional medical system. If health is socially constructed as a natural or normal state, illness is simultaneously construed as unnatural and abnormal (Lupton 2006). Foucault has studied how notions of normality and abnormality have changed through history when they concern madness, criminality and sexuality (cf. Foucault 1975, 1977/1991, 1979, 1999). In his writings he shows how truth is dynamic and changeable, a function of power/knowledge exerted through the different technologies used in a specific time and place. If illness and disease are discursively construed as abnormal conditions, they will, accordingly, require professional treatment. Since the eighteenth century 'state apparatuses such as medicine, the educational system, psychiatry and the law define the limits of behaviour and record activities, punishing those bodies which violate the established boundaries, and thus rendering bodies productive and politically and economically useful' (Lupton 2006: 25). Contemporary discourses of health promotion, whether focused on education or medicine, are thus construed as a societal necessity for the control, regulation and cure of inhabitants in the maintenance of a healthy society.

Lifelong learning policies envisage the healthy society and the characteristics of healthy and desired individuals. They portray a number of risks if the measures to achieve such visions are not adopted. Beck (1992) describes our modern society as a distinctively new type of society, the 'risk society', where individuals depend on public institutions instead of on family and kinship relations. Responsibility for controlling and avoiding catastrophe therefore is associated with the power/knowledge of experts (Turner 2001). Such risk and danger is used as a lever of persuasion for implementing national, communal or workplace-related lifelong learning systems and for emphasizing the importance of transforming individuals into so-called lifelong learners.

A healthy society is described as displaying a number of characteristics. First, it should be *a competitive society* whose inhabitants have the knowledge and skills needed for a continuously changing and increasingly globalized marketplace, a state of affairs which can be illustrated by an American example: 'While lifelong learning as leisure activity is an interesting topic … Rather, the emphasis is on economic wellbeing and competitiveness for individuals and the nation as a whole' (US Department of Education 2000: 9). The foundation for a healthy society is thus described in economic terms, focusing on the preconditions of the market place. For individuals as well as organizations or nations, competition is construed as good and desirable, and thus healthy.

Second, a healthy society is *a democratic society*. It is identified with community activities in civil society. Moreover, it is about informed citizenry, social cohesion, social inclusion and equality. The expectations that lifelong learning will build a healthy society are high. A citation from an Australian government policy text states that:

> Higher levels of literacy competence are linked to better health, more efficient consumption choices, and non-participation in criminal activities. People with more schooling are likely to make more informed choices when voting and to participate more actively in their communities through, for example, voluntary work.
>
> (Watson 2003)

A Swedish example from the Ministry of Education (ME) combines economic arguments with those of equity, democracy and personal development: 'All adults must be given the opportunity to broaden and deepen their knowledge and skills in order to promote personal development, democracy, equality of opportunity, economic growth and employment, and an equitable distribution of wealth' (ME 2001).

Third, health is thus defined in terms of *knowledge and learning*. A healthy society is construed as a 'learning society', a 'knowledge society', an 'information society', a 'learning economy' or a 'knowledge-based economy'. In a society where the construct of health is so closely related to knowledge and continuous learning it becomes acceptable to talk about and define healthy individuals as 'lifelong learners'. Being a lifelong learner is regarded as the normal, healthy and desired condition for people, irrespective of age, class, gender, ethnic background or other preconditions. Opengart and Short (2002) describe lifelong learners as active and capable 'free agent learners' who are:

> independent, highly motivated adults who take responsibility for their learning and development, utilize their spare time to learn, use new approaches to learning, and self-teach using a variety of resources. These employees are more selective and independent in the training they receive.
> (Opengart and Short 2002: 222)

To conclude, the healthy society is thus construed in terms of competitiveness and democracy. It is populated by devoted lifelong learners who as a result of adopting a learning lifestyle are competitive and contribute to democracy. Such a construction indicates that health is not conceived as a passive or stable condition. It needs to be actively and repeatedly sustained to be protected. Healthy individuals subject themselves to the logic of the learning society and become active and capable lifelong learners.

Pathology, medicine and freedom

The following section could be thought of as a renaming game where the professionals in education and learning get the medical titles, or labels, of 'doctors' and 'nurses' and the targets of policy concern are the 'patients'. Such labels are to be regarded as characteristic subject positions within the dominant lifelong learning discourse described above. Members of the learning society subject themselves to such positions and thereby in relation to others in different ways as we will see below. Through playing innovative mind-games one can open up understandings of lifelong learning, policy writing and practice to new perspectives. This approach could be described in terms of what Ulmer (1994, 2004) calls heuretics. As such it allows the researcher an inventory use of theories to critically examine the taken-for-granted truths of a discourse.

Lifelong learning policies identify the professionals of different kinds who are to be instrumental in their implementation. These comprise, for example, politicians, educators at different levels, human resource managers, career and study counsellors. Policy language works to include professional groups into the policy discourse, giving them the status of experts with the authority to govern others. They become the 'we' who have a professional and legitimate knowledge about others who then become the targets of policy. It is a specific knowledge about ' "hidden truths" within the patient to be revealed by experts' (Jose 1998: 42). Such truths define the objects to be known about the 'patient'. To put it another way, they identify what is important and relevant knowledge within an area defined by those who claim to hold the truth. In the process expert power/knowledge creates others as objects: 'the truth of the subject in the other who knows' (Jose 1998: 46). Being the 'other who knows' thus authorizes the professional to identify knowledge about other subjects and 'create the modes of self-recognition available to the subject' (Jose 1998: 46). The 'other' in this expression is the subject who is being transformed into an object of knowledge by expert power/knowledge. Who is defined as the 'other', as subject and object, is therefore a particular configuration of power and knowledge. In my renaming game the professionals can be divided into 'doctors' and 'nurses'.

The doctors

The doctors operate on two levels. On an overriding level, consisting of policy makers, politicians, educational planners, researchers and management gurus, these expert doctors set up the rules of the game by reference to their professional expertise. They have, or claim to have, the legitimate power/knowledge to distinguish the deviant from the normal, the healthy from the unhealthy. Given such legitimacy, lifelong learning policies point to competencies needed in the learning society: 'reading, writing, numeracy and at least a second language, problem-solving ability, creativity and teamwork, computing skills, ability to communicate, including in a multi-cultural context, and the ability to learn how to learn, etc.' (European Trade Union Confederation 2002). Such competencies are construed as the healthy signs of the lifelong learner.

Further than this, policies stress the importance of the lifelong learner displaying values and behaviours of 'free agency' (Opengart and Short 2002). Individuals who fail to display this are discursively diagnosed and pathologized as unhealthy and in need of treatment. Policy rhetoric portrays the healthy condition of the lifelong learner as something that can be achieved, thus, not being a lifelong learner is curable. The cure they proclaim requires education and lifelong learning activity: formal education, unemployment projects, study circles etc. The doctors on this level have a strong influence when building systems and institutions suitable for the treatment of illness. They are designed for what Foucault (1977/1999) calls hierarchical observation. Systems and institutions allow anonymous surveillance, where it is possible to watch and control individual behaviour without direct contact with those being observed. They include a technology for control of time and space. An example of this can be seen in the Swedish treatment of unemployment. The Swedish parliament establishes requirements for and levels of unemployment compensation while the labour unions are responsible for administration. The system has an inbuilt control mechanism to monitor the behaviours of the unemployed and ensure adequate treatment; it involves documentation from the job centres and lifelong learning actors working on specific unemployment projects, in vocational training and so on. It is through documentation that the patient is watched and monitored.

On an operational level, doctors make the anamnesis and diagnosis of the patients. The doctors on this level comprise, for example, career and study counsellors, human resource managers and managers of different kinds of lifelong learning activities. They ask the patients to tell their history of 'illness' and prepare written documentation of their earlier education and learning activities, reasons for not participating in lifelong learning activities, attitudes towards education and learning, in order to define their illness status. This type of examination supports what Foucault (1977/1999) calls a normalizing judgement, which seeks to measure deviant behaviour and oppositional attitudes such as disobedience, laziness, negligence, etc. Normalizing judgement 'differentiates, hierarchizes, homogenizes, excludes, in short, it *normalizes*' (Foucault 1977/1999: 183, italics in original). The normal individual is established through these techniques and, simultaneously, the normal becomes an imperative against which deviance is measured. Such examination thus brings together hierarchical observation and normalizing judgement. The examination is a highly ritualized ceremony of power where truth is established (Foucault 1977/1999: 184). An important instrument of the examination is the written document which not only measures normality but also makes each individual a 'case'. These are techniques at the heart of medicine as well as in education as they establish the norm and the individual subject.

The nurses and the patients

The nurses, often addressed as teachers, educators, trainers and the like, deal with the actual treatment and care of patients. In their service they use different disciplinary techniques as corrective measures that aim at normalizing abnormal behaviour. Returning to the example of unemployment, the treatment can be for the reinforcement of correct healthy signs, values and behaviours. Over the years the description of the correct, and thus desired, characteristics of the healthy individual has changed from someone who is reactive to authority demands, in favour of someone who is a free and active agent:

> Learning will be: Largely self-directed, internally motivated- learner driven and responsive to individual need, interest. The 21st Century learners

will construct their own courses of learning facilitated increasingly by technology – unconstrained by time, place, formal learning structures, require a generous provision of trusted learning resources. Critical thinking and information literacy skills will become very important, conducted in many styles for many reasons – multi-tasked ... also believed that the role of learning as a whole would be increasingly essential to a healthy and productive society.

(Shepard 2000)

Since such an important characteristic of the lifelong learner is to be active and self-directed the nurses' treatment has to include techniques for motivating the patients to become self-motivated.

The disciplinary techniques or projects of docility aimed at the unemployed as a collective work on the individual body. They delineate time, space and economic resources. An unemployed person is required to perform certain rituals at the job centre and unemployment agency; for example, administrative tasks such as filling out forms and sending in unemployment declaration cards. They need to be in physical attendance at the job centre; in educational or other lifelong learning activities, in job-related and job-searching activities (writing CVs, have a high job-application quota etc.). The unemployed person is required to subject her- or himself to the economic constraints of unemployment or social welfare compensation, or government contributions instead of salary. In accordance with these disciplinary techniques that function as moral imperative to delineate the body and work on it.

Policy target groups such as the unemployed represent the patients of this renaming game. They comprise those who, according to the lifelong policy rhetoric, do not want to participate in formal post-compulsory education and training or other learning activities. These qualities are described in relation to and as consequences of various factors: socio-economic grouping, low levels of formal education, gender, ethnicity, disability and so forth. Being a patient means being subject to the norms of discourses since there is no way of standing outside them. The individual subject, of Foucauldian writing, is shaped in and by the truths held within the discourses of which she or he is part. But the individual is not just the object of disciplinary concern, as in the government of others referred to above, but subjects him- or herself through the normalizing technologies.

Ideas of self-regulation have changed through history. A common feature, however, has been the moral imperative to take responsibility and work actively in the government of the self. Foucault (1988) refers to two different technologies represented by the Greek expressions: *epimelēsthai sautou*, take care of yourself (Socrates), and *gnothi souton*, know yourself (also known as the Delphic principle). 'To take care of oneself consists of knowing oneself. Knowing oneself becomes the object of the quest of concern for self.

Being occupied with oneself and political activities are linked' (Foucault 1988: 26). The Socratic idea of taking care of yourself included an imperative for young men to be concerned, politically, with themselves and the city. Later the Hellenists saw this as a duty of one's whole lifespan. The imperative was to seek permanent medical care and become the doctor of oneself. To know oneself is to be self-reflective. Through active self-exercises such as study, reading, writing, preparing for misfortune and death, the individual learns to know him- or herself.

> Since we have to take care throughout life, the objective is no longer to get prepared for adult life, or for another life, but to get prepared for a certain complete achievement of life. This achievement is complete at the moment just prior to death.
>
> (Foucault 1988: 31)

Self-knowledge is related to the cultivation of the self, both philosophically through ethical preparation and activity in real-life situations.

Another important technology of the self, *exomologēsis*, was introduced in early Christianity as a ritual of recognizing yourself as a sinner and penitent. This recognition of the self eventually came to form the foundation for the confession, a practice which also came to have significance outside the church. Self-examination and moral reflexivity are central features of the confession. Whereas *exomologēsis* was non-verbal, symbolic, ritual and theatrical, the confession remained verbal. Foucault calls this a medical model; 'one must show one's wounds in order to be cured' (Foucault 1988: 43). One must show obedience and sacrifice the self and ones own will to the master. He sees this as a political technology that became a new technology of the self. To conclude, 'Through some political technology of individuals, we have been led to recognize ourselves as a society, as a part of a social entity, as a part of a nation, of a state' (Foucault 1988: 146).

To take the prescribed medicine of lifelong learning activities and adapt to the moral rules by becoming a lifelong learner is one of the available subject positions for the patient. Since the ideas of taking care of oneself and knowing oneself is in line with the medicine prescribed by doctors, patients should subject themselves to the activities offered by nurses. In lifelong learning, patients are expected to subject themselves to the technology of both *exomologēsis* and confession. *Exomologēsis* is evident in the symbolic rituals surrounding the application for unemployment compensation. It is evident in practices of enrolment at the job centre where the unemployed has to show him- or herself to be a sinner and penitent to authority. Following such rituals the unemployed person will be 'forgiven' and restored to a healthy and desired condition through verbal confession, and by showing willingness to become a lifelong learner whose endeavour it is to both know and take care of oneself during the whole lifespan.

Freedom

Participation in lifelong learning activities is positioned as leading to rewards of employability, well-paid work, self-reliance, empowerment and flexibility of life choice. It appears as if such rewards 'should', if policy rhetoric or systems and institutions could simply dictate, trigger the patients' motivation to accept the offered treatment. Yet politicians and educational practitioners are witness to individual resistance to education and lifelong learning. Subject positions of resistance are, of course, available as response to discourses of lifelong learning. These may be positioned as undesirable and contested within discourses claiming scientific knowledge of the 'other'. Rose (1999) discusses such power/knowledge relation in terms of:

> the space between freedom as an ideal, as articulated in struggles against particular regimes of power, and freedom as a mode of organizing and regulation: freedom here as a certain way of administrating a population that depends upon the capacities of free individuals.
>
> (Rose 1999: 64)

Contemporary notions to the effect that humans are free subjects who can, and must, govern themselves can be contrasted with previous ideas about human conduct. Rose discusses the freedom of individuals in terms of changes of mentalities – ways of thinking about freedom that have changed through history. He proposes that freedom realized through the norms and principles for organizing and governing others differs from freedom realized through government of the self. The mentalities of governing in our society put the subject in a conflicting situation where it has both the freedom to adapt to the ideals of the learning society and the freedom of resistance. Perhaps the discourse conceptualizing the good and healthy society as comprising free, independent and active individuals actually fools people into believing that freedom of choice opens up all subject positions equally. The problem of resistance may, at least to a certain extent, be that such a discourse promises individual freedom. This freedom, however, may be illusionary since it is countered by the power/knowledge of professional experts. Since the discourse of lifelong learning works to include all citizens within the learning society and healthy society, there is no way of standing outside this. Individuals have to position themselves in relation to the discourse. Accordingly, freedom is not absolute, but is always a subjection to the discourse even where it is a resistance.

Summing up

This chapter has deconstructed lifelong learning as and through a pathologized and medicalized discourse. By playing an inventory renaming game, the power/knowledge relation between the different subjectivities of contemporary discourses of lifelong learning has been opened for scrutiny, using new perspectives and understandings of the mentalities surrounding the government of others and the self. The overarching idea of this chapter has been to challenge what have become normalized truths in lifelong learning policy rhetoric. That is, questioning the mentalities that have come to be taken-for-granted in the contemporary meta-discourse, which thereby exclude other possible ways of thinking and acting. One of the aspects that has been especially challenging in the process of analysing the discourse is that some medical terms operate in policy texts by explicitly referring to health and the promotion of healthy societies, but usually treat these aspects as educational, not medical, matters. This hybrid use of medical words and concepts triggered me to design a pair of medically cut glasses, using Foucauldian tools to shape them, to see if such a change of focus would allow other understandings of the construction of contemporary lifelong learning. Through these glasses the professionals of lifelong learning became doctors and nurses and the objects of their concern were patients.

The chapter has shown how lifelong learning policy speaks of a healthy society and produces a discourse pathologizing individuals who fail to live up to the expectations of lifelong learning. Within such a discourse, lifelong learning is constructed as a cure or to revisit the metaphor used at the beginning of the chapter an educational viagra that engenders potent citizens for the so-called learning society. This raises the question of individual freedom to resist the dominant position held by lifelong learning professionals: what happens to those who reject the prescribed medication? The possibility of resistance seems to be built into the discourse itself since the policy rhetoric envisions individual freedom and independence as desirable values of the free-agent lifelong learner. However, only some expressions of freedom and life choices are available.

References

Beck, U. (1992) *Risk society: Towards a New Modernity*, London: Sage.

Berglund, G. (2004) 'The discourses of lifelong learning: global, national, or?', in P.A. Danaher, C. Macpherson, F. Nouwens, and D. Orr (eds), *Lifelong learning: Whose Responsibility and What is Your Contribution?* Proceedings of the 3rd International lifelong learning conference, Yeppoon, Queensland, Australia, 13–16 June. Rockhampton: Central Queensland University Press.

Cambridge Advanced Learners Dictionary (2006) Online Available: www.dictionary. cambridge.org (accessed 1 October 2006).

Canguilhem, G. (1991) *The Normal and the Pathological*, New York: Zone Books.

Dean, M. (1999) *Governmentality: Power and Rule in Modern Society*, London: Sage.

Dewar, D. (1999) *Opportunity Scotland: A Paper on Lifelong Learning. Part 1: An Agenda for Learners.* Edinburgh: Scottish Office Education and Industry Department. Online. Available: www.scotland.gov.uk/library/documents-w1/lllgp-01.htm (accessed 1 September 2006).

European Trade Union Confederation (2002) *Framework of Actions for the Lifelong Learning Development of Competencies and Qualifications*. European agreement between: European Trade Union Confederation (ETUC), Union of Industrial and Employers' Confederations of Europe (UNICE), European Centre of Enterprises with Public Participation and of Enterprises of General Economic Interest (CEEP). Brussels: International Union House. Online. Available: www.etuc.org/a/580 (accessed 1 September 2006).

Foucault, M. (1972) *The Archaeology of Knowledge & the Discourse on Language*, New York: Pantheon Books.

Foucault, M. (1975) *The Birth of the Clinic: An Archaeology of Medical Perception*, New York: Vintage Books.

Foucault, M. (1977/1991) *Discipline and Punish: The Birth of the Prison*, London: Penguin Books.

Foucault, M. (1979) *The History of Sexuality: An Introduction*, London: Penguine.

Foucault, M. (1988) 'Technologies of the self', in L.H. Martin, H. Gutman and P.H. Hutton (eds), *Technologies of the Self: A Seminar with Michel Foucault*, Amherst, MA: University of Massachusetts Press.

Foucault, M. (1999) *Abnormal: Lectures at the Collège de France*, New York: Picador.

Jose, J. (1998) *Biopolitics of the Subject: An introduction to the Ideas of Michel Foucault*, Darwin: Northern Territory University Press.

Lupton, D. (2006) *Medicine as Culture*, 2nd edition, London: Sage.

Martin, L.H., Gutman, H. and Hutton, P.H. (eds) (1988) *Technologies of the Self: A Seminar with Michel Foucault*, Amherst, MA: University of Massachusetts Press.

Ministry of Education (ME) (2001) *Reforms in Higher Education – A More Open System. Summary of Government Bill 2001/02:15*.U01.016. Online. Available: utbildning.regeringen.se/inenglish/publications.htm (accessed 1 June 2002).

Olsson, U. (1997) *Folkhälsa som Pedagogiskt Projekt: Bilden av Hälsoupplysning i Statens Offentliga Utredningar*, Uppsala: Uppsala University.

Opengart, R. and Short, D.C. (2002) 'Free agent learners: the new career model and its impact on human resource development', *International Journal of Lifelong Education*, 21: 220–33.

Rose, N. (1999) *Powers of Freedom: Reframing Political Thought*, Cambridge: Cambridge University Press.

Shepard, B. (2000) *The 21st Century Learner: Premises and Goals. The Launch of the 21st Century Learner Initiative*. Washington, DC. November 9, 2000. Speech by Beverly Sheppard, Deputy Director, Institute of Museum and Library Services. Online Available: www.imls.gov/whatsnew/current/sp110900.htm (accessed 11 December 2003).

Turner, B.S. (2001) *Medical Power and Social Knowledge*, 2nd edition, London: Sage.

Ulmer, G.L. (1994) *Heuretics: The Logic of Invention*, London: The John Hopkins University Press.

Ulmer, G.L. (2004) *Teletheory*, Revised 2nd edition. New York: Atropos Press.

US Department of Education (2000) National Center for Education Statistics. *Lifelong Learning NCES Task Force: Final Report, Volume II*, Working Paper No.2. 2000–16b, by the NCES Lifelong Learning Task Force. Washington, DC: 2000. Online. Available: nces.ed.gov/pubsearch (accessed 8 December 2003).

Watson, L. (2003) *Lifelong Learning in Australia*. 03/13. Australian Government: Department of Education, Science and Training. Online. Available: www.detya. gov.au/highered/eippubs/eip03_13/03_13.pdf (accessed 1 October 2004).

World Health Organisation (WHO) (2006) *Frequently Asked Question: What is the WHO Definition of Health?* Online. Available: www.who.int/suggestions/faq/en/ (accessed 1 October 2006).

Chapter 12

Motivation theory as power in disguise[1]

Helene Ahl

What motivates adults to engage in lifelong learning? This is a question frequently asked by policy makers and educators. Lifelong learning is considered as the solution to several pressing problems, particularly the need to update the knowledge base of the labour force as globalization forces industry to restructure. It is seen as a route to personal growth and as a way to create active and democratic citizens and a good society. Motivation for learning is thus important.

However, all adults do not seem to share this concern. Learners do not enrol at the desired rates, and some groups seem particularly difficult to motivate. In Sweden, immigrants and men in rural areas are specific examples of unmotivated groups. The question of how to motivate people for lifelong learning is therefore urgent. This chapter reviews what motivation theory has to say about motivation and lifelong learning, but instead of taking the answers of this body of knowledge for granted, I discuss it through a Foucauldian power/knowledge lens.

Knowledge, according to Foucault, is any discourse, any version of events that has received the stamp of truth. Foucault said that knowledge is power, but he did not mean that the more knowledge a person has, the more power she has. Rather, power is inherent in knowledge, or knowledge has 'power implications', as power is exercised rather than possessed (Foucault 1995). In this view, power is exercised by drawing on knowledge that allows actions to be presented in an acceptable light, or to define the world or a person in a way which allows things to be done.

Knowledge orders people and objects, determines what is right and wrong, desirable or not, real or unreal, true or untrue, and thus acts as a way to privilege certain actions and relations, and counts others as irrelevant or illegitimate. Knowledge produces subject identities. Motivation theory, for example, produces 'motivated' and 'unmotivated' subjects. Knowledge is therefore never neutral.

The exercise of power through knowledge does not have to be done deliberately, in fact, most knowledge is taken-for-granted and never questioned

(Berger and Luckmann 1966). The more it is taken-for-granted and the more people draw on the same knowledge, the more powerful it becomes.

Foucault paid special attention to the academic disciplines as truth-producing institutions, and outlined an agenda both for studying how knowledge is produced through the disciplines and for the power effects of such knowledge (Foucault 1972). The aim of this chapter is therefore two-fold: to discuss and question how academic motivation theory is produced, and to discuss its power effects, particularly with regard to how it positions the lifelong learner.

The first section is a brief review of the literature – it summarizes academic knowledge on motivation and lifelong learning. The second section takes up a Foucauldian perspective with regard to this body of knowledge, and discusses the production and the power implications of motivation theory. The third section discusses how motivation theory positions the lifelong learner. I conclude by suggesting an alternative view of motivation, namely as a relational concept.

What does the literature say about motivation and lifelong learning?

Early theories on motivation are based in industrial psychology, as researchers were interested in what motivates workers. The theories reflect a number of different outlooks on humankind (Ahl 2004a, 2006). The earliest theories see humans as economic, rational decision makers, who choose that which gives them the highest rewards. This was, for example, the philosophy of scientific management. The Human Relations School instead proposed that humans are social beings, motivated by group norms and affiliations. The behaviourists suggested that behaviour is learned and that learning is facilitated by supplying a stimuli or a reward. If motivation is what causes behaviour, then motivation is in this case a stimuli or a reward. Need-based theories say that behaviour is partly motivated by external factors, but even more so by innate, human needs; either of a hierarchical model valid for all (Maslow 1987), of needs for achievement, power and affiliation differently distributed among people (McClelland 1961), or of the need to avoid pain and the need to grow (Herzberg 1966). Cognitive theories, however, say that people's ideas about how the world is configured influence their behaviour. Individual differences therefore become important in motivation theory (Lewin 1935; Vroom 1964/1995).

Theories that specifically address the question of how to motivate adults to take part in and complete organized further education reflect general motivation theory. There is a large cognitive element – they discuss, for example, expectations that a certain education will result in a certain outcome as a determinant of decisions to participate, building directly on Lewin and Vroom (Rubenson 1977; Cross 1981). There are concepts from behaviourist theory, as well as the theory of the economic actor, in that they discuss the role of short-term rewards, particularly a new job or a promotion (cf. Knowles 1980). The social human is present in discussions of group norms as determinants for decisions to participate, and in the role of the study group in encouraging adults to complete their education (Husén 1958; Wlodkowski 1999). Dominant by a long way, however, are need-based theories. Not all but most theories take it for granted that humans have an intrinsic motivation to learn (e.g. Husén 1958; Knowles 1980; Cross 1981; Cropley 1985; Wlodkowski 1999), building on Herzberg's theory of our need to grow or Maslow's theory about humans' innate need for self-realization.

The theories therefore see study motivation as always latent, temporarily hampered by dispositional, situational and/or structural factors. Dispositional variables are either personality traits or personal qualities acquired through upbringing and early school experiences, such as insufficient self-confidence, negative early school experiences, or identification with a social group where education is not valued (Boshier 1973, 1985; Cross 1981).

Situational variables are not as closely tied to a person, but to a person's life situation. Examples are lack of time and lack of concrete, expected results of study. Suggested barriers on the institutional or structural level are lack of availability of education opportunities, absence of child care, pedagogy not suited for adults or lack of job opportunities (Cross 1981). The work organization may be a structural barrier, where learning at work is discussed.

Once barriers are identified, the theory implies that by acting to remove them motivation will resurface. Politicians are advised to work on the institutional barriers: arrange educational opportunities reflecting the needs of the job market; arrange financing, information and child care; and provide flexible, ICT-based learning modules to overcome barriers of time and space. They are also advised to 'work on attitudes' so that education becomes desirable, and ensure that teaching is performed in such a way as not to scare people off later in life. Employers are advised to reorganize work in order to facilitate developmental learning (Ellström et al. 1996; Holmer 1996).

The majority of the advice is, however, pedagogical. There is great confidence in the ability of a suitable pedagogy to remove obstacles that originate elsewhere. Positive, new study experiences are for example held to remove the bad effects of negative, earlier ones. Good educational experiences are said to be able to raise motivation in spite of obstacles located outside of the educational situation (see Husén 1958; Knowles 1980; Dufresne-Tasse 1985; Stock 1985; Vulpius 1985; Hedin and Svensson 1997; Wlodkowski 1999).

The model is one of homeostasis. Initially, there is motivation. This becomes hampered due to various barriers. After removing these barriers motivation re-emerges, and all is well again. The model takes it for granted that it is possible to affect motivation, and hence behaviour, by amending individual, situational or structural barriers. Four assumptions are built into this model:

- that such an entity as motivation exists;
- that motivation causes behaviour;
- that it is possible to affect motivation and thus behaviour; and
- that motivation resides with the individual.

All four assumptions may be questioned, as discussed below.

A power/knowledge view on motivation theory

In his inaugural address to the *College de France*, Foucault (1972) outlines the practices through which a discourse is produced, controlled, selected, organized and redistributed. These practices dictate what can be said and what cannot, by whom and through what means. Foucault says that foremost of discursive practices are assumptions that are taken-for-granted. In motivation theory, the first such assumption is that something called motivation indeed exists, and that it is possible to identify, describe and measure it. A further discursive practice concerns the methods used for measuring motivation. Foucault writes that the discipline regulates what is necessary for formulating new statements through its 'groups of objects, methods, their corpus of propositions considered to be true, the interplay of rules and definitions, of techniques and tools' (1972: 222). The most common method of operationalizing motivation is to build a model of situational and personal variables. Situational variables may sometimes be measured by observation, but personal variables are usually measured by subjecting respondents to various questions or statements and asking them to which extent they agree or disagree, measured on a Likert-type scale. The questions are intended to measure a psychological *construct*, i.e. something which is assumed to exist by the scientist.

The problem with this is circular reasoning. The questions prove the construct. No matter the result obtained – say that one measured 'need for achievement' among male recruits on a seven point scale, and found it to be on average five point eight – then one has, by the very act of asking the questions, created a construct identified as the need for achievement. It may turn out that the recruits achieve very well, but contrary to common sense, it does not confirm that there is anything such as a need for achievement. For this conclusion to be drawn it would be necessary to demonstrate that the need for achievement came before the actual achievements, and no such thing can be shown in a correlation study.

The second basic assumption of motivation theory, that motivation causes behaviour, may also be questioned. Psychologists who have conducted systematic analyses of attitude-behaviour research (motivation here falling under the 'attitudes' category, see King and McGuinnies 1972: 8) demonstrate that even within the standard research paradigm of psychology there is very little evidence for a relationship between attitudes and action (Wicker 1969; Abelson 1972; Foxall 1984). It has been suggested that people's statements of their attitudes justify past behaviour rather than indicate future behaviour (Abelson 1972; Payne *et al.* 1992).

Moreover, and moving on to the third assumption: the practical reason for attitude research, motivation research being part of this, is that assumption that new information will influence attitudes, which in turn will influence behaviour. Abelson's (1972) review of psychological research showed that there was no correspondence between how much new information a person absorbed and any change in attitudes.

If the assumptions that motivation theory builds on are not valid, so that motivation does not exist, or if, at any rate, it is not amenable to new information, and does not affect behaviour, does this mean that the knowledge about motivation reported in the earlier section is invalid and of no importance? Invalid, perhaps, but still important. It is a body of knowledge with power implications that need to be addressed.

Most of motivation theory is framed in a humanist discourse, and seems like a benevolent undertaking. It talks about people's social needs and their needs for self-realization. However, if one looks closely at the contexts in which motivation theory has been produced, and for what reasons and for whom, another picture emerges. Foucault (1972) talks about 'the will to truth' as one of the discursive practices forming a discourse. Here 'truth' is determined in a historically contingent manner, in which the false is demarcated from the true and what counts as knowledge is decided. What becomes truth is regulated not only through the disciplines, but in terms of that which is socially required. The production of knowledge will therefore be influenced by those financing research, be they private or public institutions, and by how their questions are framed.

Who financed motivation research and what was their chief interest? The main purchaser of motivation theory was industry writes O'Connor (1999), and the explicit purpose was to increase productivity and settle worker unrest. Theories about what makes humans tick were seen as useful instruments to control people, both by industry and by government. Herman (1995) describes how psychology developed as a response to governmental needs of control and how psychology came to hold the individual accountable for societal problems. War, poverty, racial unrest, unemployment, economic growth, social problems, education problems and even revolutions were explained in terms of the self and attributed to shortcomings among individuals. These shortcomings were to be corrected by psychology. The language of psychology thus offered a way to present political initiatives as scientific and neutral, or as therapeutic, while at the same time avoiding any discussion of politics and power. Psychology was used as camouflaged direction and control.

Motivation theory is part and parcel of this package. The fourth basic assumption of motivation theory is that motivation resides with the individual. By ascribing motivation to the individual it becomes possible to blame the individual for social problems and constructs the individual as insufficient while simultaneously disregarding social circumstances and rendering government invisible. A model like Maslow's demonstrates how this works. His model is regarded as humanist, but it could well be seen as an elitist model disguised as humanism. The model explicitly states that all human beings have the potential of reaching self-realization, but only a fraction can count on achieving it. Self-realization thus becomes a false promise. If only a few can ever reach it, it constructs the rest of humanity as psychologically insufficient. Moreover, it identifies that the remedy for this insufficiency is that of working on one's self-realization, not of engaging in political or collective action to change social circumstances.

The individualist focus is framed within a Western, individualistic understanding of humans and a Western form of governance. The most influential theories privilege the self-actualized individuals. Maslow put them literally at the top of the hierarchy, Herzberg privileged self-actualization through work and McClelland focused on the need for achievement. Anything 'social' was placed further down the ladder and less valued. Maslow put social needs third from bottom in his hierarchy, Herzberg counted social needs to be hygiene factors and McClelland did not count the need for affinity as contributing to the development of society. Theories of inner and outer motivation privilege the former. These models are presented as universal, but are not consistent with, for example, Eastern understandings of the social web and the place of the individual in this web. In this sense the theories are also colonizing. They impose a Western understanding of the individual in cultures in which this is not appropriate or relevant, thus marginalizing and making other sorts of understanding of the individual invisible.

Research comparing Western and Eastern understandings demonstrate this point. Miller (1997), who researches cultural representation of duty, says that duty has a negative connotation in the West. It is about limitations and having to do things one does not want to do. The ideal is that a person does things from her own desire. This builds on the West's dualistic view of individual/society, nature/culture and duty/desire. Acting for the benefit of someone else is not compatible with the assumptions of the economic human. Hindus, writes Miller (1997), see no such sharp distinction between the individual and the collective. Acting according to one's *dharma* (i.e. fulfilling one's social duties) is simultaneously a way of actualizing oneself. The choice situation between duty and desire simply does not exist. A Western motivation theory such as Deci and Ryan's (1985) in which inner and outer motivation are compared, and where inner motivation is privileged, has no application in the society Miller describes. Similar observations were made by Iyengar and Lepper (2002) who found that the US students within their study preferred to make choices themselves, whereas the Asian students preferred others to make choices for them, but that inner motivation, measured by standardized tests, increased in both groups. The authors explain that there are different norms for action, and the self is differently constituted in these cultures. Western theories do not always apply – not even in the West. Most of the reviewed motivation theories can be criticized for neglecting or down-playing cultural and social norms and institutional arrangements, thus severely limiting their explanatory power.

Motivation theory is also androcentric. Androcentrism means, literally, the doctrine of male-centredness. It is the idea that men's experiences are generalizable to all humans. As most social science theories, motivation theories are presented as universal, but the great majority of the research is done on men, by men and with men's paid work as the unquestioned standard. The private sphere of life, with homemaking and child caring, is, if at all present, at best seen as an obstacle. The only theorist who explicitly mentioned women's work was McCelland (1961), but there was only one specific task that was deemed of importance, namely raising achievement oriented sons. Hyde and Kling (2001) reveal, however, that McClelland and his colleagues actually included women at the start of their studies, but as the women did not verify the theory, they were excluded. Women's 'need for achievement', unlike men's, was not raised when they were put in a competitive situation. McClelland therefore held that women needed an altogether different psychology from men (McClelland 1961). Women were wrong, the theory was not. Repeated studies since then show that women's average need for achievement has increased as has their participation in the work force, and today it is the same as men's (Hyde and Kling 2001). McClelland thus made a mistake when he did not incorporate cultural and social norms in his models – on the other hand, his neglect was probably also the result of a cultural and social norm, namely the idea that women raise children and men start companies.

The Human Relations School was also criticized for ignoring gender and thus misrepresenting their research results (Acker and Van Houten 1974). The finding that people who have their social needs satisfied were happier and more productive came from a several year-long experiment with six young women who were completely dependent on the discretion of the managers of their work environment and subject to a high degree of paternalistic control. They had little choice but to increase their productivity. Men in similar experiments were not individually selected, but selected as a group, they were older, less dependent and did not increase their productivity. There was no discussion of the gender aspect in the reports. The resulting reports disregard both gender and power. The conclusion that a socially satisfied worker is a motivated worker is thus highly questionable. One might as well conclude that a closely supervised and controlled worker is a productive worker. This shows the insufficiency of social theory that disregards gender and which takes gender/power relationships for granted (Ahl 2004b).

In summary, the discourse of motivation as produced and reflected in academic motivation theory is built upon certain assumptions that are highly questionable, and have certain power effects: it puts the blame for problems at the level of social structure on the individual, thereby constructing the individual as insufficient. Political and economic action may pass unnoticed. It also privileges a Western, androcentric understanding of the individual and 'his' role and place in society. In this it marginalizes cultures where this understanding is not appropriate. It also confirms and recreates the subordinate role of women.

How does motivation theory construct the lifelong learner?

In Foucault's view, a subject gets constituted through discourse. There is no 'pre-discursive' subject. A person learns what it is to be an individual by what he or she is taught that an individual is within his or her culture, or, put differently, through the discourses that are available. A discourse both restricts and enables subject identities. Foucault analysed how discourses produce subjects through 'dividing practices' (Foucault 2003). This activity of production is particularly conspicuous in theories of motivation in adult education. These theories, and most of the practical interest in such theories, concentrate on how to recruit and keep lifelong learners. This presupposes that there are some people who are not easily recruited – otherwise there would be no need for the theories. The theories postulate that (some) adults have motivation problems and suggest what these consist of and how to amend them. This takes the discourse of lifelong learning for granted – individuals are supposed to be interested in lifelong learning for their own and society's benefits and if they are not, this presents a problem, or, at best, a misunderstanding to be corrected.

The discussion of motivation theory in the previous section suggests, however, that the conception of individuals as having motivation problems is not the only possible interpretation. An alternative proposition is that 'motivation problems', if keeping to this terminology, arise only in the relationship between the recruiter and those who do not want to be recruited. If the recruiter's interest was not there to begin with, there would be no reason to talk about motivation problems. One could even assert that the motivation problem belongs to the recruiter, and not to the prospective recruited. Such a conclusion is supported by Paldanius (2002) who interviewed a group of people in Sweden who had not accepted offers of continued education. They belonged to exactly the category of uneducated people that the discourse on lifelong learning maintains must raise their level of education for their own and society's benefit. Contrary to theory, Paldanius found no latent study motivation that could be released through the elimination of barriers and obstacles. His respondents were simply not interested. Moreover, they had found no reason to articulate disinterest until Paldanius asked the question. Education was a non-choice. They were much more interested in doing something else. His respondents valued work, family and a stable, well-arranged daily routine. Education was only seen as an alternative, or a necessary evil, if, and only if, it would lead to a guaranteed job opportunity. Education *per se* was not valued, and as his respondents did not have career ambitions in the ordinary sense of the word, they did not perceive any value in education as a career step.

Given the current discourse of globalization and lifelong learning, this group of people presents a problem for policy makers, researchers and educators, but it is the discourse, and the policy makers, the researchers and the educators who make them a problem. Paldanius writes that this group is in a position characterized by symbolic violence, in that they are first defined by society's institutions and structures and then presented as a solution to the problem they have become (Paldanius 2002). By the very act of categorizing these unwilling learners they are also stigmatized and marginalized. Seeking to assimilate the uneducated among the educated through lifelong learning programmes 'heightens awareness of difference and social exclusion' (Edwards *et al.* 2001: 426), denies diversity and constructs the devalued 'other'.

The discourse on lifelong learning, and the theories concerning motivation that serve this discourse, therefore construct the unwilling lifelong learner. The 'unwilling learner' is both the reason for and the solution to societal problems, while those who formulate the problems, and the basis for the formulation of the problem, remain invisible. They are made invisible because they represent normality, the ideology in power and knowledge that is always taken-for-granted.

This construction of the lifelong learner is concordant with research findings on how, for example, the techniques of need assessment, curriculum development and examination in the US create a dependent, disciplined subject and recreate prevailing power regimes (Wilson 1999). It is resonant with how the discourse on lifelong learning in the UK places the responsibility for the smooth functioning of society on the individual instead of on society's structures, thereby distributing blame to those who do not make it (Martin 2003; Crowther 2004). It is also congruent with how Swedish adult education policy through its governance techniques of guidance and risk calculation tries to make people take the 'right' decisions by 'themselves' and excludes those who do not (Fejes 2005). There are many good arguments for taking a critical stance towards the discourse of lifelong learning, how it is used and how it constructs the lifelong learner. Motivation theory is an important and integral part of this discourse. However, from a critical scholarly viewpoint, it has so far been neglected. There is also reason to try to assess how motivation theory or everyday understanding of motivation in adult education is reflected in practice. It may put the adult educator in an impossible hostage position, as an actor who is supposed to deal with the so constructed 'unmotivated adults' in order to fulfil governments' expectations and projections of economic growth. Furthermore, any educational policy that assumes and takes for granted motivation as residing with the individual may be quite inefficient. Perhaps it is not the individual that is 'wrong', but rather that the educational policy is unsuitable. Instead of trying to change people, perhaps policies should be reviewed and reassessed.

Motivation as a relational concept

The point of departure for this chapter was the question 'What motivates adults to continue their education' but resulted and ended in another question, namely, 'Who says that this is a problem, why, and on what grounds?' I would suggest taking the latter question as the point of departure for future research. For this to make sense, however, motivation must be conceptualized in a different way. Instead of regarding it as an entity, residing within the individual, I suggest seeing it as a relational concept. It is hardly possible to speak about motivation without relating it to something – one can be motivated to work, to study, to play and so on, but never just 'motivated' (unless using it as a synonym for energetic). By using the word 'unmotivated', which is of greater practical interest for educators and policy makers, this becomes even clearer. The person who does not want to study, and therefore does not participate, has no problems, and no need for an explanatory theory, or for a policy to do something about it. It is when someone wants someone *else* to do something and this person does not, that the problem arises. The problem then becomes located in the relation between these two people. Even 'personal' motivation problems may be regarded as relational. For example, someone who wants to lose weight but does not go on a diet may have internalized a message that he or she weighs too much, from the doctor or, perhaps, from advertising, and has motivation problems in relation to this internalized other. In both cases, motivation is all about discipline and power. It is easier to resist in the first case, when 'the other' is external and identifiable, than in the second case, when the disciplinary power is internalized (Foucault 1995).

Abandoning the search for motivation as essence, and looking at it instead as a relational and discursive concept, opens up new vistas for social science and adult education research. It reveals the operation of power and shows how the discourse on lifelong learning, as a necessary response to economic and technological determinism, constructs the lifelong learner as insufficient or inadequate. It challenges normality, prevailing ideologies and the assumption that education is the most obvious response to societal problems. It also places the responsibility for the success of educational policies where it belongs, namely with the policy makers.

Using a Foucauldian approach further presents a way to theorize resistance. The 'unmotivated adults' referred to earlier who valued work and a stable family life before education clearly drew on other discourses that produced other subject identities than the discourse of lifelong learning. Such discourses are perhaps marginal in relation to the dominant ones, or at least seen as marginal by the researchers and the policy makers, but they are obviously around, and they provide a solid base for resistance. Looking more closely at such discourses rather than simply making individuals 'wrong' would, I believe, be productive for research.

Notes

1 This chapter is an edited version of an article originally published in *International Journal of Lifelong Education* (Ahl 2006). I thank Taylor & Francis for permission to use the copyright material.

References

Abelson, R.P. (1972) 'Are attitudes necessary?' in B.T. King and E. McGinnies (eds), *Attitudes, Conflict, and Social Change*, New York and London: Academic Press.

Acker, J. and Van Houten, D.R. (1974) 'Differential recruitment and control: the sex structuring of organizations', *Administrative Science Quarterly*, 19: 152–63.

Ahl, H. (2004a) *Motivation och Vuxnas Lärande: En Kunskapsöversikt och Problematisering*, Stockholm: Myndigheten för Skolutveckling.

Ahl, H. (2004b) *The Scientific Reproduction of Gender Inequality: A Discourse Analysis of Research Texts on Women's Entrepreneurship*, Copenhagen: CBS Press.

Ahl, H. (2006) 'Motivation in adult education: a problem solver or a euphemism for direction and control?', *International Journal of Lifelong Education*, 25: 385–405.

Berger, P. and Luckmann, T. (1966) *The Social Construction of Reality: A Treatise in the Sociology of Knowledge*, London: Penguin Books.

Boshier, R. (1973) 'Educational participation and drop-out: a theoretical model', *Adult Education*, 23: 255–82.

Boshier, R. (1985) 'Motivation for adult education', in J.H. Knoll (ed.), *Motivation for Adult Education*, München: Saur.

Cropley, A.J. (1985) 'Motivation for participation in adult education', in J.H. Knoll (ed.), *Motivation for Adult Education*, München: Saur.

Cross, P.K. (1981) *Adults as Learners*, San Fransisco: Jossey-Bass.

Crowther, J. (2004) ' "In and against" lifelong learning: flexibility and the corrosion of character', *International Journal of Lifelong Education*, 23: 125–36.

Deci, E.L. and Ryan, R.M. (1985) *Intrinsic Motivation and Self-determination in Human Behavior*, New York: Plenum.

Dufresne-Tasse, C. (1985) 'Eleven propositions and certain considerations concerning adult student motivation', in J.H. Knoll (ed.), *Motivation for Adult Education*, München: Saur.

Edwards, R., Armstrong, P. and Miller, N. (2001) 'Include me out: critical readings of social exclusion, social inclusion and lifelong learning', *International Journal of Lifelong Education*, 20: 417–28.

Ellström, P.-E., Gustavsson, B. and Larsson, S. (eds) (1996) *Livslångt Lärande*, Lund: Studentlitteratur.

Fejes, A. (2005) 'New wine in old skins: changing patterns in the governing of the adult learner in Sweden', *International Journal of Lifelong Education*, 24: 71–86.

Foucault, M. (1995) *Discipline and Punish*, trans A. Sheridan, New York: Random House.

Foucault, M. (1972). 'The discourse on language (L'ordre du discourse)', in *The Archaeology of Knowledge and the Discourse on Language*, New York: Pantheon Books.

Foucault, M. (2003) 'Governmentality', in P. Rabinow and N. Rose (eds), *The Essential Foucault: Selections From the Essential Works of Foucault 1954–1984*, New York: The New Press.

Foxall, G. (1984) 'Evidence for attitudinal-behavioral consistency: implications for consumer research paradigms', *Journal of Economic Psychology*, 5: 71–92.

Hedin, A. and Svensson, L. (eds) (1997) *Nycklar till Kunskap*, Lund: Studentlitteratur.

Herman, E. (1995) *The Romance of American Psychology: Political Culture in the Age of Experts*, Berkeley: University of California Press.

Herzberg, F. (1966) *Work and the Nature of Man*, New York: World Publishing.

Holmer, J. (1996). *Opportunities to Learn and Motivation for Lifelong Learning*, Karlstad: Jämställdhetscentrum, Arbetsvetenskap.

Husén, T. (1958) *Vuxna Lär*, Stockholm: Ehlins.

Hyde, J.S. and Kling, K.C. (2001) 'Women, motivation and achievement' *Psychology of Women Quarterly*, 25: 364–78.

Iyengar, S.S. and Lepper, M.R. (2002) 'Choice and its consequences: on the costs and benefits of self-determination', in A. Tesser, D.A. Stapel and J.V. Wood (eds), *Self and Motivation: Emerging Psychological Perspectives*, Washington, DC: American Psychological Association.

King, B.T. and McGuinnies (1972) 'Overview: social contexts and issues for contemporary attitude change research', in B.T. King and E. McGuinnies (eds), *Attitudes, Conflict, and Social Change*, New York and London: Academic Press.

Knowles, M.S. (1980) *The Modern Practice of Adult Education: From Pedagogy to Andragogy*, New York: Cambridge.

Knowles, M.S. (1989) *The Making of an Adult Educator*, San Fransisco: Jossey-Bass.

Lewin, K. (1935). *A Dynamic Theory of Personality*, New York: McGraw-Hill.

McClelland, D.C. (1961) *The Achieving Society*, New York: Van Nostrand.

Martin, I. (2003) 'Adult education, lifelong learning and citizenship: some ifs and buts', *International Journal of Lifelong Education*, 22: 566–79.

Maslow, A.A. (1987) *Motivation and Personality*, New York: Addison Wesley Longman.

Miller, J.G. (1997) 'Cultural conceptions of duty', in D. Munro, J.F. Schumaker and S.C. Carr (eds), *Motivation and Culture*, London: Routledge.

O'Connor, E. (1999) 'The politics of management thought: a case study of the Harvard Business School and the Human Relations School', *Academy of Management Review*, 24: 117–31.

Paldanius, S. (2002) *Ointressets Rationalitet: Om Svårigheter att Rekrytera Arbetslösa till Vuxenstudier*, Linköping: Linköping University.

Payne, J.W., Bettman, J.R. and Johnson, E.J. (1992) 'Behavioral decision research: a constructive processing perspective', *Annual Review of Psychology*, 43: 87–131.

Rubenson, K. (1977) 'Participation in recurrent education: a research review', paper presented at the Meeting of National delegates on Developments in Recurrent Education, Paris, March 1977.

Stock, A. (1985) 'Adult education for special target groups', in J.H. Knoll (ed.), *Motivation for Adult Education*, München: Saur.

Wicker, A.W. (1969) 'Attitudes v. actions: the relationship of verbal and overt responses to attitude objects', *Journal of Social Issues*, 25: 41–78.

Wilson, A.L. (1999) 'Creating identities of dependency: adult education as a knowledge-power regime', *International Journal of Lifelong Education*, 18: 85–93.

Wlodkowski, R.J. (1999) *Enhancing Adult Motivation to Learn: A Comprehensive Guide for Teaching All Adults*, San Fransisco: Jossey-Bass.

Vroom, V.H. (1964/1995) *Work and Motivation*, San Fransisco: Jossey-Bass.

Vulpius, A. (1985) 'Work with target groups and marginal groups in continuing education with special consideration of the unemployed', in J.H. Knoll (ed.), *Motivation for Adult Education*, München: Saur.

Chapter 13

Discipline and e-learning

Katherine Nicoll

This chapter draws on resources from the work of Michel Foucault to begin an examination of the influence of e-learning on the disciplines and disciplinary practices within universities. These explorations are guided by the view that discussion of e-learning within the education literature remains overwhelmingly positioned within a modernist metanarrative (Lyotard 1979) of contributing to 'truth' and 'emancipation', enabling learners to become more 'autonomous', where autonomy is assumed unproblematically to be a good thing. Even where a potential for computerized information technologies to transform learning is posited, arguments tend to be underpinned by an assumption that the rest is business as usual. For example, e-learning is argued to increase the speed of communication and interaction, its 'volume', 'variety' and 'value' (Garrison and Anderson 2003), but analysis does not go further than this. Lyotard, of course, saw wider implications in the increase in computerized forms of communication and information technology for the kinds of knowledge that would be legitimized within an information age. Debates elsewhere about education and the university suggest that there may be more to say about what goes on through e-learning (Usher and Edwards 1994; Lankshear *et al.* 2002; Lea and Nicoll 2002). These are suggestive of the need to re-evaluate modernist stances and to examine e-learning as a far more ambivalent set of cultural practices.

The intention in writing this piece has been to draw on Foucault's thoughts on pedagogical practices and discipline as both a systematic body of knowledge and an exercise of power to look at the way in which disciplinary practices are being influenced through the proliferation of e-learning. The university is a specific and significant site in its involvement in disciplining activities. It is the place where people learn to become active subjects with particular knowledge, norms of behaviour and social roles. In adopting a Foucauldian stance, discourses of e-learning emerge from within those of the wider human sciences, as both disciplinary practices and knowledge of those practices. They are an emerging 'power-knowledge' *formation* (Foucault 1980), both effecting change and providing the knowledge to effect change. They are therefore supportive of changing disciplinary formations and govern that change in particular directions, but at the same time are formed within the changing disciplinary practices that they seek to explain and effect. Therefore, they are themselves subject to change, as with the emerging discussion of the significance of globalization and the postmodern for e-learning.

The chapter is in three sections. First, views of the disciplines as 'disinterested' bodies of knowledge of the world are examined. These are contrasted with Foucault's notion of discipline as a body of knowledge and exercise of power. Second, the techniques of discipline – observation, normalization and examination – and their role in disciplining the subject within the university are explored together with an examination of how the practices of e-learning might be said to be resulting in a reconfiguration of discipline. Does e-learning subvert the disciplines and disciplining practices? Or, does it continue to exert discipline even if it is no longer contained within the boundaries of the traditional disciplines and the physical boundaries of the university? A third section turns briefly to the reflexive issue of the changing discourses of e-learning and their ambivalent position as being part of and at the same time contributing to change. It touches on questions of identity and the way in which the inter- and multi-disciplinarity associated with e-learning in the university context can be construed as contributing to multiple identities and multi-centred selves.

The discipline as body of knowledge and exercise of power

The idea of the disciplines as disinterested and bounded bodies of knowledge is one at the heart of the modern idea of the university. In many ways it is central to the legitimation of universities as 'above', separate from, the exercise of power, and with that the necessity for academic freedom. It is an idea that provides a legitimation for universities to function in specific ways. Disciplinary boundaries demarcate what is considered to be knowledge within a particular domain and through their discursive practices the criteria by which claims are established as 'true' or 'false' and legitimate or illegitimate. 'Disciplines are a way of carving up areas of study and regulating what constitutes proper investigation in each area' (Elam 1994: 95). Truth is knowledge untainted by the distorting effects of exercises of power or the embellishments of rhetoric. Knowledge is disinterested in that it is concerned only with truth. As Usher (1993: 17) suggests, we are 'enfolded in an implicit conception of disciplines as neutral bodies of knowledge with enlightening and empowering effects that enable us to act effectively in the world'. The modern disciplines thus maintain themselves by defining truth and claiming it as their own. In this way they exclude the question of power from their own discourses – a question over the conditions for their own existence and possibility as bodies of knowledge.

This notion of the disciplines and disciplinarity has been much debated (Messer-Davidow *et al.* 1993). From a Marxist perspective, the knowledge produced and conveyed through the disciplines is part of the dominant ideology and serves the interests of capitalism. Feminists contest the epistemological assumptions underpinning the disciplines as embodying masculinist norms, similarly; deconstruction challenges epistemological assumptions and institutional authority. These critiques re-introduce questions of power in relation to knowledge – as the truth and disinterestedness of disciplinary practices are brought into question, questions of whose power and whose truth emerge to be addressed. For some time now we have understood the university as the means for the constitution of knowledge and differential allocation of that knowledge to groups and individuals within societies:

> [W]e have to recognize the great cleavages in what one might call the social appropriation of discourse. Education may well be, as of right, the instrument whereby every individual, in a society like our own, can gain access to any kind of discourse. But we well know that in its distribution, in what it permits and in what it prevents, it follows the well-trodden battle-lines of social conflict. Every educational system is a political means of maintaining or of modifying the appropriation of discourse, with the knowledge and the powers it carries with it.
>
> (Foucault 1996: 351)

For Foucault (1977), discourses of right, associated with sovereign power, afford us our understanding that individuals 'should' have equal access to education and thus to discourse. But it is disciplinary power, operating in its most intense form within educational institutions, including the university, which acts to allocate discourses differentially to individuals as subjects and subjects them to these. From the beginning of the modern state there has existed a relation between sovereign and disciplinary power from which they are dissociable. For Foucault, it was the emergence of disciplinary practices that made it possible for the modern juridical notion of 'right' to emerge: 'The real, corporal disciplines constituted the foundations of the formal, juridical liberties' (Foucault 1977: 222). In this chapter, it is Foucault's notion of disciplinary power and disciplining practices that are drawn upon extensively to examine discipline both as a body of knowledge and as an exercise of power. Foucault's work helps us to challenge modern assumptions of the separation of knowledge from power and to examine their relationships. For him, 'power and knowledge directly imply one another ... there is no power relation without the relative constitution of a field of knowledge, nor any knowledge that does not presuppose and constitute at the same time power relations' (Foucault 1977: 27). Power and knowledge are therefore correlative and are found together in 'regimes of truth'. Within this analysis, disciplines emerge as 'power-knowledge formations' with their own 'regimes of truth'. There is then a co-implication of disciplinary truth and disciplining power.

In the university context, disciplinary power is exercised effectively through the production of those that are 'educated'. Learners are required to bring forth their subjectivities for disciplining, to become a particular type of person. People become active subjects in becoming subject to particular disciplines. For instance, in learning to become a lawyer, scientist, biochemist, accountant or teacher, one becomes a particular type of subject with a repertoire of understandings, predispositions and ways of doing things. The body is improved and transformed so as to become capable. In order to produce useful bodies, '... a technique of overlapping subjection and objectification' (Foucault, cited in Dreyfus and Rabinow 1982: 160) is exercised. Students are made subject to requirements that they are active in learning and demonstrate their learning to observers. Through observation and the recording of their capacities, students become objects of knowledge. Agency then does not entail an escape from power but a specific exercise of it. Capacities are evaluated through processes of observation and examination, the criteria and methods which are provided by the discipline (e.g. law, biochemistry etc.). These methods are made more efficient, critiqued and re-disseminated through the discipline of education. As knowledge (in both the discipline and education) changes, so do the disciplining practices aimed at framing behaviour. Here

> [T]he chief function of the disciplinary power is to 'train', rather than to select and to levy; or, no doubt, to train in order to levy and select all the more ... Discipline 'makes' individuals; it is the specific technique of a power that regards individuals both as objects and as instruments of its exercise.
>
> (Foucault 1977: 170)

In this sense educational discourses, together with those of the disciplines, can 'create' a range of embodied subjectivities. Rather than being regulated externally, subjects regulate themselves through principles of, for example, autonomy and self-reflection, themselves disciplinary effects.

Disciplinary knowledge is never entirely discrete. Although the boundaries are 'fuzzy' and shift there is a difference between those who attempt to 'police' – to confine what is to 'count' as knowledge – and those who attempt to transgress the boundary so as to redefine what is constituted as legitimate knowledge (Thompson Klein 1993). There is a debate over what constitutes 'the disciplines' and whether certain bodies of knowledge such as education are disciplines, or sub-, inter- or multi-disciplinary fields of knowledge, which draw upon disciplines in constituting themselves and the practices they legitimize. On this reading they would be seen as second-order knowledge, dependent on the 'foundational' knowledge of the disciplines (in the case of education, for example, particularly on psychology). However, despite such uncertainties over status, bodies of disciplinary and other knowledge derived from and within them are both subject to and subject others to disciplinary practices. 'Situated within the university and regulated in much the same way as any other discipline, interdisciplinary studies ... operate on principles of identity, admitting only that which is recognized as proper to the particular interdisciplinary area' (Elam 1994: 96). Fields of knowledge are as defensive of their territory and identity as the foundational disciplines. Their rationale remains foundational, even if they are not disciplines in any 'pure' sense.

Changes in knowledge within a discipline can have an effect on practices within that discipline but can also impact on other disciplines. And, the relationship between education as a set of disciplinary practices and other disciplines is particularly significant, as the latter entail ranges of pedagogical practices and require conceptions of education in order to effect and be effective. Shifts within education, such as those towards and within a framing of lifelong learning, workplace or e-learning (or an emphasis on increasing choice, autonomy and self-reflection), therefore provide the possibility for disturbing the pedagogical practices for the formation and maintenance of other disciplines and, with that, the subjectivities of learners. What then are we to make of these shifts, as they are:

> [E]ver and more subtle refinements of technologies of power based upon knowledge which has itself been produced within or used by the discipline of education ... Power is still exercised in the search for normal and governable people. If it is more humane, it is more subtle; if it is less overt and involves less violence to bring power into play, it may be more dangerous because of its insidious silence.
>
> (Marshall 1989: 108–9)

Extending access and opportunity through discourses of e-learning may signify a more extensive achievement of an active, productive and governable positioning of subjects, where learners may literally and metaphorically be 'kept in their place' – a maintenance, if reconfiguration, or even extension, of discipline.

E-learning and disciplinary techniques

How do the different practices of e-learning support the reconfiguration of discipline as exercise of power? Here some ways are sketched in which the techniques of discipline (hierarchical observation, normalizing judgement and the examination) may be reconfigured within e-learning, and with that can result in a changing of the subject – both bodies of knowledge and the subjectivities of learners.

Foucault (1977), in his analysis of the emergence and spread of disciplinary techniques since the seventeenth century, 'mapped' out 'tactics' in the support of their diffusion. He did not intend us to read any deep underlying meaning into such a spread. Rather, as a precautionary measure he urged us to look to their functioning and coherence in operation:

> Describing them will require great attention to details: beneath every set of figures, we must seek not a meaning, but a precaution; we must situate them not only in the inextricability of a functioning, but in the coherence of a tactic.
>
> (Foucault 1977: 139)

A sketch of the reconfiguration of disciplinary techniques in relation to e-learning is here then an exploration, an initial descriptive tracing, of some nuances of techniques whereby disciplining practices may be reconfigured and a tentative exploration of the possibilities of their functioning in this.

Within the 'traditional' university (I use this word to indicate a university where face-to-face teaching is the norm, and teaching and learning is typically carried out through lectures, seminars, assignment tasks and examination) it might initially appear that a set of enclosures – the lecture theatres, seminar rooms and library – order bodies and make them available for disciplining. Disciplinary practices in some cases are partly built on a requirement of bodily presence. However, it is not sufficient in itself that this be the case for disciplinary power to function. And, within e-learning it is precisely that physical presence which is lacking. It would be understandable to assert therefore – as is often done in the discourses of learner-centredness of e-learning (cf. Garrison and Anderson 2003) – that the individual is 'freer', has more autonomy and is less subject to discipline within e-learning. However, the lack of physical presence does not mean that the 'sites' required for discipline are absent. Although physical spaces within traditional universities have been necessary for the effective transmission of disciplinary knowledge (lecture theatres and libraries), enactments of the appropriate norms of discipline (seminar rooms) and in examination (lecture halls), they have their virtual corollaries. These are found within electronically presented module materials with their hyperlinks to sites and search engines on the internet, in discussion forums and through e-readings and e-databases within libraries and elsewhere. To make e-learning possible as an alternative to a traditional university system of learning is to set up a productive network of e-locations wherein subjectivities can be enclosed in order that they can then be mobilized; identifying necessary subject knowledge, communicating and being communicated with, and thus being brought forth for active practices of observation, normalization and examination. This is no different from that of a traditional system. The aim in design is

> ... to establish presences and absences, to know where and how to locate individuals, to set up useful communications, to interrupt others, to be able at each moment to supervise the conduct of each individual, to assess it, to judge it, to calculate its qualities or merits.
>
> (Foucault 1977: 143)

Thus, although physical enclosures typify our understanding of traditional pedagogy as disciplinary practice, it is not these that are central for it to function. Rather, it is the capacity to capture individuals in their specificity, to ensure that they do not disappear, to channel their movements, and to keep them separate in order that they can be controlled. Rather than a set of physical enclosures, '[d]iscipline organizes an analytic space' (Foucault 1977: 143) as a means for the exercise of power. Thus both traditional university and e-learning environments are organized as analytic spaces.

In tracing tactics and functioning of mechanisms within e-learning it becomes apparent that there arises the opportunity for an intensification and extension of discipline that is unavailable through practices mediated by traditional means. We can begin to see this possibility if we consider the e-environment as a *rhetorical place*, a place for the making of meaning, rather than a physical or virtual space. 'A place is a socially or subjectively meaningful space', which is made place in two ways (Burbules 2002: 78): first by a designer and then again by the learner. Thus, 'maps' of meaning are in part drawn up in advance, mediated and controlled as course materials and their virtual connections within a web of locations. They make and control meanings and their 'appropriate' connections, but at the same time create boundaries around a place that 'buffers us [the student] from a world of choices, affirms identity and independence, and offers a progressive disclosure of zones of potential activity in lieu of predetermined (and in the case of computer interfaces thus windowed) choices' (Joyce 2002: 85, in parenthesis inserted). Such maps are then places through which the learner is located and heavily regulated in the making of meaning, even where the individual appears to be engaged through their own active construction of meaning, further exploration and mapping (for example, through identifying 'favourite places'). It is through such mappings that places of e-learning emerge as the 'architecture' that then transform patterns of traditional university activity into those of extended and intensified sites of disciplinary practice.

In describing such architecture, Burbules (2002) identifies patterns of virtual activity as widely controlled through prior design in terms of five polarities:

- the control and facilitation of movement;
- the communication of assumptions and expectations of interaction;

- the extent to which participant disclosure is necessary;
- the extent to which architectures disclose their own design; and
- who is allowed in and who kept out.

However, it is not only the e-learning designer who is involved in this case, as each web location is also purposefully pre-designed around these same polarities. The description of polarity begins perhaps to articulate a particular fluidity and utility in the architectures of e-environments, and point to their potential in the intensification of disciplinary processes, even though they are not completely controllable. Traditional university environments by comparison are not able to be so densely designed as places through their architecture, controlling and directing bodies, subjecting them to mechanisms of discipline, and so controlling and channeling meaning. To some extent you could say therefore that traditional university courses may be more 'open' in disciplinary terms than e-learning.

We can see a potential intensification and extension of disciplinary power again in relation to the additional opportunities afforded for observation. Lecturers and learners are brought into a place where they can observe one another more intensively than through learning designed for lecture theatres, seminar rooms and the physical and temporal 'spaces' between these. The lecturer has various electronic tools available for the observation and recording of the location and action of bodies within virtual spaces – the watchful eye is ever-present through the permanent record of textual 'talk' as rhetorical work within computer-mediated communications, in the potential to track student activity within course sites and on websites from web logs, and in the diverse opportunities afforded in this for analysis (Garrison and Anderson 2003). Discipline is intensified in e-learning as subjects (students and the lecturer) are made more 'visible' and 'permanent' in what they say, and thus more open to correction and ranking.

Discipline through observation and recording may be exerted not only by the lecturers and students, but by other lecturers, support staff, researchers and even employers of students. As the panoptic cell is not simply visible from a central point but is capable of being observed through a wider network or web of surveillance, this intensifies an awareness, by the subjects (both student and teacher) that they might be being observed, although they can never be sure whether or not this is the case. The mere possibility of being observed may be sufficient to tailor behaviour to what is believed to be required.

These practices of observation and recording are not neutral as they work through norms; they mark out which actions are included and excluded from the norm. For Foucault, normalizing judgement fills the gaps that judicial law leaves empty. It serves to create a distinction between 'good-bad', 'normal-abnormal', and make infinitesimal gradations and distinctions of these. The mere fact that observation is possible, acts to incite the teacher to monitor student conversation and engage with encouragements or otherwise.

Indeed, it is this opportunity for the intensification of observation and recording in e-learning that supports possibilities for the intensification of examination; distribution of individuals according to ranks or grades through their contributions to virtual discussions and activities and a marking of the gaps and hierarchies of qualities, skills and aptitudes. The norms provide the basis for sorting and classifying, creating boundaries and exclusions. They are not then simply descriptive, as they embody the exercise of power: 'The power of normalization imposes homogeneity; but it individualizes by making it possible to measure gaps, to determine levels, to fix specialties and to render the differences useful by fitting them one to another' (Foucault 1977: 184).

The use of regulations to enforce visible attendance and in some cases also the examination of appropriate participation in this way appears to be a product for many of a shift to e-learning. Garrison and Anderson (2003: 96) identify e-learning courses as offering as much as 40 or 50 per cent of the overall course grade for participation, and this of course is an extension of the disciplinary techniques of normalization and examination (Foucault 1977); practices of observation and normalization are brought together, intensified and made more productive through examination. But even without this extension of examination to what is after all an equivalent to the seminar discussion within a traditional university environment, the extended and intensified capacity for observation and normalization in e-learning, when coupled with the requirement for student presence, suggests the intensification of disciplinary effects.

Educators argue that the textual communication of e-learning has distinct advantages over spoken learning in the promotion of self-disciplining practices: 'writing intensifies the sense of self and fosters more conscious interaction between persons' (Ong, in Garrison and Anderson 2003: 26). From this perspective e-learning can be seen as an extension of wider moves towards a harnessing of the subject to discipline itself and not an achievement of freedom, choice or emancipation for the individual as humanist discourses of e-learning would suggest. Rather than power being exercised through the direct presence of lecturer and learner, the power of observation becomes exercised by the learner upon themselves. Here lecturers 'have been *dis*embodied by educational jargon that is increasingly dominated by the mutually informing vocabularies of business and cognitive science, as well as the dictates of "learning at a distance"' (McWilliam 1996: 312). The absent presence of the lecturer is, however, still to be found embedded if not embodied within the architecture of the place of e-learning, where learning activities require textual communications that are aligned with the explicit achievement of outcomes. Foucault talks about an increasing social requirement for self-discipline as a 'self-surveillance' – an active subject but still enmeshed within exercises of power, what Miller and Rose (1993) refer to as an aspect of 'governing at a distance'. This textual (rather than verbal) rehearsal of the disciplined subjectivity is a reconfiguration that intensifies effect; it increases self-scrutiny and the governing of the self as it develops these capacities.

With the 'opening' of the possibilities for observation in e-learning is an accompanying possibility for the unsettling of previous norms and knowledge of the discipline. Normalizing judgements are spread wider than the more traditionally conceived relationship between individual learner and lecturer (we have considered this already in relation to a rather diffused control through the architecture of websites) and they easily include, for instance, the workplace supervisor and mentors in workplace learning. And, this suggests shifting roles as well as norms:

> The distributed nature of workplace learning implies that different aspects of the learning process will need to be shared between different actors. A changing division of labour in supporting learning will have implications for the roles of academic staff based in higher education and of 'workplace' based staff.
>
> (Harris 2006: 80)

This introduces complexity and potential conflict into normalization processes, as there may be different categorizations arising from the parties involved in making judgements. It provides the basis for an explicit politics about the norms inscribed in disciplinary practices; they can no longer be taken-for-granted to reside in certain bodies of knowledge. The body of knowledge and the norms of the discipline are no longer so closely controlled by a lecturer without the direct influence of others. This may reinforce normalization within a traditional view of the discipline, as is the case through practices of peer scrutiny of the design of e-learning course materials. However, the norms may be challenged by the introduction of the wider interests of employers and learners into the evaluation of what constitutes the body of knowledge.

Norms would therefore seem to be diffused through e-learning, even though the possibilities for normalizing judgement are to some extent intensified as we saw above. However, the power of disciplinary practice is not lost but is reconfigured, re-embedded and intensified across other architectures and relations. Lecturers may become 'process- and system-oriented professionals' (Miller and Xulu 1996, in Harris 2006: 97). And, knowledge emerges in hybrid forms between that of the workplace, disciplinary knowledge and that identified by learners through their own web searches. Harris (2006) argues a likely lack of parity of esteem between workplace and disciplinary qualifications, which, she suggests, is overlooked in discourses of workplace learning. For example, Boud and Solomon (2001, cited in Harris 2006) suggest a trend towards a co-validation of knowledge within workplace learning: 'the workplace, the individual learner and the university have to work together to produce and validate a non-disciplinary yet still "legitimate" knowledge'. However, it is through such processes, whereby workplace knowledge and norms become legitimized through the university, that a wider shift to the valuing of knowledge for its capacity to improve system efficiency is supported (cf. Lyotard 1984; Lankshear *et al.* 2002). Through reconfiguration that extends university disciplinary practices into the workplace, disciplinary knowledge itself is unsettled and its boundaries become less clearly defined, as it becomes open to discussion. The possibilities afforded by e-learning support this unsettling of the discipline.

The subject of e-learning

There is a reflexive difficulty in putting forward the argument above. In attempting to chart some of the changing disciplinary practices within the university under the influence of trends towards e-learning the very discourses of e-learning are largely generated from within the institutional contexts where these processes are at work. Indeed, this very chapter has been subject to disciplinary practices through peer review in a previous version as an article (Nicoll and Edwards 1997) and, again, through a colloquium where colleagues specializing in Foucauldian scholarship gave critical and normative comment (see reference to the genesis of this collection in the Preface). What can then be said of this chapter and the wider subject of e-learning as a body of knowledge? Or perhaps more tellingly even, what and who is the subject of e-learning?

Discourses of e-learning have tended largely to construct the area of study as about the mechanics of its implementation (the appropriate use of technology in education, the effective delivery of educational messages, the efficient systems for materials production and so on). Liberal, humanistic and radical values – of individual autonomy, personal development and access and equity – justifying educational practice were seen to legitimize e-learning also. For some e-learning offers a way of more fully embedding those values. E-learning offers a more 'learner-centred', 'empowering' and 'progressive' approach to education and training. Such discourses construct e-learning practice as unproblematic in relation to the disciplines and discipline. The focus is on the how of e-learning rather than the more precautionary kind of exploration of tactics and their functioning that Foucault suggests. In providing access and opportunity, e-learning 'empowers' individuals and the power of e-learning is left unexamined.

E-learning is not a discipline. It does not have its own rules of knowledge formation as do the established disciplines and reflexively it exemplifies the multi- and inter-disciplinarity it tends to support. Like its bigger sister, education, it draws together people with interests in, for instance, the media, psychology, sociology, computer science, language and communication. However, as Elam (1994) suggests of many similar bodies of knowledge, the principle of identity has been to the fore in e-learning's formulation as a subject. Here the 'field' of e-learning with its implicit metaphor of boundedness constitutes a regime of truth through which boundaries begin to be established and 'policed'. Yet these boundaries are inherently 'fuzzy' and constantly transgressed, indefensible.

In other words, the very demise of discipline as bodies of knowledge to which e-learning can be said to be contributing may also be impacting upon e-learning itself as a body of knowledge. However, because these different discourses of e-learning are themselves constituted within disciplinary frameworks, they also suggest different forms of observation, norms and examination for those who study. They may even be said to offer a more 'complete' regime of truth for the developing practices of e-learning, and even while the e-learning practices that they legitimate may also be said to be resulting in a reconfiguration and extension of discipline. Therefore the discourses of e-learning are themselves subject to diffusion, fragmentation and reconfiguration, even through the work of this chapter. At the core of each is the attempt to provide knowledge, which, whether or not this was intended, becomes implicated in the exercise of power through disciplinary mechanisms, and the intensification of effects in the control and production of ever more useful subjects.

Who are those educated subjects, constituted at the intersection of disciplinary knowledge and new forms of learning mediated by e-technology? First, they are disciplined subjects, skilled in the navigation of rhetorical places and in their mobilization in practices of meaning making. Lankshear et al. (2003) draw on the work of Gilster (1997) to talk of the tools and procedures of knowledge assembly that are increasingly required within the information age, customizing personal newsfeeds for the receipt of information on topics of interest, searching for background information, drawing together useful information and relating these to that from more traditional sources. These resonate with earlier discussion within the chapter of the e-environment as a rhetorical place where students learn to make meanings within places that partially enclose. Whether these practices support identities that are 'instrumental' or 'intuitive' in their engagements in e-learning (Heim, in Lankshear et al. 2003), such as in the proliferation of blogs, will depend in part on the normalization processes to which they are subject. These will be formed not only through those embedded within the e-learning architectures designed for their use, but also through wider and intersecting architectures. Such subjects are likely to be skilled in practices of self-discipline and self-examination, as has been seen. However, the possibility for a range of learner identities, and identity as a learner, may be both troubling and pleasurable. The modern bounded subject is displaced by the multi-centred subject, produced at the intersection of a relative profusion of architectures of place, and across the boundaries of a variety of knowledges, a process supported through the practices of e-learning.

Conclusion

Conclusions suggest closure and for this chapter this would be singularly inappropriate. What can be said is that practices of e-learning take up and reconfigure mechanisms whereby 'discipline' is a modality for the exercise of power. Disciplinary practices are already those drawn upon by universities as specialized institutions of the sort examined by Foucault, and as an 'essential instrument for a particular end' (Foucault 1977: 215). But in e-learning they are taken up within the institution by university staff as a way of reinforcing and reorganizing mechanisms of power internally – within the institution. In so doing, these mechanisms become reconfigured; the nuances and qualities afforded their expression and function alter disciplinary mechanisms. Here we might then talk about a tactic in the generalization of 'panopticism' as a metaphor for disciplinary mechanisms, as they reach out from the enclosed walls of the university. The university has, as Foucault calls it, been a place exercising 'a sort of social "quarantine"' (1977: 217), but through e-learning it reaches out and infiltrates other such institutions and mechanisms, in an extension and intensification of the wider disciplinary society. This kind of infiltration acts on and within other disciplinary mechanisms:

> [S]ometimes undermining them, but serving as an intermediary between them, linking them together, extending them and above all making it possible to bring the effects of power to the most minute and distance elements. It assures an infinitesimal distribution of the power relations.
>
> (Foucault 1977: 216)

It distributes those mechanisms specific to the university, so as to allow them to join up with others, to make them possible within other places.

A network of disciplinary practices is extended throughout the social formation introducing different norms and hierarchies. Thus, although e-learning may be a force towards the demise of the traditional power-knowledge formations of the university and towards the production of autonomous and reflective learners, it would not appear to signal a demise of discipline as such. As suggested, e-learning signals a power to constitute multi-centred subjectivities with diverse capacities and the potential to legitimate different knowledges, though this is by no means an inevitable or unified outcome.

References

Burbules, N. (2002) 'The web as a rhetorical place', in I. Snyder (ed.), *Silicon Literacies: Communication, Innovation and Education in the Electronic Age*, London: Routledge.

Dreyfus, H. and Rabinow, P. (1982) *Michael Foucault: Beyond Structuralism and Hermeneutics*, Hertfordshire: Harvester Wheatsheaf.

Elam, D. (1994) *Feminism and Deconstruction: Ms. en Abyme*, London: Routledge.

Foucault, M. (1996) 'Discourse on language', in R. Kearney and M. Rainwater (eds), *The Continental Philosophy Reader*, London: Routledge.

Foucault, M. (1977) *Discipline and Punish: The Birth of the Prison*, London: Penguin Books.

Foucault, M. (1980) *Power/Knowledge: Selected Interviews and Other Writings 1972–77*, Brighton: Harvester Press.

Garrison, D. and Anderson, T. (2003) *E-Learning in the 21st Century: A Framework for Research and Practice,* London: RoutledgeFalmer.

Harris, J. (2006) 'Annex A: Review of the literature on academic literature on workplace learning', in J. Brennan and B. Little with H. Conner, J. de Weert Egbert, Harris, B. Josselyn, N. Ratcliffe and A. Scesa (eds), *Towards a Strategy for Workplace Learning*, a report to the Higher Education Funding Council for England by CERI & KPMG: www.hefce.ac.uk/pubs/rdreports/2006/rd09_06/rd09_06.doc (accessed 25 September 2007).

Heim, M. (1993) *The Metaphysics of Virtual Reality*, New York: Oxford University Press.

Joyce, M. (2002) 'Then again who isn't: post-hypertextual rhetorics', in I. Snyder (ed.), *Silicon Literacies: Communication, Innovation and Education in the Electronic Age*, London: RoutledgeFalmer.

Lankshear, C., Peters, M. and Knobel, M. (2002) 'Information, knowledge and learning: some issues facing epistemology and education in the digital age', in M. Lea and K. Nicoll (eds), *Distributed Learning: Social and Cultural Approaches to Practice*, London: RoutledgeFalmer.

Lea, M. and Nicoll, K. (eds), *Distributed Learning: Social and Cultural Approaches to Practice*, London: RoutledgeFalmer.

Lyotard, J.F. (1979) *The Postmodern Condition: A Report on Knowledge*, Manchester: Manchester University Press.

McWilliam, E. (1996) 'Touchy subjects: a risky enquiry into pedagogic pleasure', *British Educational Research Journal,* 22: 305–17.

Marshall, J. (1989) 'Foucault and education', *Australian Journal of Education*, 33: 99–113.

Messer-Davidow, E., Shumway, D. and Sylvan, D. (eds) (1993) *Knowledges: Historical and Critical Studies in Disciplinarity*, Charlottesville: University Press of Virginia.

Miller, P. and Rose, N. (1993) 'Governing economic life', in M. Gane and T. Johnson (eds), *Foucault's New Domains*, London: Routledge.

Miller, C. and Xulu, S. (1996) *Final Report: Contexual Analysis (Cluster 1 – Universities and Technikons)*, South Africa: Education, Training and Development Practioner Project, GTZ.

Nicoll, K. (2006) *Flexibility and Lifelong Learning: Policy, Discourse and Politics*, London: RoutledgeFalmer.

Nicoll, K. and Edwards, R. (1997) 'Open learning and the demise of discipline', *Open Learning*, 12: 14–24.

Thompson Klein, J. (1993) 'Blurring, cracking and crossing: permeation and the fracturing of discipline', in E. Messer-Davidow, D. Shumway and D. Sylvan (eds), *Knowledges: Historical and Critical Studies in Disciplinarity*, Charlottesville: University Press of Virginia.

Usher, R. and Edwards, R. (1994) *Postmodernism and Education: Different Voices, Different Worlds*, London: Routledge.

Usher, R. (1993) 'Re-examining the place of disciplines in adult education', *Studies in Continuing Education*, 15: 15–25.

Chapter 14

Academic work and adult education

A site of multiple subjects

Nicky Solomon

Research into academic writing has typically focused on writing practices in specific disciplines, particularly in terms of students' induction into a disciplinary area. In this chapter I take a different focus. The focus is on academic writing in terms of a relationship between programmes of governing and the construction of knowledge and academic identities. Drawing on Foucault's theorization of governmentality (Foucault 1991) together with the Canadian work on genre theory (Freedman and Medway 1994; Freadman 1994, 1998, 2000) I examine a number of my own academic publications.

The publications that I have selected vary in genre and content and I am using this variation to draw attention to the complexity and diversity of the textual practices of contemporary academics. As a tactical move I have grouped my publications according to 'genre' categories. These are not necessarily 'perfect-fits', but they are groupings that foreground particular kinds of 'textual uptakes'. The concept of 'uptake' draws on the genre work of Freadman (2000). Each group of publications can be understood as a textual uptake that does particular kinds of work within its institutional location. It is an uptake that constructs particular kinds of 'plausible' knowledge and writing subjects (Edwards *et al.* 2004). The term *subject* captures two overlapping sets of meanings: one relates to the content of the text, that is, the knowledge that is produced, while the second is to do with the person who is being actively constructed through the writing and the reading of the text. The second meaning draws on Foucauldian understandings of the 'subject' as discussed in the next section.

The publications in group one (Hood and Solomon 1985; Hood *et al.* 1996) are instructional texts, written for adult English as a second language (ESL) teachers working in an adult migrant English programme in Australia. Group two publications comprise two occasional papers (Brown *et al.* 1994; Cope *et al.* 1994) and a government report (Gibb *et al.* 1996) on language and cultural matters. The occasional papers and government report are the outcomes of commissioned projects. These publications are 'hybrid' texts as they are constructions of knowledge that have been subjected to multiple disciplinary practices and do not conform to any single text shape. Group three publications are academic book chapters (Solomon 1996, 1999; Scheeres and Solomon 2000a, b) and refereed journal articles (Garrick and Solomon 1997; Usher and Solomon 1999) theorizing workplace learning and the nature of collaborative research. These 'disciplined texts', considered to be more conventional academic writings, have been subjected to the requirements of a disciplinary community within the academy.

In the next section, I briefly describe some aspects of governmentality and genre theory that I have taken up to explore the way these publications have produced particular kinds of subjects within and through programmes of governing. I then focus on each group of publications and the particular programme and set of discursive sequences through which each subject has been constructed.

Theorizing the subject

Governmentality provides a way of understanding the complex socio-political mechanisms of governing that help to produce programmes which govern contemporary academic work. These programmes include programmes of the State and those beyond the State to include

> all endeavours to shape, guide, direct the conduct of others, whether these be the crew of a ship, the members of a household, the employees of a boss, the children of a family or the inhabitants of a territory ... [and] ... embraces the ways to govern ourselves.
>
> (Rose 1999: 3)

I use governmentality to examine how academic conduct is governed locally (that is within a higher education institution) and at a distance by the State and other governing bodies.

Each group of publications is located within an institutional site that is connected to a particular programme of governing in Australia. The programmes are: the Adult Migrant Education Program (AMEP), the National Workplace and Training Reforms (hereafter referred to as National Reforms), and what I am naming as the 'Globalizing Disciplinary Communities'. I suggest that each programme, in one shape or form, is a pedagogical intervention – a technology of government – whose purpose is to construct particular kinds of 'productive' subjects in a country's population, in this case Australia: in the AMEP it is English language-speaking subjects; in the National Reforms programme it is a linguistically and technically competent workforce; and in the Globalizing Disciplinary Communities it is academic subjects whose work is consonant with the diverse knowledge needs of the global economy.

Miller and Rose's (1993) examination of the technical devices for governing the population draws attention to the key role language plays in the establishment of networks and the workings of 'action at a distance' that make possible the alignment of government, institutions and subjects. It is this discursive character of governing which is particularly interesting. It is through language that governmental fields are composed, rendered thinkable, 'sayable' and manageable. It is language that constructs knowledge, relationships and alliances. In other words, the relationship of power and knowledge and self is brought about through discursive practices (Dreyfus and Rabinow 1982; Foucault 1991). It is through these discursive practices that programmes of governing are constructed and elaborated and that 'specify the appropriate basis for the organization and mobilization of social life … (for) it is in language that programmes of government are elaborated' (Miller and Rose 1993: 80). Language is seen as a technology for producing social realities, for creating domains of thought and for making these domains of thought 'actionable'. Language renders aspects of existence amenable to inscription, recording and calculation and thus amenable to regulation and also to intervention. Language is a site, not just for knowing and calculating what is, but a site that sets up conditions of possibility (Rose 1998).

Genre theory, a theory about language and social processes (Miller 1994), offers the possibility of understanding 'genre' as one of the discursive mechanisms through which government, institutions and subjects intersect and operate. Genres can be understood as sites of inscription and also as processes for inscribing subjects in such a way that their goals are aligned with institutional goals and programmes of governing.

In order to explain the range, scope and potential freedom that is possible within genre, Freadman (1994) uses the metaphor of a game to correspond with the notion of genre. Importantly for Freadman, genres/games are located within multiple social activities and the term *ceremony* is used to capture the broader discursive space.

> Ceremonies are games that situate other games; they are the rules for the setting of the game, for placing and timing it in relation with other places and times. They are the rules for playing the game, but they are not the rules of the game. Games, then, are rules for the production of certain acts in those 'places'. That there may be 'play' at both these levels is important: knowing the rules is knowing how much play the rules allow and how to play with them.
>
> (Freadman 1994: 47)

I take up this concept of a 'ceremony' to describe the discursive location for each group of publications. As indicated earlier, I locate the publications within each of their programmes of governing. These programmes, as discursive constructions, can be understood as ceremonials. Each ceremonial or ceremonial place is constituted by various rituals, regulations and participants. Programmes unfold through sets of discursive sequences that construct and reconstruct particular kinds of genres that themselves position and reposition the participating subjects. In other words texts, in Freadman's terms, arise within ceremonials and their form is determined by their ceremonial place and function. The ceremonial is framed by and frames a time and space, setting it apart from others and marking its specificity. Genre is therefore constituted by its ceremonial place. In these terms, each group of publications can be understood as both constituting and constituted by a ceremonial place.

Genres for Freadman (1998, 2000) are constituted in ways that set up particular kinds of uptakes:

> 'Uptake' names the bi-directional relation between a text and what Peirce would call its 'interpretant': the text is contrived to secure a certain class of uptakes, and the interpretant, or the uptake text, confirms its generic status by conforming to this contrivance. The uptake text (also) has the power not to confirm this generic status, which it may modify minimally, or even utterly, by taking its object as some other kind.
>
> (Freadman 1998: 1)

Each of the publications is therefore a textual uptake within a particular discursive sequence. A discursive sequence refers to the relationship between texts and the 'typical' unfolding of texts within particular cultural and discursive locations. In other words the moves between texts are predictable and not arbitrary ones that take account of texts as practices with a history and within a sequence that works towards a desired outcome (Edwards *et al.* 2004). Within this sequence the writing of the publication is subjected to, and a subject of, the conventions, regulations and expectations of its discursive location. Yet importantly, at the same time, unanticipated uptakes may occur. The taking up of the various groups of my publications for this chapter is an example of an unanticipated uptake. The discursive sequences of this 'new' uptake positions the subjects (the texts and the writer) in a different way to the intended uptakes of the publications, when each was written.

I am suggesting that the placement of genre into a governmental framing 'takes-up' the challenge posed by Freedman and Medway:

> Genre studies are a particularly promising instrument for illuminating the social process in its detailed operation, and afford an opportunity we should not refuse of examining what it means to be part of an institutional process. What does participation in a genre do to, and for, an individual or group? What opportunities do the relationships reflected in and structured by a genre afford for human creative action, or, alternatively, for the domination of others?
>
> (Freedman and Medway 1994: 12)

Each group of publications (instructional texts, hybrid texts, disciplined texts) realizes the relationship between programmes of government, institutional locations and the position (and positioning) of the writer. This complex relationship can be usefully located within Freadman's notion of 'ceremonial place'. In this way 'ceremonial place' can be understood as a set of discursive sequences that positions the writings within a particular set of programmes of governmentality. Both the 'programme' and the 'ceremonial place' have rules and conventions that are, at the one time, constitutive and regulatory, as well as open to play and disturbance. Understanding ceremonial place as a programme of governmentality draws attention to the possibilities of using the concept of genre as a kind of inscription that contributes to the construction of particular kinds of subjects. In summary, I use the term 'uptake' to understand the active positioning of subjects within the discursive sequences as the programmes of governmentality unfold in both predictable and unanticipated ways.

Exploring the subjects: instructional texts

The AMEP is a programme of the Commonwealth Government of Australia, within which group one publications (two editions of *Focus on Reading,* a professional development text for adult ESL teachers) are located. These two editions can be understood as specific kinds of textual uptakes within a ceremonial place. This ceremonial place comprises sets of discursive sequences that have helped to construct English language teaching as a field of practice, together with English language learners and teachers as particular kinds of productive Australian subjects.

The AMEP is a complex political and social activity that focuses on a normalizing of the relationship between living in Australia with the speaking of English in order to help realize the social and economic goals of governing. The AMEP can be seen as a pedagogical technology of power designed to construct an English-speaking and thus productive population. The making of these productive subjects was not through imposition, force or coercion. Indeed, migrants chose whether or not to take up English language learning opportunities. Governing was such that migrants saw English language fluency as a primary personal goal – a goal that helped them gain independence and enabled them to participate actively as Australian subjects. The AMEP therefore made possible an alignment of government and individual goals, which in turn contributed to the construction of productive English speaking migrant subjects.

Within this ceremonial place teachers are another set of productive subjects. Productivity for these teachers is in terms of being able to meet the range of English language learning needs of the migrants, as well as to develop a professional face for the Australian public and the international English language teaching world. The complex discursive and political framings of the AMEP were, to a large extent, unnoticed by English language learners and their teachers. The classroom and the educational institution were the significant sites. While it was 'known' that the programme was publicly funded, learners' and teachers' practices were directly framed by the 'physical' walls of the classroom and by the regulations of the educational institution. Their focus was on the practicalities of 'how to teach English' (in the case of the teachers) or 'learning English' (in the case of the learners).

Each edition of *Focus on Reading* has been generated within the same ceremonial place as both are located within the same macro-level objective to produce English language speaking population and, to a certain degree, are subjected to shared rituals and regulations. However the constituents of the ceremonial place varied with each edition. These variations relate to the different times (1985 and 1996) and places (an ESL educational provider and a university) of their writing. These time and place differences locate each within similar yet different sets of discursive sequences.

The writing of the first edition of *Focus on Reading* was located within various institutional and professional discursive sequences. These sequences were linked to an emergence in the government consciousness of the significance of reading and writing for participating productively in Australia. Within governing discourses education was understood to be an important site and a technology in this venture. An accompanying set of discursive sequences was within education institutions where there was a growing understanding of the need to professionalize English language teaching at a time when few teachers had English language teaching qualifications. This was taken up within institutions by the provision of resources for professional development activities. Importantly, I, the writing subject, together with the co-author, was in an institutional position that provided the opportunity to write the first publication in Australia on the teaching of reading to adult ESL learners.

The decision to write a handbook as a professional development resource was a deliberate one. It was a conscious textual uptake within the prevailing professional and institutional discourses. A 'how to' book was a genre that reflected the knowledge resources of the time. These included the writers' knowledge and experience, their status in the institution (peers) as well as the teachers' disinterest in engaging with 'theories'. An instructional book for teachers sat comfortably as a companion to student textbooks that teachers used. However, unlike students' textbooks, this handbook was not a step-by-step prescription. While it was an instructional text with 'do this and do that' advice, it also had a broader curriculum application. In other words it played with the rules of the instructional genre.

By 1996 the constituents and discursive location of the AMEP ceremonial place differed significantly and this was realized in a second edition of *Focus on Reading* that was similar yet different to the earlier edition. A sign of the different conditions is the title change. The subtitle *Handbook for Teachers* is no longer included and, as such, the book no longer signals itself as an instructional text. The location, desires and position of the writers, the links with a more sophisticated adult ESL and literacy theoretical and curriculum discourses, and the qualifications of the readers resulted in a different text. In this uptake, the writers were inscribing and constructing a different kind of knowledge that was reaching out to a wider range of audiences and possible uptakes. The audiences included teachers in the field and the international and local academic community, but it was also written to give the writers a scholarly publication that 'counted' in the Australian research assessment exercise.

The text had to serve practitioners' interests and provide practice-based orientation. It did this by retaining some of the features of the first edition, such as pre-reading questions inviting readers to examine their own teaching experiences, as well as chapter summaries that drew together main concepts and themes. But there are also significant differences in content, particularly in terms of the balance of 'theory' and 'practice'. An additional chapter was included on 'Reading Theory' and the first chapter on 'Understanding Reading' included sections on 'critical reading and reader positioning', 'reading as a social and cultural practice' and 'comparing spoken and written English'. In addition there was a 'Reference' section in each chapter as well as 'Further Readings'. These inclusions signal the field's growing relationship with the academy.

It would be misleading to suggest that the increased theoretical weight was written only for academic valuing. While the text was contributing to the writers' construction of themselves as academics, the shift was also related to changing discursive locations of both the teachers and the students. Teachers not only had an abundance of teaching materials but also their teaching work had changed. The student profiles were more varied and also the institutional rules and regulations were more complex. The language learning needs were diverse and teachers were working in very different institutions and their everyday work required many kinds of knowledge.

In summary, both editions of *Focus on Reading* (as instructional texts) were produced within the AMEP ceremonial place and played a pedagogical role in realizing one of the programmes of government, that is, the construction of literate English-speaking citizens whose individual goals were aligned with broader socio-economic objectives. As one of these citizens, in the writing of these books, I was actively inscribing myself as a productive subject.

Exploring the subjects: hybrid texts

Group two publications comprise two occasional papers and a government report. Each publication is one of the outcomes of a collaborative research project commissioned by the Australian government and/or industry bodies in the 1990s. The collaborative research projects were connected to two related sets of government programmes – national workplace reforms and training reforms. These national reforms brought together the academy, industry and government into a new programmatic relationship. While industry, government and the academy had been familiar research partners

(Godin 1998), the distinctive nature of these alliances in Australia in the 1990s draws attention to a relationship between the characteristics of contemporary governing and modes of knowledge production. As an academic working on projects commissioned by government and industry bodies, I was part of the discursive unfolding of these programmes. Through this process I was constructed as a commissioned writing subject, which differed from the English language writing subject constructed through group one publications.

In the national reforms ceremonial place, as in the AMEP ceremonial place, the programme was concerned with the construction of 'competent' 'productive' subjects, but in this place the reach was broader. It encompassed education and training programmes for all workers (and potential workers) regardless of their language background. This difference is manifested in and constituted by the complex set of participants, networks of power, rules and regulations and discursive sequences. Therefore while it was a highly regulated policy-driven site, it was also constituted by unfamiliar and not well-rehearsed rules and conventions. There were new alignments between academics, policy makers, unions, professional and employment bodies as well as private organizations. These alignments required different spoken and written conversations. In other words there were new discursive sequences through which new genres and new subjects emerged.

Although different to the AMEP ceremonial place, there were some overlaps. Indeed, in part, the effectiveness of the national reforms ceremonial place had been dependent on particular kinds of expertise, including expertise in 'language teaching and learning'. Academic subjects who had participated in the AMEP ceremonial place, such as myself, had a place. Knowledge about language was needed to make explicit the new language practices that had become integral to contemporary work and training. In the contemporary workplace, competence referred to linguistic and cultural competence as well as technical competence (NTB 1992). The ability to work productively in the 'sexualized' workplace, the ability of individuals to align their own goals with those of the organization, the ability to learn, all require the worker to be linguistically competent. Therefore subjects with 'knowledge about language', and 'knowledge about the language of learning', were desired in the national reforms ceremonial place.

Academics participating in collaborative commissioned research projects were subjected to various institutional regimes of the academy, the commissioning body and other participating institutions. Each had its own discourses, conventions and regulations, yet at the same time attempted to settle into a new alignment. In this contested area, academics took up ambivalent subject positions as they actively self-regulated into the new networks and power relations. They performed as an academic with 'worthwhile' expert knowledge, which would contribute to the construction of productive subjects (Australian population), and as an academic whose goals aligned with those of the academy, industry and/or government.

The national reforms ceremonial place generated a commissioned research process as a predictable staged set of discursive sequences. The unfolding collaborative knowledge producing process revolved around a sequence of written and spoken texts and accompanying actions. The written texts include an advertisement in national papers inviting expressions of interest or submissions; a brief outlining the objectives and parameters of the project; a tender (submission) document outlining expertise, methodology, anticipated outcomes, budget details; a number of reporting texts; and a range of publications whose purpose was to disseminate the new knowledge. Each written text was constructed in dialogue with a number of spoken texts including spoken interactions and negotiations during the construction of the submission and during the empirical research stage. Together these spoken and written texts established the social relationships and textual boundaries. The texts served to discursively mediate the historical and hierarchical differences of the various participants. Each written text was inscribed as an accountable boundary marker representing a stage in the process of knowledge production. It was through the textual practices of the research that academics took up various positions within the new hybrid spaces that cross-over institutional and disciplinary boundaries.

The opening up of the boundaries is indicated in the variations in the textual shape of the three publications in this group. Their lack of compliance to any one genre is in sharp contrast to the structured process within which they were constructed. They exemplify the contradictions of the workings of governmentality. On the one hand, collaborative research projects generated within this ceremonial place are centrally programmed, managed and directed and highly regulated, while on the other hand, the knowledge produced is often unanticipated and diverse. Stronach and Maclure (1997) use the term 'unruly' to capture this kind of knowledge, that is, knowledge produced outside the rules of disciplinary methodology and not in the service of disciplinary truth.

The three publications place the 'new knowledge' into the public domain, subjecting it to a number of potential uptakes including scrutiny and debate. The publications themselves are a particular uptake within various discursive sequences. For example Brown *et al.* (1994) was an occasional paper that drew on a final report of a project that was commissioned by a government department. The report itself was a textual uptake of a number of other textual practices within the project. The project involved developing a literacy strategy for a large workplace where the literacy skills of its mainly migrant workforce were investigated and where various training strategies for the employees were recommended. The writing and publication of the occasional paper was part of a legitimizing process of knowledge production that repositions knowledge produced in a particular context to other potential sites and audiences.

Occasional papers and government reports represent different kinds of textual uptakes with each positioning the subjects in a particular way. In terms of the occasional paper, this is a position outside the rules and regimes of the commissioning body and the collaborative partners. It shifts both the knowledge and the writers to a less regulated space – one that isn't clearly located within any conventional generic form. An occasional paper is a written performance that does not regulate to conventional academic criteria associated with refereed writings or to criteria regulated by explicit instrumental performative objectives. It is as if the occasional paper occupies a discursive space that attempts to sit outside convention.

The government report sits within a more regulated set of discursive sequences and therefore positions the subjects in a different way. The publication, and thus the knowledge, is government 'owned'. The authors, the experts commissioned by the government, are either invisible or downgraded as the government positions itself as the knowledge producer and as the authority. The experts employed to help the government meets its objective have all but disappeared, with their expertise infused and diffused in the text. The publication acts as a marker of the government's performance for its own accountability purposes. Academics, as active subjects with different accountabilities, inscribe their performances in these projects in other textual uptakes (Scheeres and Solomon 2000a, b) and the occasional paper, a text that re-establishes their authorial role, is one such site.

The publications are textual uptakes that could be understood as characteristic of Mode 2 knowledge (Gibbons *et al.* 1994), knowledge that is produced outside the academy, and is transdisciplinary, transient and heterogeneous. However these uptakes sat uncomfortably with the rules of the games of the globalizing disciplinary community ceremonial place. The disciplinary practices of that community call for a different textual uptake, an uptake that positions the subject in an academically disciplined way. And that is the subject of next ceremonial place.

Exploring the subjects: disciplined texts

Group three publications (disciplined texts) can be understood as textual uptakes involving the disciplining of the subject required within globalizing academic communities. These publications construct a different kind of academic subject to those inscribed in groups one and two publications. This ceremonial place shares the same broad global conditions through which the national training and workplace reforms have emerged. Yet the specificity of the sets of technologies and disciplinary pressures within this ceremonial place produce distinctive discursive sequences and rituals.

As a writing subject in the national reforms ceremonial place I enjoyed the idea that I was contributing to government policy, and I enjoyed the legitimacy of being 'so close to the action'. However, I sought other kinds of legitimacies in order to position myself as a scholar – just one of my multiple subject positions as a 'productive' academic. Academic publications, as in this group, are an active 'signing on' as a disciplinary academic (Edwards and Usher 1999: 269).

This is in contrast to the inscriptions and subject positions constructed through collaborative research project work with government and industry (group two publications).

Within this ceremonial place there are a number of intersecting discursive sequences, including the government research assessment exercise, that influence the writing of group three publications. The published research reports based on industry, government and/or enterprise partnership projects (located in the national reforms ceremonial place) do not 'count' in research assessment exercises in Australia. In order to be counted a different textual uptake is needed. A different textual uptake is required. Group three publications exemplify the written subject that has been constructed through the discursive sequences that are shaped by (and shaping) globalizing disciplinary communities.

Unlike the other groups of publications, scholarly book chapters and journal articles are a 'transparent' demonstration of productive scholarly work. Therefore, they can be seen to exemplify Mode 1 knowledge (Gibbons *et al.* 1994). They have been produced within the disciplinary sequences of the academy and they are accountable to the regimes of the disciplinary fields of knowledge (as well as to the disciplinary practices of programmes of the government's research assessment exercise). As such they already have a legitimacy within the academic community and therefore require less explanation and theorization. The publications speak for themselves.

Taking up multiple writing subjects

The discussion above has conceptualized the multiplicity and complexities of textual practices of the contemporary academic subject as a consequence of the intersection of a number of political and social discourses. It has argued that the multiple textual practices have not been generated arbitrarily but are connected to specific programmes of governmentality that focus on the construction of 'productive subjects'. These programmes are explained as particular kinds of ceremonial places, each of which comprises specific rituals and discursive sequences that produce specific textual uptakes. These uptakes are mediated through institutional practices and contribute to the construction of particular kinds of legitimate knowledge. It is by participating in these places that academics inscribe themselves as active subjects.

I have also drawn attention to the dynamic that operates between the ceremonial places. While a ceremonial place may be characterized by specific discourses, each influences the other. In part this explains the reasons for the changes in the contemporary academic subject. Previously, academic subjects may have understood themselves to be constructed within a single ceremonial place that comprised the disciplinary community and its institution locations. However, the conditions of contemporary society have meant that this understanding is difficult to sustain. The boundaries between the ceremonial places and discursive sequences are blurred and this is evident in current changes in academic practices. A variety of textual practices now constitute knowledge produced in and with the academy. Moreover, this chapter is an example of just one of the varieties of textual practices that constitute academic writing.

I have taken up a theoretical position that can help to explain the link between the broad and local conditions of academic work with variations in typical academic writing, as exemplified in my own writing. This position suggests that academics through their writing produce not only ideas and knowledge but also their identities and at the same time this writing contributes to and is produced by multiple global and local conditions and discourses.

References

Brown, K., Prince, D. and Solomon, N. (1994) 'Literacy issues in a restructuring workplace', *Occasional Paper No. 2*, NLLIA/Centre for Workplace Communication and Culture, UTS.

Cope, B., Solomon, N., Prince, D. and Kalantzis, M. (1994) 'Communication, collaboration and culture: meeting the communication demands of the restructured workplace', *Occasional Paper No. 4*, NLLIA/Centre for Workplace Communication and Culture, UTS.

Dreyfus, H.L. and Rabinow, P. (eds) (1982) *Michel Foucault: Beyond Structuralism and Hermeneutics*, Chicago: University of Chicago Press.

Edwards, R. and Usher, R. (1999) 'Society of Signs? Mediating a learning society', *British Journal of Educational Studies*, 47: 261–73.

Edwards, R., Nicoll, K., Solomon, N. and Usher, R. (2004) *Persuasive Texts? Rhetoric and Educational Discourse*, London: Routledge.

Foucault, M. (1991) 'Governmentality' in G. Burchell, C. Gordon and P. Miller (eds), *The Foucault Effect: Studies in Governmentality*, Chicago: University of Chicago Press.

Freadman, A. (1994) 'Anyone for tennis?' in A. Freedman and P. Medway (eds), *Genre and the New Rhetoric*, London: Taylor & Frances.

Freadman, A. (1998) 'Uptake', paper presented at the International Symposium on Genre, Simon Fraser University, Vancouver, Canada, January 1998.

Freadman, A. (2000) 'Uptake' in R. Coe L. Lingard and T. Teslenko (eds), *The Rhetoric and Ideology of Genre: Strategies for Stability and Change*, New York: Hampton Press.

Freedman, A. and Medway, P. (eds) (1994) *Genre and the New Rhetoric,* London: Taylor & Francis.

Garrick, J. and Solomon, N. (1997) 'Technologies of compliance', *Studies in Continuing Education,* 19: 71–81.

Gibb, J., Keenan, M. and Solomon, N. (1996) *Literacy at Work: Incorporating English Language and Literacy into Industry/Enterprise Competency Standards*, National Board of Employment, Education and Training, Australian Language and Literacy Council, Commonwealth of Australia.

Gibbons, M., Limoges, C., Nowotny, H., Schwartzman, S., Scott, P. and Trow, M. (1994) *The New Production of Knowledge: The Dynamics of Science and Research in Contemporary Societies*, London: Sage.

Godin, B. (1998) 'Writing performative history: the new *new* Atlantis?', *Social Studies of Science*, 28: 465–83.

Hood, S. and Solomon, N. (1985) *Focus on Reading: A Handbook for Teachers*, Sydney: National Curriculum Resource Centre.

Hood, S., Burns, A. and Solomon, N. (1996) *Focus on Reading*, 2nd edition, Sydney: Macquarie University, NCELTR.

Miller, C. (1994) 'Genre as social action' in A. Freedman and P. Medway (eds), *Genre and the New Rhetoric*, London: Taylor & Francis.

Miller, N. and Rose, N. (1993) 'Governing economic life' in M. Gane and T. Johnson (eds), *Foucault's New Domains*, London: Routledge.

National Training Board (NTB) (1992) *National Competency Standards and Guidelines*, 2nd edition, Canberra: ACT.

Rose, N. (1998) 'An interview with Nikolas Rose', *Arena Journal*, 11: 83–96.

Rose, N. (1999) *Powers of Freedom: Reframing Political Thought*, Cambridge: Cambridge University Press.

Scheeres, H. and Solomon, N. (2000a) 'Whose text? Methodological dilemmas in collaborative research practice' in A. Lee and C. Poynton (eds), *Culture and Text*, St Leonards New South Wales: Allen & Unwin.

Scheeres, H. and Solomon, N. (2000b) 'Research partnerships at work: new identities for new times' in J. Garrick and C. Rhodes (eds), *Research and Knowledge at Work: Perspectives, Case-studies and Innovative Strategies*, London: Routledge.

Solomon, N. (1996) 'Plain English: from a perspective of language in society' in R. Hasan and G. Williams (eds), *Literacy in Society*, New York: Addison Wesley Longman.

Solomon, N. (1999) 'Culture and difference in workplace learning' in D. Boud and J. Garrick (eds), *Understanding Workplace Learning*, London: Routledge.

Stronach, I. and Maclure, M. (1997) *Educational Research Undone: The Postmodern Embrace*, Buckingham: Open University Press.

Usher, R. and Solomon, N. (1999) 'Experiential learning and the shaping of subjectivity in the workplace', *Studies in the Education of Adult*, 31: 155–63.

Section 3

Governing subjects

Chapter 15

Encountering Foucault in lifelong learning

Gert Biesta

> The only important problem is what happens on the ground.
>
> (Foucault 1991a: 83)

The chapters in this book stage a range of different encounters with the work of Michel Foucault. Through them we not only gain a better understanding of the potential of Foucault's work but at the same time the chapters shed a different light on policies and practices of lifelong learning. There is, therefore, a double encounter in this book: we encounter Foucault in lifelong learning and we encounter lifelong learning through the eyes of Foucault. Both encounters are, of course, important. Whereas the stated purpose of this book is to gain a new and different understanding of lifelong learning and, through this, to contribute to a reconceptualization of lifelong learning, the book also functions as a 'test' of Foucauldian ideas. It reveals strengths and weaknesses of using Foucault to analyse and understand educational practices and processes and the wider strategies and techniques of governing in late-modern, neoliberal societies. For this final chapter this raises two questions: What has this book achieved in understanding and conceptualizing lifelong learning differently? And what does this tell us about the significance of Foucault's work for this particular endeavour? To address these questions I will focus on three issues:

- the nature of Foucauldian analysis;
- the question of normativity; and
- the opportunities for change.

In what follows I will first try to characterize the main thrust of the chapters against the background of Foucault's ideas on governmentality and power. I will then focus on what I see as one of the most interesting dimensions of this book, viz., the question as to what follows from Foucauldian analysis. I will first characterize how the different authors answer this question. I will then discuss what I see as the specific 'nature' of Foucauldian analysis, particularly with respect to the relationship between power and knowledge. This will provide the background for my reflections on the strengths and weaknesses of the contributions in this book which, finally, will bring me back to the question of normativity in Foucauldian analysis and the question as to how such analysis can support change.

The governmentality of lifelong learning

What unites the chapters in this book is that they all analyse policies and practices of lifelong learning with reference to the idea of 'governmentality'. 'Governmentality' – a neologism introduced by Foucault to refer to 'governmental rationality' (cf. Foucault 1991b; Gordon 1999: 1) – refers 'to the structures of power by which conduct is organized and by which governance is aligned with the self-organizing capacities of individual subjects' (Olssen this volume: 35). What Foucault was after with the idea of governmentality was an understanding of practices of governing – and more generally an understanding of the 'exercise' of power – which was not based on the idea of power as coercion or violence. Foucault argued that we should see power as a relationship, but not simply as 'a relationship between partners', but rather as 'a way in which certain actions modify others' (Foucault 1982: 219).

> In effect, what defines a relationship of power is that it is a mode of action which does not act directly and immediately on others. Instead it acts upon their actions: an action upon an action, on existing actions or on those which may arise in the present or the future.
>
> (Foucault 1982: 220)

A relationship of violence 'forces, it bends, it breaks on the wheel, it destroys, or it closes the door on all possibilities' (Foucault 1982: 220). A power relationship, on the other hand, 'can only be articulated on the basis of two elements which are indispensable', namely that the one over whom power is exercised 'be thoroughly recognized and maintained to the very end as a person who acts' and that, 'faced with a relationship of power, a whole field of responses, reactions, results, and possible interventions may open up' (Foucault 1928: 220). To govern, therefore, means 'to structure the possible field of action of others' (Foucault 1982: 221) which, in turn, implies that power as a mode of action upon the actions of others does not do away with freedom but rather presupposes it. 'Power is exercised only over free subjects, and only insofar as they are free' (Foucault 1982: 221).

This way of understanding power allows for a new kind of analysis of practices of governing, an analysis which does not simply look at the activities of those 'in power' and the ways in which they force others into particular actions, but which rather focuses on the ways in which power 'circulates' in relationships and social networks and on how the circulation of power is the *result* of what free subjects do to others and to themselves, not its precondition.

This is why Foucault emphasized that the analysis of power relations within a society 'cannot be reduced to the study of a series of institutions, not even to the study of all those institutions which would merit the name "political" ' (Foucault 1982: 224). The reason for this is that power relations 'are rooted in the system of social networks' (Foucault 1982: 224). This means that we shouldn't simply look for those who 'steer' those networks; it is rather that a particular configuration puts some in the steering position or gives the impression that some are 'in control'. The actual workings of power are thus quite messy. As Foucault (1982: 224) put it: 'The forms and the specific situations of the government of men by one another in a given society are multiple; they are superimposed, they cross, impose their own limits, sometimes cancel one another out, sometimes reinforce one another'. This is not to say that the state is no longer important or no longer powerful. But this is not because power in some original form belongs to the state, but 'because power relations have come more and more under state control (although this state control has not taken the same form in pedagogical, judicial, economic, or family systems)' (Foucault 1982: 224). This is what Foucault referred to as the *governmentalization* of the state (cf. Foucault 1991b: 103; Simons and Masschelein this volume).

Whereas the analysis of power and of practices of governing plays a crucial role in Foucault's work, he has made it clear that ultimately 'it is not power, but the subject, which is the general theme of my research' (Foucault 1982: 209; see also Biesta 1998a). For Foucault, the point is not simply to find an answer to the question of how power is exercised and what happens when individuals exert power over others and over themselves. Foucault seeks to answer these questions because he wants to understand how particular subjectivities, particular ways of being, are 'produced' through these processes and, also, how other subjectivities and identities are made difficult or impossible. Whereas in his earlier analyses Foucault explored this through the examination of disciplinary power and pastoral power, governmentality, as Nicoll and Fejes make clear in the introduction, combines the two perspectives in the study of the rationality of governing, thus foregrounding the *active* contributions individuals make to the circulation of power relationships and have to make in order for particular modes of governing to become possible. As Edwards in his chapter explains, governing 'does not so much *determine* people's subjectivities, but rather elicits, fosters, promotes and attributes [them]' (Edwards this volume: 26). Or, in the words of Dean: 'to analyze government is to analyze those practices that try and shape, sculpt, mobilize and work through the choices, desires, aspirations, needs, wants and lifestyles of individuals and groups' (Dean 1999: 12). This line of thought is particularly prominent in the Foucauldian analysis of the governmental rationality of neoliberalism in which the self is configured as an 'entrepreneurial self' or an 'entrepreneur of the self'. The entrepreneurial self, as we can read in the chapter by Simons and Masschelein, is not simply – or perhaps we should say: not only – a free subject; the entrepreneurial self is also a *governable* subject, that is, a subject that is of 'strategic importance for advanced liberal government' (Simons and Masschelein this volume: 56).

Against this background it is now possible to characterize the contributions in this book in a more precise manner. What all the authors in their own way show is that lifelong learning is not a 'natural' phenomenon that exists outside of the circulation of power and beyond the influence of neoliberal governmentality, but that it is rather closely tied up with the neoliberal governmentality. The chapters show the different ways in which the field of action of lifelong learning is structured. The point of making this visible is not only to show 'the structures of power by which conduct is organized' (Olssen this volume: 35); it is also to reveal the ways in which 'governance is aligned with the self-organizing capacities of individual subjects' (Olssen this volume: 35). The chapters show, in other words, that the governmentality of lifelong learning as it manifests itself in contemporary neoliberal societies, calls forth a particular *kind* of subjectivity called the 'lifelong learner'. Lifelong learners are not only *condemned*, so we might say, to a never-ending life of learning. Under the neoliberal governmentality of lifelong learning, lifelong learners have also become increasingly *responsible* for their own learning. The chapters thus show how the neoliberal governmentality of lifelong learning has turned learning from a right into a duty (cf. Biesta 2006). This reveals that the neoliberal governmentality of lifelong learning is bound up with particular power relationships and particular ways of being, and it is in this 'assemblage' that we can find what Simons and Masschelein refer to as the *governmentalization* of learning itself.

The consequences of Foucault

Whereas most of the chapters in this book follow a similar – though definitely not identical – pattern in their *analyses* of the governmentality of lifelong learning, the *conclusions* they draw from their analyses are quite different. Olssen suggests, for example, that a Foucauldian analysis should be complemented with a *normative* argument which would allow us to 'safeguard learning from neoliberal appropriation' (Olssen this volume: 44). He argues for a democratic conception of lifelong learning and suggests that in order to bring this about we need 'a theory of learning that teaches how powers are formed, harnessed and sustained; how compositions are brought into being, or avoided; how encounters are influenced and how institutional and collective politics are negotiated productively' (Olssen this volume: 44). Edwards takes a more 'modest' approach, highlighting the fact that 'attempts to mobilize lifelong learning in specific ways' will never be 'perfect' since they will always be subject 'to diverse and unexpected shifts and changes' (Edwards this volume: 32). But he also calls for a more active decentring of the 'regime of truth' of lifelong learning 'in order that we can look again at the meanings it has and the work it does' (Edwards this volume: 32). Simons and Masschelein take, in a sense, a more radical approach in that they argue for the need to reject learning altogether – 'freeing ourselves from learning' as they call it. Their reason for this is that as long as we try to 'improve' learning itself we remain caught up in the 'current governmental regime' of which learning is part (Simons and Masschelein this volume: 57).

Whereas the aforementioned authors draw explicit implications and recommendations from their analyses, Olsson and Petersson seem to refrain from doing so. They present their analysis without drawing any conclusions from it and seem to want to leave it to the reader to do this. Popkewitz is slightly more explicit about the way in which his analyses might be used in that he argues that a historicizing analysis as the one he provides in his chapter might help to 'unthink' particular fixed oppositions and thus might lead to different ways of thinking and being. Fejes takes a similar approach in his attempt to historicize the figure of the lifelong learner, but draws more explicit conclusions from his analysis by arguing that different 'configurations' of the lifelong learner all result in particular exclusions, sometimes even in the name of inclusion. He summons his readers to 'take a critical attitude towards the narratives of lifelong learning, to try to understand what kinds of subjects are their effects' (Fejes this volume: 98). Fogde's detailed analysis of the ways in which contemporary job-search practices 'regulate' the subject in a particular way again remains on the side of analysis, without drawing any specific lessons. Like Edwards, Zackrisson and Assarsson emphasize the fact that the workings of power are never perfect. Participants in adult education use such education in ways that fit their own patterns of life, which makes it difficult to understand these processes as a one-sided exertion of power. They suggest that it is always possible 'to act defiantly' (Sipos Zackrisson and Assarsson this volume: 123). Their optimistic conclusion therefore is that 'the normalizing techniques of power not only produce obedient and predictable people but also those whom we might label 'disobedient and unpredictable' (Sipos Zackrisson and Assarsson this volume: 123).

The more descriptive analysis provided by Anderson, another example of an author whose analysis does not lead to any specific conclusions or recommendations, stands in stark contracts to the way in which Berglund draws conclusions from her research. Like Simons and Masschelein she is acutely aware of the fact that the 'freedom of choice' that can be found in the neoliberal governmentality of lifelong learning is part and parcel of this governmentality and should therefore not be simply seen as a point from which resistance can emerge. As long as subjects do not become aware of the ways in which power/knowledge operates through these practices, they will be fooled into believing 'that such freedom of choice opens up all subject positions equally' (Berglund this volume: 147). Berglund thus seems to suggest that an understanding of the workings of the neoliberal governmentality of lifelong learning might be a way to overcome or counter some of its power effects. This way of thinking can also be found in Ahl's contribution as she argues that the kind of analysis that she has conducted makes it possible to question what is considered to be normal and what is considered to be deviant. In this way, Ahl suggests, it can support the resistance of those who, from the dominant or 'normal' perspective, appear as a problem. Nicoll does something similar in her analysis of e-learning, in that she presents different ways to understand e-learning and its implications for disciplines and subjectivities. Her conclusion is that e-learning in itself does not determine a particular 'use'. Therefore, whether it will lead to more discipline or more freedom crucially depends on the uptake. The analysis itself can be seen as making readers – including those who use e-learning – aware of these different options. Solomon's discussion, the last one in the row, shares most with those chapters which aim to analyse the neoliberal governmentality without articulating any specific lessons or drawing any specific conclusions.

When we look at the chapters in this way, that is, by focusing on the conclusions and recommendations that the authors draw from their analysis, we can roughly discern three different approaches. Some authors just present an analysis of policies and practices of lifelong learning, highlighting, for example, how such policies and practices call forth particular subjectivities and create particular subject positions, but they leave it to their readers to draw any conclusions from this. Others are more explicit in their conclusions and suggest more or less explicitly that Foucauldian analysis can help us to unveil the workings of power, and that it is because of this that such analysis help individuals to be less determined by power. They emphasize, in other words, the emancipatory potential of Foucault. A third group of authors is more reluctant to 'translate' their analyses into recommendations for action because they seem to acknowledge that Foucauldian analysis has implications for the very practice of analysis itself as well. (This is what Nicoll in her chapter refers to as the 'reflexive difficulty'.) I am inclined to agree with the third group of authors because in my view Foucault has not only provided us with a different way to analyse power and governing, his work also implies a different understanding of what the analysis of power itself can achieve. This has everything to do with the way in which we understand the relationship between power and knowledge. 'After' Foucault, so I wish to suggest, we have to understand this relationship in a fundamentally different way than 'before' Foucault, and this has important implications for what Foucauldian analysis can achieve and how it might be utilized to effect change. In order to appreciate what the difference is that makes this difference, I need to say a little more about Foucault and (the) Enlightenment.

Stop making sense? The question of method

Many would argue that Foucault has helped us to understand the workings of power in a new and different way. At one level this is, of course, correct. But what complicates the matter is that for Foucault a better understanding of the workings of power does not automatically put us in a position where we can free ourselves from the impact of the workings of power. Foucault has explicitly rejected the idea that we can use knowledge to 'combat' power. He has rejected the Manichean foundations of the Enlightenment in that he has challenged the idea that power and knowledge are separate 'entities' and that emancipation consists in the 'victory' of knowledge over power (cf. Pels 1992). For Foucault power and knowledge always come together – something which is expressed in his notion of 'power/knowledge'. This is why he has argued that we should abandon 'a whole tradition that allows us to imagine that knowledge can only exist where the power relations are suspended' (Foucault 1975: 27). This is not to say that change is no longer possible or that knowledge has become futile. But what it does signify is the end of the 'innocence' of knowledge, the end of the idea that knowledge is 'pure', 'simple' and uncontaminated by power and thus can be used to reveal how power operates. Foucault urges us to acknowledge that we are always operating *within* fields of power/knowledge – of power/knowledge against power/knowledge, not of power against knowledge or knowledge against power. What is 'new', therefore, about Foucault's analysis of power – and hence should be taken into consideration in any Foucauldian analysis – is that he does not see this analysis as the way in which we can escape and overcome the workings of power (cf. Biesta 1998b).

Does this mean that for Foucault we live in an iron cage from which escape is impossible? Is it the case, as some of Foucault's critics have argued, that his work has an 'anaesthetizing effect' because the 'implacable logic' of it leaves 'no possible room for initiative' (Foucault 1991a: 82)? These questions only make sense as long as we assume that it is possible to occupy a place outside of the system from which we can analyse and criticize the system. They only make sense, in other words, as long as we assume that knowledge is 'outside' of or 'beyond' power. But what Foucault has urged us to do is precisely to move beyond this inside-outside thinking. There is, therefore, potential for action, change and critique in Foucault's 'universe', but it requires an approach that is distinctively different from the modern Enlightenment approach. According to Foucault it is true 'that we have to give up hope of ever acceding to a point of view that could give us access to any complete and definitive knowledge of what may constitute our historical limits' (Foucault 1984: 47). But this doesn't mean that there is nothing to do. Foucault agrees with Enlightenment thinkers such as Kant that criticism 'consists of analysing and reflecting upon limits' (Foucault 1984: 45). He argues that

> if the Kantian question was that of knowing what limits knowledge had to renounce transgressing, it seems to me that the critical question today has to be turned back into a positive one: in what is given to us as universal, necessary, obligatory, what place is occupied by whatever is singular, contingent, and the product of arbitrary constraints?
>
> (Foucault 1984: 45)

In some of his work Foucault has referred to this approach as 'eventualization' (Foucault 1991a). Eventualization comes down to a 'breach of self-evidence'. 'It means making visible a singularity at places where there is a temptation to invoke a historical constant, an immediate anthropological trait, or an obviousness which imposes itself uniformly on all' (Foucault 1991a: 76). Rather than looking for a single explanation of particular 'facts' or 'events', eventualization works 'by constructing around the singular event ... a "polygon" or rather a "polyhedron" of intelligibility, the number of whose faces is not given in advance and can never properly be taken as finite' (Foucault 1991a: 77). Eventualization thus means to complicate and to pluralize our understanding of events, their elements, their relations and their domains of reference. Looked at it in this way, eventualization does, therefore, not result in a 'deeper' understanding, an understanding of underlying 'structures' or 'causes' and in this respect eventualization does not generate the kind of knowledge that will set us free from the workings of those structures or causes. But Foucault has been adamant that this does not mean that such analysis is without effect. What eventualization does *not* generate, so he has argued, is advice or guidelines or instructions as to what is to be done. But what it can bring about is a situation in which people ' "no longer know what they do", so that the acts, gestures, discourses which up until then had seemed to go without saying become problematic, difficult, dangerous' – and this effect is entirely *intentional* (Foucault 1991a: 84). Foucauldian analysis therefore doesn't result in a deeper or more true understanding of how power works – it only tries to unsettle what is taken-for-granted – nor does it aim to produce recipes for action. This kind of analysis is therefore not meant to 'solve' problems and is not meant to give ideas to reformers to make the world a better one. In relation to this, Foucault has emphasized that this kind of knowledge is not meant for the 'social workers' or the 'reformers' but rather for the subjects who act.

> Critique doesn't have to be the premise of a deduction which concludes: this then is what needs to be done. It should be an instrument for those who fight, those who resist and refuse what is. Its use should be in processes of conflict and confrontation, essays in refusal. It doesn't have to lay down the law for the law. It isn't a stage of programming. It is a challenge directed to what is.
>
> (Foucault 1991a: 84)

What Foucault is arguing for is not only a different 'style' of critique but also a different 'audience' for critique, not the ones who try to solve problems and make things better, but those who are struggling to make possible different ways of being and doing – which lies behind Foucault's claim that in a sense '(t)he only important problem is what happens on the ground' (Foucault 1991a: 83). What this entails is a '*practical* critique that takes the form of a possible transgression' (Foucault 1984: 45; emphasis added). The critical practice of transgression is not meant to overcome limits (not in the least because limits are not only constraining but always also enabling) (cf. Simmons 1995: 69). Transgression rather is the practical and experimental 'illumination of limits' (cf. Foucault 1977: 33–8; Boyne 1990).

Foucault's rejection of the modern approach to Enlightenment, where emancipation is seen as the process in which we overcome the workings of power through our understanding of how power works, therefore does not mean the end of any critical work. It rather opens up a new domain for critique and a new critical 'style' or practice called 'transgression'. Transgression, understood as the *experimental* illumination of limits, can take the form of what I have elsewhere called a counter-practice (cf. Biesta 1998b). Counter-practices should not be designed on the basis of the assumption that they will be better. What matters only is that counter-practices are different. The critical 'work' of counter-practices consists in showing (or proving, as Foucault would say) that the way things are, is only one (limited) possibility. Yet this tiny step is crucial, since it opens up the possibility 'of no longer being, doing, or thinking what we are, do, or think' – and in precisely this sense 'it is seeking to give a new impetus ... to the undefined work of freedom' (Foucault 1984: 46).

Encountering Foucault in lifelong learning

As I have suggested above, there are roughly three ways in which the authors in this book approach Foucauldian analysis. Some just present an analysis of policies and practice of lifelong learning without drawing any particular conclusions or formulating any specific recommendations. Others present their analysis as a way to unveil the workings of power in the neoliberal governmentality of lifelong learning and aim to use this understanding to indicate ways in which the effects of the workings of power can be resisted or overcome. The third group, as I have argued, shows more reluctance in formulating recommendations for change as they seem to be aware of some of the reflexive difficulties that follow from using Foucault. Against the background of what I have said in the previous section, I am now in a position to comment on these three different usages of Foucault in a more precise manner. Before I do so, I wish to emphasize that most chapters do not neatly fall within just one of the groups. In most cases authors rely on at least two of these approaches. My comments are therefore not aimed at particular chapters in this book, but focus on the different approaches or strategies that can be discerned in the chapters. What they reveal, however, are distinctly different ways to use Foucault and conduct Foucauldian analysis. My point is, however, that there are tensions between some of the uses of Foucault and what I see as the specific character of Foucauldian analysis.

With regards to the first group I am inclined to say that they only use 'half' of Foucault in their analyses. They use Foucault's understanding of power and the product of subjectivities/subject-positions predominantly as a theory to describe and analyse policies and practices of lifelong learning. What is lacking in this approach is an awareness of the methodological aspects of Foucauldian analysis. As a result, the authors give the impression that their analyses have to be accepted as a true or accurate account of what is going on in the field of lifelong learning. Such an approach not only lacks the reflexivity Foucauldian analysis would call for. Because of the absence of specific recommendations it also remains unclear where these authors stand politically. It is, in other words, not clear what the normative agenda of these authors – if any – exactly is.

This is not the case with the contributions in the second group where it is quite clear what the motivations for the engagement with Foucauldian analysis are. Here, the main impetus of Foucauldian analysis is to achieve an understanding of the workings of power that can help individuals to overcome some of the impact of the workings of power. Authors in this group thus clearly identify with an emancipatory agenda. But whereas the authors in this group are much more explicit about their motivations and, as a result of this, much more reflexive about both the content and the method of their analysis, the problem, as I see it, is that they combine a post-Foucauldian analysis with a pre-Foucauldian methodology. This is a tempting strategy, not in the least because the Foucauldian analysis of the neoliberal governmentality of lifelong learning makes a lot of sense and to a certain extent even rings true and such insights might help individuals to do things differently. The problem here, from a Foucauldian perspective, is that it spurs individuals into action on the basis of what we might call a new 'self-evidence', a new and better way to understand what is 'really' going on. Such an approach lacks reflexivity as well, because it is neither able to problematize the self-evidence that should lead to emancipation and freedom nor able to acknowledge the extent to which such a strategy would itself rely on the operation of power, that is, on the structuring of the possible field of action of others on the basis of a certain self-evidence.

This is where the third approach which I have discerned in the contributions to this book remains closer to Foucault, not only because they combine Foucauldian theory – a Foucauldian understanding of the workings of power and the constitutions of subjectivities and subject-positions – with a Foucauldian methodology, but also because in their analyses they aim to breach the self-evidence of particular practices and policies of lifelong learning without claiming to generate a deeper truth about what actually is going on. Such an approach is not without what we might call 'emancipatory effect'. But it is first of all important to see that this is a different *kind* of emancipation; not an emancipation that tries to escape power but rather one that allows for a different power/knowledge constellation – a different way of being and doing. It is, therefore, not emancipation in the 'traditional' sense as liberation from power, but more something that is akin to what Foucault has so aptly referred to as the undefined work of freedom. It is also important to see that the emancipatory effect of these kind of analyses is not based on the construction of a new self-evidence, but on the transgression of existing self-evidence in order to show that other subject-positions are possible; subject-positions that, in a sense, are located outside of existing and predominant discourses and, in a sense, cannot be captured or articulated within them. This is very well captured in Ahl's remarks on the 'unmotivated adult' where she shows that the person who does not want to study, and in this respect appears as 'unmotivated' in an 'official' perspective, actually has no problem and hence has no need for an explanatory theory or for a policy that does something about it. It is, as she writes, 'when someone wants someone *else* to do something and this person does not, that the problem arises' (Ahl this book: 160).

Conclusions

In this chapter I have aimed to provide a perspective on the contributions in this book. I have argued that Foucauldian analysis should not only be characterized by a usage of Foucault's theories of power and subjectivity, but also be informed by his ideas on method and methodology because it is there that, in my view, has made a major intervention in modern philosophy. I have suggested that some of the contributions in this book predominantly focus on Foucault's theories. Others display an awareness of methodological issues, particularly in relation to the question as to what can be 'done' with or on the basis of Foucauldian analysis. Whereas some of the latter approaches give an answer to this question through the adoption of a 'pre-Foucauldian' framework – relying upon a modern understanding of emancipation and Enlightenment – other contributions have been more successful in combining a Foucauldian approach at the level of both content and method. I wish to emphasize, however, that most of the chapters combine elements of these three approaches, which means the distinctions I have introduced run through the chapters rather than that they organize the chapters in clear groupings. My comments are, therefore, mainly intended as a reading guide, but I leave it to the readers to judge to what extent they feel that the distinctions I have introduced are helpful in their own encounter with Foucault in lifelong learning.

The chapters in this book do indeed provide a different way to understand aspects of the policies and practices of lifelong learning in contemporary neoliberal societies. They also show the fruitfulness of a Foucauldian approach, although I have argued that a consistent use of Foucault in the encounter with lifelong learning is more difficult than it may seem, not in the least because Foucault urges us to resist our 'modern' inclinations to come up with better understandings, solutions and plans for action. What Foucault asks us to do is first and foremost to breach self-evidence as this opens up opportunities for doing and being differently. Many of the chapters in this book are successful in questioning the self-evidence of lifelong learning even up to the point where the self-evidence of learning itself is called into question. In this respect the chapters help us to de-naturalize – or eventualize, as Foucault would call it – lifelong learning.

Who is to benefit from all this? Again, Foucault helps us to resist the temptation to assume that analysis should lead to suggestions for policy and practice, to suggestions for improvement and the solution of problems. As some of the chapters in this book show what is a problem for policy makers is not at all a problem 'on the ground' and to make this visible can help those 'on the ground' to resist adopting the problem perspective of policy makers. This is not, as I have argued, a strategy that allows them to escape the workings of power. But it does provide opportunities for different ways of doing and being and thus can provide support for resisting or even refusing particular subjectivities or subject-positions. It is important to bear in mind, however, that contrary to what seems to be the emphasis in Foucault, it can also provide support for the *adoption* of particular subjectivities and subject-positions, particularly where individuals come to the conclusion that the adoption of such positions might well be beneficial to them. This requires judgement, and it is important to see that such judgements cannot be made in the abstract or at the level of theory; they have to be made 'on the ground' as well. Whether we adopt or reject the subject-position of the lifelong learner is therefore, at the end of the day, open to us. What the contributions in this book have helped to make visible is that there is at least this choice. In this respect the chapters have made an important 'opening' in the policies and practices of lifelong learning.

References

Biesta, G. (1998a) 'Pedagogy without humanism: Foucault and the subject of education', *Interchange* 29: 1–16.

Biesta, G. (1998b) ' "Say you want a revolution ..." Suggestions for the impossible future of critical pedagogy', *Educational Theory* 48: 499–510.

Biesta, G. (2006) 'What's the point of lifelong learning if lifelong learning has no point? On the democratic deficit of policies for lifelong learning', *European Educational Research Journal* 5: 169–80.

Boyne, R. (1990) *Foucault and Derrida: The Other Side of Reason*, London: Routledge.

Dean, M. (1999) *Governmentality: Power and Rule in Modern Society*, London: Sage.

Foucault, M. (1975) *Discipline and Punish: The Birth of the Prison*, New York: Vintage.

Foucault, M. (1977) 'A preface to transgression', in D.F. Bouchard (ed.), *Language, Counter-Memory, Practice. Selected Essays and Interview by Michel Foucault*, Ithaca: Cornell University Press.

Foucault, M. (1982) 'Afterword: The subject and power', in L. Dreyfus and P. Rabinow (eds), *Michel Foucault: Beyond Structuralism and Hermeneutics*, 2nd edition, Chicago: The University of Chicago press.

Foucault, M. (1984) 'What is Enlightenment?' in P. Rabinow (ed.), *The Foucault Reader*, New York: Pantheon.

Foucault, M. (1991a) 'Questions of method', in G. Burchell, C. Gordon and P. Miller (eds), *The Foucault Effect. Studies in Governmentality*, Chicago: The University of Chicago Press.

Foucault, M. (1991b) 'Governmentality', in G. Burchell, C. Gordon and P. Miller (eds), *The Foucault Effect. Studies in Governmentality*, Chicago: The University of Chicago Press.

Gordon, C. (1991) 'Governmental rationality: an introduction', in G. Burchell, C. Gordon and P. Miller (eds), *The Foucault Effect. Studies in Governmentality*, Chicago: The University of Chicago Press.

Pels, D. (1992) 'Kennispolitiek: Een gebruiksaanwijzing voor Foucault', *Kennis & Methode*, 16: 39–62.

Simmons, J. (1995) *Foucault & The Political*, London and New York: Routledge.

Index